RELIGION AND CULTURE IN THE MIDDLE AGES

Shadows of Mary

T0083636

RELIGION AND CULTURE IN THE MIDDLE AGES

Shadows of Mary

*Reading the Virgin Mary
in Medieval Texts*

TERESA P. REED

UNIVERSITY OF WALES PRESS
CARDIFF
2003

British Library Cataloguing-in-Publication Data
A catalogue record for this book is available from the British Library.

ISBN 0–7083–1797–9 paperback
    0–7083–1798–7 hardback

Typeset at the University of Wales Press
Printed in Great Britain by MPG Books Limited, Bodmin, Cornwall

CONTENTS

In memory of my father, Nathaniel E. Reed,
whose love and guidance made this possible

SERIES EDITORS' PREFACE

Religion and Culture in the Middle Ages aims to explore the interface between medieval religion and culture, with as broad as possible an understanding of those terms. It puts to the forefront studies which engage with works that significantly contributed to the shaping of medieval culture. However, it also gives attention to studies dealing with works that reflect and highlight aspects of medieval culture that have been neglected in the past by scholars of the medieval disciplines. For example, devotional works and the practice they infer illuminate in remarkable ways our understanding of the medieval subject and its culture, while studies of the material space designed and inhabited by medieval subjects yields new evidence on the period and the people who shaped it and lived in it. In the larger field of religion and culture, we also want to explore further the roles played by women as authors, readers and owners of books, thereby defining them more precisely as actors in the cultural field.

The series as a whole investigates the European Middle Ages, from *c.*500 to *c.*1500. Our aim is to explore medieval religion and culture with the tools belonging to such disciplines as, among others, art history, philosophy, theology, history, musicology, the history of medicine, and literature. In particular, we would like to promote interdisciplinary studies, as we believe strongly that our modern understanding of the term applies fascinatingly well to a cultural period marked by a less tight confinement and categorization of its disciplines than the modern period. However, our only criterion is academic excellence, with the belief that the use of a large diversity of critical tools and theoretical approaches serves for a deeper understanding of medieval culture. We want the series to reflect this diversity, as we believe that, as a collection of outstanding contributions, it offers a more subtle representation of a period that is marked by paradoxes and contradictions and which necessarily reflects diversity and difference, however difficult it may sometimes have proved for medieval culture to accept these notions.

ACKNOWLEDGEMENTS

For gracefully balanced support and guidance, I thank R. Allen Shoaf, Daniel Cottom and James Paxson who have seen me and this project through from the beginning. For faith and friendship (and lots of good food), I especially thank Marlene, Susan, Trish, Glenn, Gina, Suzanne, Kelly and Karen. Their being there in every hour and a half of need made possible every word of this project. To all at the University of Wales Press, particularly Duncan Campbell and Ceinwen Jones, many thanks for their patience and care in dealing with this first-time author. For never doubting that I would accomplish whatever I set out to do, I thank my parents Violet and Nathaniel Reed. Finally, for loving me with a perfect indifference to work or anything else, I thank Catherine, Michael, Laurie, Louis, Fantsy and Ellie.

Chapter 1 has appeared in different form in *Mediævalia*, Volume 21.2 (Spring 1997).
An earlier version of Chapter 4 appeared in *South Atlantic Review*, Volume 65.2 (Spring 2000).
Unless otherwise indicated, translations are my own.

Going by Contraries:
Eve, Mary and Meaning in the Medieval Church

In medieval narrative practices and the reading habits that accompany them, we can recognize what is at stake as a culture (re)constructs itself discursively. To begin to grasp what is at stake, ethically, spiritually and materially, in the process of representation, it is necessary to understand how and why the category of 'the feminine' comes to play such a large and largely overwritten role in various literary conventions. In the Middle Ages, what it meant to be a woman was filtered through that culture's epitome of womanhood, the Holy Virgin Mary. It is little wonder, then, that all kinds of texts concerning women, from those of popular, secular culture to those dealing with the intricacies of theology, invoked the Virgin's name as an aid in defining femininity. In texts as generically different as Chaucer's *Man of Law's Tale* and the thirteenth-century *Seinte Marherete, þe Meiden ant Martyr*, readers encounter a wide variety of female bodies: dead, living, painful, pregnant, menstruating, lactating, sealed, sliced open, sublated and sensible. Ultimately these bodies represent a lack of plenitude and transcendence. At the same time, they become the tropes through which timeless concepts can be predicated.

Though the primary texts upon which I focus are medieval, more precisely Middle English, I am concerned not with some simplistic uncovering of the past but rather with coming to a broader understanding of the ways in which such texts played a part in a culture's process of making truths for itself and in grasping a specific understanding of the role of 'the feminine' in such an overdetermined undertaking. My concern is to look at some standard texts about Mary that nevertheless operate in ways that are not always acknowledged within official models of discursive practice. The various cultural forces of the past that I investigate continue to captivate every aspect of our being even today, for our reliance on transcendent truths has persisted even though the terms of those truths have changed. If what Jean de Meun wrote in his portion of *Le Roman de la Rose* contains any truth –

> Thus things go by contraries; one is the gloss of the other. If one wants to define one of the pair, he must remember the other, or he will never, by any intention, assign a definition to it; for he who has no understanding of the two will never understand the difference between them and without this difference no definition that one may make can come to anything.[1]

– then any investigation of the past is already tinted by present concerns. If there is any truth to Jean's words from this perspective, we see that understanding some of our present reading practices will necessarily involve retrospective analysis of previous epistemologies and modes of representation. Similarly, any view of the past is bound to be tinted by every aspect of our present being. What is at stake currently in investigations in medieval studies, then, is both a tangible and historical foundation of ideas and a more evanescent investigation into the interrelatedness of present-day and past ways of thinking. What interests me in the texts that I choose and the details upon which I focus is not determining the accuracy of the historical data or providing an overarching history of Marian theology and its practice but the written representation and illustrations of Mary's body as a primary trope, the presentation and ordering of information included in often very different texts and the establishment of narrative authority through the process. For these things reveal much about the logic that established tenets of the medieval church. Ruth Morse has similarly written 'An inevitable intertextuality pervades the . . . texts' of the Middle Ages[2] and 'At the simplest level, "truth" means something at least as much like "exemplary" or "representative" as it does "what really happened so far as it can be ascertained".'[3] Writers, Morse determines, make claims to tell the truth and be strict about its representation but then immediately jump into conventional rhetorical habits.[4] In effect Morse illustrates the way that intertextuality worked as a regular productive, though anxiety-producing, part of writing, but

this anxiety, this deference to past authority or some supposed earlier
or pre-text also allowed 'authors to exploit a rich narrative uncertainty
and to create a space within which they could manipulate their true
tales about the past'.[5]

My interest leads me to examine aspects of the history and literature
of the church in the context of various and often mercurial forces such
as death, sexuality and law; repetition, stereotyping and parody; racial
and cultural heritage and prejudices; and concepts of sin, redemption
and salvation. In this investigation, a basic argument at work is that
history, more particularly the history of the church, is an epistemo-
logical category itself and, as such, must be considered as bound up in
representation's problems and plenitude. Unveiling some of the presuppositions by which medieval literary and devotional texts could be
imagined and brought into representation (as well as interpreted by
later scholars) will illustrate some of the culturally bound forces at
work in producing church doctrine and practice. The principal mode
of construction was based on a binary model. In medieval literature
and criticism, the difference between humanity and divinity and, more
fundamentally, between good and evil, parallels sexual difference. By
exposing this underlying aspect of representation, this book comprises
an exploration and, at times, a critique of ways of conceptualizing
differences of all kinds, including that between the past and the
present.

One site around which the contingent nature of the church's truths
becomes apparent is in the figure of the Virgin Mary, who was both
alone of all her sex and the inheritor of a culture's anxieties over
excessive, repulsive, yet life-giving female flesh as well as an exemplum
for all of humanity. Describing the Virgin's exemplary functions Ann
W. Astell writes:

> In the Marian exposition [of the Song of Songs], the fusion of two
> histories – the evangelical biography of Mary and the Song's literal
> meaning ('historia') – emphasizes the typological implications of the text
> as a prefigurement not only of Christ's life, but also of every Christian's
> . . . Mary's voice becomes the exemplary utterance of the devout.[6]

The contradictions comprehended in the figure of Mary – the
spiritually necessary body, the immaculately menstruating woman and
the godly human and human piece of divinity, to name but a few –
focus medieval Christianity's anxieties and desires and more generally

those of the culture at large. Gail McMurry Gibson argues that
emphasis on Mary was even greater in England:

> In the Middle Ages, it was not primarily continental theologians but
> English ones who were so eager to proclaim Mary's powers and her saving
> grace, her freedom from original sin; not French exegetes but English
> Benedictines like Anselm of Canterbury, Eadmer, William of Newburghe
> and the Cistercian abbot Aelred of Rievaulx, who were in the twelfth
> century arguing passionately for the doctrine of Mary's Immaculate
> Conception . . . English theologians were those who were insisting upon a
> kind of quaternity of heaven, writing emotional prose that amounted to a
> feminization of divinity.[7]

Shadows of Mary traces the shadows of Mary in five 'characters' –
Chaucer's Constance, his Wife of Bath, the medical woman of the
English Trotula, Saint Margaret of Antioch (both in Chapter 3) and the
Pearl maiden. The differences among these five are great: three are
positive exempla and one negative, while the medical woman is simply
infirmity personified; three are virtual human characters, one is a
medical effigy and one is an allegorical ideal. Yet together with Mary –
shadowed by her opposite, Eve – these five chart an ontological
sequence illustrating the figurative existence of this thing called 'the
feminine' and its employment in more extensive agendas of medieval
culture.

While my understanding of this figuration comes from careful,
contextual and close reading of medieval historical and literary texts, it
is also indebted to recent work in post-structuralist theories of
language, subjectivity and gender proposed by literary theorists such as
Jacques Derrida, Luce Irigaray, Julia Kristeva and Judith Butler. In
her essay '*Stabat Mater*' Kristeva writes:

> Christianity is doubtless the most refined symbolic construct in which
> femininity . . . is focused on *Maternality*. Let us call 'maternal' the
> ambivalent principle that is bound to the species, on the one hand and on
> the other stems from an identity catastrophe that causes the Name to
> topple over into the unnameable that one imagines as femininity, non-
> language or body.[8]

Kristeva's inferences suggest the often bewildering articulations
between language, identities and female flesh with which this project
will be concerned at large. Similarly, I am interested in those parts of

Irigaray's writings that point to a materialistic basis of semiotic systems and disturbing consequences of re-membering this materialism. Derrida's focus on the materiality of language itself[9] and of the supplementary nature of representation to ideas reminds us of another facet of the matter of writing.

Bringing such theories to bear upon texts of Marian devotion affords the unique opportunity for investigating the cultural matrix that Mary represents. Post-structural theory provides insight into the idiosyncrasies of the diverse and contradictory nature of figures of Mary in medieval literature and subsequent responses to them. Study of the figure that Mary becomes reveals the idiosyncratic essence of figuration itself. Even more basically, this project struggles to understand how Mary's body and the female body itself provide the palimpsest of medieval Christian faith. What must be clarified within this conglomeration is the difference between a ubiquitous cultural matrix that might be labelled 'Marian figuration' and the specific characteristics of its application in a particular text or work of art. Bringing together a diversity of texts, from the canonical Chaucerian texts and *Pearl*, to the cycle dramas and religious lyrics and the more marginalized *English Trotula* and *Seinte Marherete*, provides me with the chance to make this clarification. This unique blend of texts allows me to explore this cultural matrix more fully than a look only at canonical texts would, while the inclusion of texts considered to be at the centre of medieval literary studies illustrates that the idiosyncrasies I investigate are characteristic of cultural construction and not in opposition to dominant ideologies. Such idiosyncrasies, then, are endemic even to normative discourses and are, in fact, constitutive of them and the rhetorical power they hold.

The notion of the interrelatedness between past and present, texts and lives, truths and idiosyncrasies, rings abundantly true for the unique character of Mary, whose death was made into an element of eschatology before her birth became a topic over which disputes raged, while questions surrounding her birth were decided before those concerning her conception, as will be seen in later chapters of this book. Significantly, Mary's carnal state and, more specifically, her sexuality become issues in her story as the mother of God incarnate. Because of this her 'tale' was intimately tied to her 'tail'. Intrinsic to both tale and tail was Mary's rhetorical association with her opposite, Eve, the most deviant and tempting of women. Regardless of her eschatological status as queen of heaven and bride of Christ, Mary's

status as inheritor of cultural anxieties about the errancy of female
flesh remained in even the most standard retellings of her story. Several
detractors in the *N-Town* 'Trial of Joseph and Mary' comment on the
pregnant Mary's apparent promiscuity:

> Such a ȝonge damesel of bewté bryght
> And of schap so comely also
> Of hire tayle ofte-tyme be lyght
> And rygh tekyl vndyr þe too.[10]

(Such a young damsel of beauty bright and of shape so comely also will be
playful with her tail [pudendum] and easily swept off her feet.)

Even if only to be dramatically disproved later, this passage effectively
sexualizes the Virgin and puts her sexuality outside the bounds of
propriety and into the prurient, specular arena. This passage provides
an erotic vision of the Holy Virgin, her shapely body 'ticklish' under-
neath her lover. How could the devotional playwright picture Mary
in such vulgar hues – the hues of a common whore? How could the
audience view their spiritual queen as the wanton girl down the street?
Only against this backdrop of the expectation of sin can the miracle of
the Virgin's pregnant body hold its full salvational significance. As the
play uses the technique of reversal to instruct its audience, so the
church turned the story of Mary into doctrine by playing her exceptional characteristics against the stereotypically negative perceptions of female sexuality.[11]

Another example that illustrates the idiosyncratic nature of figures
of Mary is the 'Madonna of Humility'.[12] Even though she sits on a
stool or the ground and holds the Christ child, she is crowned not only
by a rayed halo but also by twelve stars, the crown of the Apocalyptic
woman of Revelation 12:1–5:

> And a great sign appeared in heaven: a woman clothed with the sun and
> the moon under her feet, & on her head a crown of twelve stars: & being
> with child, she cried also travailing and is in anguish to be delivered. And
> there was seen an other sign in heaven and behold a great red dragon
> having seve[n] heads, & ten horns: and on his heads seven diadems . . . and
> the dragon stood before the woman which was ready to be delivered: that
> when she should be delivered, he might devour her son. And she brought
> forth a man child, who was to govern all nations in an iron rod.

Exegetically, this passage was understood to refer to Mary's role in salvation[13] and examining Schiller's figure 106 with this tradition in mind reveals the authority of even this humble figure of Mary. Even though this is a picture of Mary as mother, holding the Christ child, it depicts a subject with considerable presence. With his back towards the lower left-hand corner of the frame and showing only two-thirds of his face to the viewer, the Christ child is not the dominant figure, although he is at the picture's centre. Instead, Mary forms a triangle that encompasses him physically, while the triforium-shaped frame mimes the shape of Mary's head and left shoulder (the third scallop mimes the top of the Christ child's head). This physical comprehension parallels Mary's temporal and spiritual comprehension of the Christ child, sucking his thumb and infantilized in the image, as it brings together many elements of the cultural matrix that Mary represents. She is crowned by stars as queen of heaven, prefiguring salvation for all humanity, as well as the Second Coming, while she holds the vehicle of that salvation in her lap. In Mary's holding the Christ child, the painting recalls the *sedes sapientiae*: the crowned Mary is also the throne of Jesus, wisdom.[14]

Additionally, the title 'Madonna of Humility' and the figure's close proximity to the ground should remind us of another aspect of Marian imagery – the cultural inheritance of being female. 'Humility' is from the Latin *humilis*, meaning 'lowly, mean, base', but more originally from *humus* or 'ground'. This virtuous humility seems to be the recuperated form of the otherwise threatening fecund maternal matter of the earth. Like the excessive matter sloughed from a woman's body each month, Mary's humility, even from her position of the crowned and enthroned queen of heaven (albeit a different type of enthroning as she becomes the throne), points towards the very material basis of an ostensibly transcendent salvation and system of virtue. In this project I investigate the relationship between such figurations of the church and the female body, specifically Mary's and Eve's bodies, as a way to understand the rhetorical practices that legitimize Christian authority.[15]

And yet, the humanity of the Holy Virgin's body is not always apparent. Various thinkers and theologians, including Bede, Alcuin, Pope Gregory the Great, Augustine of Canterbury, Richard of St Lawrence, Thomas Aquinas, Gratian and Hugh of St Victor, have dealt with the exceptional quality of Mary's body and the particular place it must hold in human society, law and convention. As the history of a mother in Judaea turned into a story of a miraculous Virgin and the queen of heaven, the church solidified its position on certain tenets of faith and the social behaviors extrapolated from them. Yet, as we will see most particularly in Chapter 1, Mary's typological connection to Eve returns in these figurations in startling ways. Even as Mary transcends the concupiscence of conception, the pain of childbirth and the fear of death, in many instances her exceptional nature is based upon an opposition to the errancy of Eve's flesh. Such opposition often sets up a relationship to Eve and the stories told about her, and this relationship to the most negative of women imaginable is never far from of any reference to Mary, even in the most holy of circumstances.

In the tropologies of the Christian tradition, Mary's relationship to Eve is central for two interrelated reasons. The traditional misogynistic reading of Genesis provides the basis of the Augustinian model of semiotics – a model of language that informs medieval poetics as much as it does theology. This system connects Eve with metaphor itself, the loss of direct access to things in themselves necessitating language as a medium between people and between them and God as the condition of a post-lapsarian existence. Countless literary, theological and philosophical texts from the period connected Eve's sin to mis-representation and misreading. The Pauline woman, commanded to save herself through procreation and modest attire,[16] inherits the recuperated repercussions of Eve's ancillary existence and mis-interpretations. Against this backdrop of social, seemingly natural and rhetorical categories – indeed, produced by them – Mary rights humanity and redeems femininity. Mary turns the sinful body of 'Eva' into the 'Ave' of the prayer of blessing. This graphic re-turning or boustrophedon[17] – employing reflection and comparison or *ratio*, paradigmatic of metaphoricity itself – embodies not only a poetics but also the very ontology and epistemology that Jean de Meun describes throughout his portion of *Le Roman* and that comprise the foundation of medieval Christianity.

Another way to understand this mode of representation is to understand it as a yoking of opposites. In such a trope, the opposites are turned away from each other but also towards each other, connected in the very statement that brings their meaning into being by setting them at odds. This was one important way in which the era conceptualized its ethic of transcendence. Yet, the yoking of Eve and Mary illustrates the figural existence of this ethic and its dependence on a belief in the errancy of female physiology. The condition of this ethic as both assumed and contentious underlies my interest in the figuration of the Eve/Mary binary because the intertextuality of the Eve/Mary story reveals what Julia Kristeva, in *Revolution in Poetic Language*, calls thetic breaks, or those places where a lapse in the signifying system occurs. These breaks are, at base, revealing because 'positionality . . . is structured as a break in the signifying process, establishing the *identification* of the subject and its object as preconditions of propositionality'.[18] Such a theoretical perspective allows one to glimpse portions of the semiotic processes that propose truths, processes that are usually so taken for granted as to seem common-sensical, natural or God-given. Thetic breaks, then, throw into question the idea of transcendence as absolute by allowing readers to investigate the semiotic processes that produce the idea of transcendence, the identity of the church and the faithful. The Eve/Mary binary constitutes such a break because it so effectively illustrates both the propositions of the church and their semiotic inheritance: the re-turn to propriety that Mary instigates must always be in response to Eve's turning away from the same. In other words, Mary is responsible *for* returning humanity to its rightful inheritance only by being responsive *to* the errancy of Eve.

In looking at the consequences of such re-turns and responses, the project also inquires into the powers of narrative to form the truths held by the church as self-evident. Inherently, the church is a normalizing institution. The Christian narrative effectively takes categories of gender and rules about life and death, social class and class markers, ethnic identity and rhetorical practices and through various discourses makes them seem natural and God-given. The secular texts that I examine in this book employ many standard repetitions of church dogma and Marian doctrine and yet each contains – as, being part of a semiotic system, each must – a break: a textual, often intertextual, site where can one see beneath the veridical veil and can find, most of the time, some female flesh.

The literary texts I have chosen are various and variously framed by the history of their composition and reception. Each foregrounds a different portion of the semiotic process of Marian figuration. Chaucer's *Man of Law's Tale* provides the opportunity to study connections between law, death and propriety while *The Wife of Bath's Prologue* and *Tale* illustrate the powerfully interconnected relationship between bodies and (pre-)texts and where each exceeds the other. The Middle English *Seinte Marherete*, found in two manuscripts dating from early in the thirteenth century, uses the metaphor of virgin motherhood, a trope with much currency in medieval Christianity, to reproduce faith. Finally, the interdependence of faith and matter, of Word and flesh, God and mother, provides me with a frame for investigating the effects of the formal and metonymic qualities of *Pearl* in making God apprehensible to the earthbound.

Stories of Mary's relation to law and her death share some striking resemblances to the *Man of Law's Tale* in which the heroine's death is narrated over and over again and yet never occurs. In Chapter 1, I begin by providing a framework for understanding the reinscriptions, fulfilments and substitutions that produce Mary's death as exemplary of narrative design moving towards a teleological, indeed eschatological, conclusion. In light of certain theoretical writings about death, including works by Elisabeth Bronfen, Jacques Derrida and Herbert Marcuse, I investigate the social uses and implications of death in general and stories about Mary's death more particularly. Her body is completely human, a fallen body – and must be if the Incarnation is to signify for humanity's salvation at all – yet her death is not a given in the church's systemic rhetoric. In fact, her death story grows with time,[19] predicted by the bodily assumptions of Enoch, Moses, Elijah and even her own son.[20] Even as it assumes miraculous qualities, her body and its passing take on an increasingly normalizing function as they become enmeshed in the Christian narrative of eternal salvation. What we will come to understand is the discursive existence of Mary's flesh, at once constrained by the prophecies of the Old Testament and the expectations of contemporary believers and yet still spilling over the boundaries placed by any single discourse of the church.

Like Mary's death story, told again and again, Constance's death recurs throughout the Man of Law's narration even though this heroine never dies. The potential for her death is one basis upon which the story works to sustain its sense of propriety in such matters as religious devotion, marriage and relation to one's society. Yet, the constant renarration of Constance's death illustrates the evanescent quality of the bulwark that sustains such propriety. In the same way that Mary's death legitimizes the Christian narrative while also ultimately confounding its closure, Constance's death (story) exemplifies the Man of Law's faith while haunting it with a filmy shadow that reminds us of how his logic produces his truths. This Man of Law's story of a woman is explicitly concerned with questions of law and yet the repeated narration and deferral of her death brings into question the precedent-based process of making law. With each example he employs to illustrate his laws, the errancy of figurative language is also brought into focus as each example suggests the infinite possibility of iteration and of rhetorical and cultural contexts without absolute anchor.[21] The Man of Law's logic of repetition becomes a shadow that darkens and permeates the narratively inscribed boundaries of Christianity and the narrator's sense of propriety. Thus, it is no wonder that Constance cannot be differentiated from her ghosts, the repetitions of the telling of her story. In this tale, the exemplary ghost that haunts Constance is the shadowy rhetorical strategy by which the Man of Law attempts to control his world. This Man *of* Law, indeed, belongs to the law and, further, is constituted by it and yet mistakes his rhetorical order for the fundamental order of the world.

Repetition, often self-aware and self-contradictory, provides the main investigative strategy for my reading of another work by Chaucer. In this second chapter, the distinction between texts and bodies is thrown into question by the Wife's intertextual life story. Even though this tale is remarkable for not mentioning the Holy Virgin's name, the stories of Mary and Alisoun nevertheless parallel each other in some revealing ways. Just as Mary represented a unique coincidence of flesh and spirit, human and divine law, body and word, the coincidence of texts constituting the character the 'Wife of Bath' calls to mind the discursive processes used by a society to describe itself and its members. Ultimately I suggest that the Wife and Mary reflect each other, or more precisely, the one acts like the negative for the other's photograph.

Additionally, the confusion and contradiction apparent in the Wife's prologue suggest a parodic strategy of self-definition, very similar to the idea of performativity posited by Judith Butler in *Gender Trouble*. The character of Alisoun is designed to show a marked awareness of contradictory roles that texts representative of mainstream culture and values call on her to perform. Several times she reminds her audience that her 'entente nys but for to pleye',[22] calling readers' attention to her performance and what might or might not be the difference between a serious life story and a staged, played-out one. At each moment when the Wife makes fun of what the 'oold' 'clerk[s]' say (fragment 3, line 707) or contradicts something she has just said, her words suggest the decontextualizing effects of even a staged or joking repetition of various discourses. Alisoun of Bath says things that her listening audience and, no doubt, much of her reading audience, would find patently ridiculous. But in putting forth her opinion, she uses rhetorical techniques of the pulpit, often preaching and providing exempla, both personal and biblical, to support the choices she has made about the way she lives her life. Similarly, she manifests much of the anti-feminist dogma against which she rails. Such contradictions in Alisoun's prologue highlight what Judith Butler might refer to as the performative structure of the church's position on gender.[23] This Wife reminds us not only of the social identity of gender but also and more interestingly of the social significance of bodies within her Christian culture. She reminds us of and interrogates the rules of her society that produce the most troubling of all signs – human bodies. She begins her prologue by setting experience and authority at odds and she manœuvres within a binary gender system. Yet her prologue destabilizes binary categories as it and her tale suggest polyvalent categories of gender and also of propriety by repeating and varying – playing with – standard, normative discourses of gender. In this way her words enter into social debate.

The belief in Mary's perpetual virginity and simultaneous mother-hood similarly pressures categories of existence and morality. The third chapter investigates the use of the paradox of the virgin mother in the reproduction of faith. Margaret, like Mary, was a virgin associated with childbirth. Margaret survives being eaten by a dragon while im-prisoned. Before being swallowed she makes the sign of the cross over her virgin body, an action that subsequently causes the dragon's stomach to burst open so that the saint can walk out unscathed. Many who witness this miracle are converted and borne into heaven by their newly found faith. Like all hagiographies, this thirteenth-century Middle English version of Margaret's life appropriates the suffering of a character for the purposes of reproducing faith. This plot element connected Margaret to medieval representations of birth – most specifically Caesarean birth – and during the period this virgin martyr was esteemed as a patroness of childbirth. Calling on Margaret's name during childbirth was also an avenue for calling on the power of God to protect one from pain and to prevent the child from being 'misbilimet' or deformed.[24]

Faith and faithful are reproduced and yet, in her torture, Margaret's story is one that is constituted by pain; prayers to her were employed, not after a happy birth, but in times of parturitive threat. This constant re-emergence of fleshiness in the figurations that reproduce faith must call our attention to the substitutional processes – substitutions of bodies one for another and of bodies for acts, gestures and texts and the faith they represent – that produce Margaret's story as exemplary of parturition, specifically and of ideal behaviour more generally. I bring to bear upon this investigation of bodies, the text of the Middle English redaction of the *De passionibus mulierum curandarum*, or the *English Trotula*, which provides insight into common, vernacular medical practice and presuppositions about women's bodies. The pain represented in this hagiography is one way by which medieval English Christianity participated in what Elaine Scarry calls 'world-making' throughout *The Body in Pain*.[25] In this vein I investigate the liminality of the painful body and of the reproductive, specifically the maternal, body and the ways in which this liminality legitimizes and divides Christian faith. Ultimately this chapter posits the idea that *Seinte Marherete* does two things simultaneously. It does what Gayle Margherita argues about hagiography in general: 'it represents the sacrifice of the feminine or feminized body that enables the transcendence of the *logos*, or, in Lacanian terms, of the paternal metaphor'.[26] Yet, the intertextuality of Margaret's story and its use in a parturitive arena suggest that the signifier 'Margaret's body' and physiology in general exist also somewhere outside (intersections of) discourse. Seeing this fleshy, intertextual excess we must additionally recognize that any truth this signifier claims to hold must be, must always have been, dispersed in an unknowable web of semiotic practices, lost moments of time and forever-decaying bits of flesh.

Finally, the interdependence of faith and matter, of Word and flesh, of God and mother, provides me with a frame for investigating the effects of the repetition and formal qualities of *Pearl* in making God apprehensible to the earthbound. This final chapter explores the obvious logic of metaphor employed in the poem, a logic enabled by an underlying, concomitant logic of metonymy. The poem teaches its readers to look for this metonymy, which is also a logic of contiguity, and to understand it as predicative of the Christian logic of dualism that would set soul and body at odds. *Pearl* uses changes to and varied perspectives on the eponymous jewel to instruct readers about the powers of repetition and variation of tropes in naming the unnameable. The recapitulative form of the poem, reflecting the perfect roundness of the pearl itself, the hundreds of pearls and pearl maidens that suffuse the poem and the ultimate view of the New Jerusalem, reflecting so closely the ultimate biblical vision of heaven in Revelation, all indicate a belief in the plenitude of heaven and a human metaphorical relation to it. In the same way that Mary was corporeally assumed into heaven to be its queen, perfect in body and soul, the Pearl

maiden reigns in heaven as 'quene by cortaysye',[27] 'wemlez' or
'immaculate' (737). But the chapter also investigates ways in which the
sublation of Mary remains incomplete and the ways in which,
similarly, the Pearl maiden reminds the narrator and the careful reader
of that which lies outside the salvational narrative, of myriad other
public and private narratives, overdetermined and ever present. As the
poem comes to rely more and more heavily on the image of the pearl in
representing the ineffable, the pearl remains immaculate and regal, but
with shifts in context the image changes. The chapter focuses on some
of these shifts as a way to investigate the poem's presentation of
differences within discursively constructed categories of the same. In
this way, the chapter provides some insight into the poem's self-
reflexive awareness of the limits of metaphorical categorization in
recreating the plenitude of heaven.

Such a reflexive attitude marks both *Pearl* and *The Wife of Bath's
Prologue* and *Tale*, whereas the Man of Law and Teochimus, the
narrator of *Seinte Marherete*, present tales much more invested in
maintaining dominant ideologies of Christian virtue. As this project
alternates between investigations of texts that are markedly self-
reflexive and those that are less so, it provides various avenues for
understanding the intricate nature of the relationship between texts
and bodies, particularly feminized bodies and texts concerned with the
rules of cultural identity. What we will come to realize is a tendency
towards categorization in general, and binarism more specifically, in
medieval Christianity's search for identity: inappropriate/appropriate,
sin/salvation, evil/good, mundane/transcendent, woman/man, Eve/
Mary, to name but a few with which this project grapples. Yet more
revealing is the careful investigation of specific moments of transgression of categorical boundaries in particular texts and contexts and
the import of such sites of permeability.

By examining texts that profess respect for the dominant ideologies of
the Middle Ages and those that overtly challenge it, *Shadows of Mary*
is situated in such a way that it can provide insight into discourses
that we take for granted about the period, that presently dominate our
understanding and seem to have had a similar effect on medieval
readers. Each chapter highlights aspects of cultural concern that
continue to captivate our attention: the social employment of death, the
semiotics of sexuality and maternity and the potential and pitfalls of
figuration itself as embodiment. At the same time, this book provides a
way to understand the limits of those discourses. Its focus on gender and

figuration foregrounds what Teresa de Lauretis calls in *Technologies of Gender* 'the constant slippage between Woman as representation, as the object and very condition of representation and . . . women as historical beings'.[28] The practice of reading for the cooperation and tensions between these poles, and the practice of reading the contingencies of a culture on a larger scale, opens a space within theology and ideology. By refusing to allow the semiotic processes of culture to be repressed, this space confronts the idea of truth as a form external to specific moments in history, particular applications of language and singular conglomerations of flesh and subjectivity. Mary is a mother, a virgin, a wife, a lover, a slut, a priestly figure, a queen, a body, a soul; just like the literary characters that reflect her, Mary's textual existence is rife with paradoxes. The contrary space that surrounds this woman is often taken for granted but constitutes the material on and from which a belief system was built.

1

Shadows of the Law:
Death in *The Man of Law's Tale*

Part of the Christian context of the Man of Law's story of Constance is the body of Marian imagery so popular in the Middle Ages. Mary is never far away in this story of a woman's trials and triumphs. Constance suffers forced marriages, murders of friends and attempted rape but ultimately triumphs in her faith, converting others along the way. She lives up to her name in all ways: she is constant in her devotion to her God, steady in her emotions and faithful to the people in her life. This behaviour is one way in which she is like the Holy Virgin Mary, the ultimate example of female virtue in the period.

But the parallels between the two women run deeper – to the level of narrative strategy – in a way that can call to our attention some disturbing implications of the Man of Law's exemplary mode. As it presents an example of ideal behaviour, *The Man of Law's Tale* represents Constance, as well as her mothers-in-law, via metaphors of death. The ghosts of these women reveal the limits of the Man of Law's precedent-based narrative strategy in controlling its world.[1] However, before we turn to an investigation of the links between narrative and death in this Man of Law's recounting, we need to consider how Mary's story came to be one increasingly concerned with law, human and divine. In the crossings, reinscriptions, fulfilments and substitutions that produce Marian devotion and through which it is enacted, we can begin to see the divisiveness of figuration that must confound narrative closure.[2]

The Middle Ages produced Mary's body in specifically legal, narrative ways. Her corporeal relation to law was one of prophecy and its fulfilment. By the thirteenth century it was common to see representations of her reading Isaiah 7:14, the prophecy of her own life: 'Behold a virgin shall conceive and bear a son and his name shall be called Emmanuel.' Growing from apocryphal stories of her childhood,[3] beliefs arose which held her to have been learned in Jewish law and the seven liberal arts. Representations of her education, in turn, fed the tenet that only as a woman aware of the (pre-)text of her own life and responsibilities in salvational law is she qualified to conceive (of) Christ.[4]

Mary's conception was similarly constrained by prophecy, by the double-natured position the human *specula sine macula*[5] must hold if the salvational process is to be effective. The doctrine of the Immaculate Conception, made official dogma only in 1854,[6] began with the *Protevangelium*'s description of Anna and Joachim's miraculous procreativity.[7] The book begins by relating the story of how the couple is kept from participating in religious rites due to their barrenness. In grief, Joachim exiles himself to the mountains and Anna begins to pray while walking in her garden. An angel appears to her saying 'the Lord hath hearkened unto thy prayer and thou shalt conceive and bear and thy seed shall be spoken of in the whole world' (4:1). At the same time, an angel visits Joachim and tells him to come home because his wife will conceive. The two meet and chastely embrace at the gate of Jerusalem. This moment was widely recreated in pictorial images in churches and books and became the representation of Mary's conception, Giotto's fourteenth-century images in the Scrovegni Chapel in Padua being prime examples.[8] The eastern church celebrated this day with a feast as early as the tenth century, while such a celebration was first known in England just before the Norman conquest,[9] held at two important churches, Canterbury and Winchester.[10] In the twelfth century, however, Bernard of Clairvaux brought up the main objection to celebrating a human's conception: doing so goes directly against dogma in that it has the potential to be a celebration of concupiscence. Bernard had previously addressed a similar issue when his concern arose over the feast celebrating the Virgin's birth. Only one other saint, John the Baptist, received such an honour. According to the Gospel of Luke, John's intra-uterine sanctification marked him as specially blessed and 'replenished with the Holy Ghost even from his mother's womb' (1:15). Bernard assumed – logically, as a good Neoplatonist would – that God would give to his own mother the same blessing.[11]

The history of disputation over these topics pointedly illustrates the process by which the period manufactured the Virgin Mary. That the question of the holiness of her birth was decided before that concerning her conception indicates a recursive process that attempts to write history to match popular and theological standards. However, Bernard remained firm in his belief that Mary was released from original sin only when God became incarnate within her, not at her own conception. In fact, throughout the period many scholastics and theologians were of the same opinion as the master of Clairvaux, but the feast was so popular that eventually doctrine caught up with practice.

The resulting doctrinal explanation is a mixture of scholasticism and mysticism. The scholastic part describes a notion of two conceptions, the natural and the spiritual. The first is the process by which the organism is materially put together. The second, called the 'animation', occurs when the soul unites itself to the flesh of the embryo and is the ultimate goal of conception. Since the notion of a soul pure from birth would not challenge the church's doctrine of original sin, this scientific view allowed Mary to be born pure in body and soul, the former having been purified by the latter at the moment of animation.[12] This scientific, scholastic view dovetailed with the already popular festival, which itself was based upon and further fostered the idea that Mary had been conceived during Anna and Joachim's chaste embrace at the gate. By the thirteenth century, believers embraced the idea of the *Praeredemptio*, or the 'Preredemption'. This theology took for granted that original sin was something inherent in the soul and not necessarily the body and so God must have made an exception when providing his mother with a soul; or, in Marina Warner's words, 'As the perfect intercessor and the perfect filial son, Jesus could hardly have failed to obtain moral purity for his Mother.'[13] Indeed, this notion of prevention of sin in Mary enhanced the mediation and sacrifice of Christ since preventing illness is better than having to cure it once it has occurred.

Popular literature and its accompanying images reinforce the notion of a sinless Mary and take it one step further to remove concupiscence from her conception. The image of Joachim and Anna's meeting at the gate is often paired with images of the Annunciation of Gabriel to Mary, marking the understanding of both incidents as moments of conception as well as greeting. A common iconographical represent-ation of the Annunciation contained the Christ child in body or soul, often already within the Virgin's body.[14] In *The Sacred Shrine: A Study of the Poetry and Art of the Catholic Church*, Yrjö Hirn describes a similar fifteenth-century Italian picture of Anna and Joachim at the gate. In this image the couple embraces as a small female figure clad in white, Mary, approaches them.[15] Such an illustration suggests the common belief that Mary was conceived with a loving and blessed hug.

The logic of such arguments illustrates how the body of Mary was a vehicle for salvational law, which it simultaneously represented and legitimized for the purpose of Christian narrative. Her body as representative of the fallen human condition reveals the purpose of salvational law, while her exceptional circumstances underscore the promise of the law's fulfilment in the Incarnation of Christ. Similarly, in Mary's role as the fleshly portion of the Incarnation, contradiction is written over so that law may be fulfilled. However, as is evident in texts as various as apocryphal works, theological writings and cycle dramas, at the same time that contradictions are elided, anxieties remain, revealed in the very law meant to transcend them. Thus, the evident anxiety over Mary's conception finds a parallel in the threat that the Incarnation poses to the discursively established boundaries of the human body.

Mary's place in a human law that protects such boundaries was questioned as early as the apocryphal works that describe her life prior to marrying Joseph. The Gospel of Pseudo-Matthew underscores her unique status, saying that 'Mary had vowed virginity' (chapter 8) whereas the other virgins of the temple were to be married when they came to be of age. Yet because of Levitical law, she has to leave the temple and be married so that her menstruating body cannot 'pollute the temple of the Lord' (*Protevangelium*, 8:2). Despite her vow of virginity, she must live under Levitical laws because her body is exemplary, a typical female's.[16] In the Middle Ages, when these Judaic proscriptions moved from the realm of law into the realms of philosophy, theology and science, the menses were understood as the formless matter of the world waiting to be shaped by the semen, the pure male form, containing the image of God. Menstruation becomes, then, the sign of excess, of matter not given form. As such it is a mark of Eve's original sin, a bodily defect *all* women inherit – one that produces their typical inferior status. All this, in turn, was supported and made material by empirical data and medical advice. For instance, couples who wished to have children were advised to have intercourse during the week after the woman's period when the menses would be as fresh as possible and more likely to take the form that the semen carried.[17]

So, like the other virgins in the temple, Mary had to leave when she began menstruating. According to the Gospel of Pseudo-Matthew, Joseph was not even meant to be Mary's husband, but only a protector for her (chapter 8). The *Protevangelium* is not so clear on what role Joseph was chosen to play in Mary's life. However, the text's repeated description of her as one of the 'pure virgins of the tribe of David' (10:1) and Joseph's own confusion over how to record Mary under Augustus's decree – as wife or daughter (17:1) – suggest that Mary did not leave the temple to become Joseph's wife. Again, these contentions illustrate Mary's unique relation to the law as it developed through the period. She is the exemplary outcome of prophecy and the instigation of yet further prophecy, but she also creates confusion in the worldly functioning of the very laws that she is meant to exemplify.

The *N-Town* cycle drama focuses on Mary – her conception, birth and life – in much more detail than do other English cycles.[18] In the *N-Town*, the confusion over law is evident when Mary finds herself between church law and a vow to God:

> A-ȝens þe lawe wyl I nevyr be
> But mannys felachep xal nevyr folwe me
> I wyl levyn evyr in chastyté
> Be þe grace of goddys wylle.[19]

(I will never be against the law but the fellowship of man shall never follow me; I will live ever in chastity, by the grace of God's will.)

Here Mary expresses knowledge of her place within salvational law and strives to protect it. This knowledge intimates the story of her parents' barrenness, their petition to the Lord, her miraculous conception, her birth and the fulfilment of the vows accompanying her parents' petition when she was brought to the temple to become *the* model of 'Clennesse *and* chastyte' (l. 70). I quote the bishop's response to Mary's words at length (ll. 79–91) because it represents so fully the troubling confusion over how to make sense of the extraordinary set of circumstances related to this young woman:

> A mercy god þese wordys wyse
>   Of þis fayr made clene
> Thei trobyl myn hert in many wyse –
>   Her wytt is grett and þat is sene!

> In clennes to levyn in godys servise
> No man here blame, non here tene
> And ʒit in lawe þus it lyce,
> Þat such weddyd xulde bene.
>   Who xal expownd þis oute?
>   Þe lawe doth after lyff of clennes;
>   Þe lawe doth bydde such mayndenes expres
>   Þat to spowsyng they xulde hem dres.
> God help us in þis dowhte.

(God's mercy on the wise words of this fair, clean maiden; they trouble my heart in many ways. Her wit is great as anyone can see! In cleanness to live in God's service – no one can blame her or her troubles. And yet the law goes thus: That such young women should be wedded. Who shall explain this? The law is about a life of cleanness; the law bids such maidens as these to address themselves to getting married. God help us in this doubt.)

Mary's very existence brings doubt into a system of law, a system in which she is remarkably a key term both as a human and as the mother of God. The passage suggests the common medieval belief that Mary was aware of her place in salvational history. Twice the bishop remarks upon the young woman's intelligence (ll. 79 and 82) and on the aptness of her words in that no man can blame someone for wanting to live a holy life (l. 84). Yet the law says maidens must marry 'after lyff of clennes' (a statement that will affect Constance in some very revealing ways also). The 'trobyl' arises in the question of which law to follow, for the passage points out the anagogical incompatibility between ways of making meaning. The bishop simply does not know how to deal with a wise, clean woman who wishes to live a holy life. Neither empirical experience nor law provides him with a context for making sense of this situation. Ultimately, the bishop must call for divine intervention to solve the interpretative dilemma that he faces in the example of Mary. An angel appears and, in the following scenes, the elderly Joseph is chosen as Mary's husband when his wooden staff begins to bloom.

Mary, however, is conspicuously absent for the next 200 lines. Sense is made of her and for her through articulation of various discourses – from the announcement of the messenger to all people about what is to be done, to Joseph's embarrassment over the social impropriety of taking a young wife; from the characters *generacionis David* that remind Joseph of his proper place and responsibilities in patrilineal descent, to the mysticism of the moment when the dead wood begins to bloom. She and her 'wordys wyse' and great 'wytt' disappear and are replaced by the very production of faith of which she is the prime marker. This production is characterized by a specific gendered and generational emphasis, which is ironically taken out of Mary's hands only to be laid at her feet. Narratological production under the guise of divine grace replaces and then recreates who Mary is and what she signifies.

As the bishop finds, the medieval concept of Mary proves troubling in part because Mary was closely associated with texts that were held to presage her life. Even before the bishop begins to deal with her, her life story consists of traces of law, prophecy, texts and writings. Considering Mary's biography in relation to a passage from Alan of Lille's *Plaint of Nature* (written sometime between 1160 and 1172), describing the Neoplatonic version of how the goddess Nature creates human beings, reveals a striking difference between ideal notions of identity and Mary's vestigial existence: 'with the aid of a reed-pen, the maiden [Nature] called up various images by drawing on slate tablets. The picture, however, did not cling closely to the underlying material but, quickly fading and disappearing, left no trace of the impression behind' (Prose 2).[20] Notice how the ideas expressed in the above quotation protect the notions of absolute presence and self-identity both of created and of creator, whereas Mary's life story is beginning to suggest that such unity is only apparent. And so the *N-Town* bishop is bound to find that underlying the apparent unity of medieval Christianity is an untraceable web of often contradictory intentions, readings and contexts. The troubling consequences of this situation, which are evident in medieval attempts to eliminate confusion from the narratives of the Immaculate Conception and the Incarnation, show up as well in medieval representations of the relation between Mary and Eve.

Mary shares a unique relationship with Eve. That Mary righted humanity and femininity with her actions was a popular trope in the Middle Ages, present in learned writings and popular literature. Mary changed 'Eva' – the first defect of the flesh – to the 'Ave' of blessing and faith. By thus 'turnand þe name of eve again' – 'turning the name of Eve again,'[21] – Mary represents the original and continuing need for salvation as well as the promise and fulfilment of salvational law. The unity broken by one woman is recreated through another.

The medieval reading of Eve's sin and, indeed, of her very coming into being connects her with a loss of the literal, with the process of naming things that is also a turning away from things. Adam, the first human, is a sexless creature hardly differentiated from its surroundings, clay pulled from the earth by Jahweh and enlivened by Jahweh's divine breath. Made in the image of God to mirror his reason and love,[22] the first human's relationship with God and the book of creation is one of unity, exact expression and replication. In direct line from its creator, it possesses form, idea, substance, being, singularity, 'oneness'.[23] However, 'if Adam is the first namer, associated with a language that is unified, perfectly expressive of intent or spirit, Eve is associated with fallen language . . . with division, difference, fragmentation and dispersal that characterize the condition of historical language'.[24] In contrast to that of the first human, the second human's relationship to its god is one of contingency, derivation, accident, supplement, helper. The second human is the inexactitude of duplication. Philo Judaeus (c.30 BC–AD 45) gives an early example of what was to become a widespread and virtually transparent mode of describing the relationship between the genders:

> But since no created thing is constant, and things mortal are necessarily liable to changes and reverses, it could not but be that the first man too should experience some ill fortune. And woman becomes for him the beginning of a blameworthy life. For so long as he was by himself . . . he went on growing . . . like God.[25]

The writers of the fifteenth-century treatise on witchcraft, the *Malleus Maleficarum*, describe woman's formation as follows: 'And it should be noted that there was a defect in the formation of the first woman, since she was formed from a bent rib . . . bent as it were in a contrary direction to man.'[26] This passage presents a typical Christian outgrowth of hierarchical Platonic duality fostered in the early church. Earlier, Paul had set the stage for such readings, echoing the Genesis creation myth in a collocation of language, bodily activity and supplementarity:

> Let a woman learn in silence with all submissiveness. I permit no woman to teach or to have authority over men; she is to keep silent. For Adam was formed first, then Eve; and Adam was not deceived, but the woman was deceived and became a transgressor. Yet woman will be saved through bearing children. (1 Timothy 2:9–15)

In other words, Eve's sin has to do with both her apparent inability to comprehend words and her facility in using them on another. And it is this use that culminates in sexual and nominal differentiation generally in the world, for when the first humans eat some fruit from the tree of knowledge of good and evil, 'the eyes of both were opened and they knew that they were naked' (Genesis 3:7). The superfluity – which is the danger – of Eve's words to Adam culminates in the awareness of sexual difference and the no-longer-superfluous addition of clothing. Philo distinguishes between the Adam of the first chapter of Genesis and the Adam of the second chapter who has fallen 'from innocence and simplicity of character to all kinds of wickedness.'[27] Again, Eve is responsible for man's movement – in language and clothing – further from unity with the book of creation.

Yet Eve's very entrance into the world was 'fallen' in this sense because her relationship to God was always one of derivation, supplement and 'helper'.[28] She never had the one-to-one connection to God with which Adam was privileged. As R. Howard Bloch asserts: 'her coming into being is synonymous . . . with a loss – within language – of the literal . . . [T]he creation of woman is synonymous with the creation of metaphor.'[29] The second human is the inexactitude of duplication, something said again, though said differently, something said 'in other words'. She is the corporeal copy of the incorporeality of truth, much as language copies ideas as Augustine intimates in his *Confessions*.[30] She is the trope, the turning away, that Mary must re-turn through spotless reflection of the divine. Indeed, Gail McMurry Gibson argues, 'the cult of the Virgin is about the meaning – and the sensuously evocative power – of words and images'.[31]

The collocations, in other words, between woman's original nature and the nature of her original sin are even more insidious. As a copy, her language cannot contain the one-to-one correlations that the first human's had and so her language marks the loss within that original language. Her sin with the serpent, then, becomes one of language, misinterpreted, missed, an attempt at communication from outside the unity that the garden is supposed to hold for Adam. And this sin becomes located in her body – eating of the tree of knowledge leads to knowledge of sexual differentiation. Adam's paradisaical unity is split by the defective, deficient copy of his body, of his intellect, of his soul and he enters the world of toil and constant (Neoplatonic) struggle to regain what he once had[32] through activities at least one step removed from those he had enjoyed in the garden: he now must toil to make the soil produce his existence, instead of merely tending the garden and receiving the direct blessings given him by God. Only Adam will remember this prior unity and suffer the full consequences of its loss, of course, because Eve never enjoyed anything but a mediated relationship to her creator.

Therefore, according to the typical medieval reading, as such an imperfect extrapolation from the first human, woman seems fated from inception to be a threat to paradisaical unity. Yet the desire present in the Garden of Eden even before the second human's wish to eat of the fruit of knowledge indicates that the narrative unity of the garden is not the transcendent, natural creation that materializes in the corpus of Christian history. Instead we see a series of substitutions. 'It is not good that the man should be alone' declares God, and begins to make the animals, and then 'The man gave names to all cattle and to the birds of the air and to every beast of the field; but for the man there was not found a helper fit for him' (Genesis 2:18 and 20). This story posits a God whose world is not complete – therefore he makes the earth – but the story immediately writes over this incompleteness by displacing it on to the human. The perfection of the unfallen garden is shown to be a myth by Adam's desire, which is an indication of lack. This incompleteness is then displaced on to and creates the inferiority of Eve. So even in this supposedly unsullied original – Adam – lies the potential to produce the inexactly copied second human. Eve and her tempter are blamed for what is revealed in this reading to be a pre-existing narrative condition. The serpent marks a mimetic break in the creation myth, similar to Eve's. The first human is given dominion over all creatures on earth (Genesis 1:28 and 2:20), yet the serpent still represents a threat. Described as 'more subtle than any other wild creature that the Lord God had made' (Genesis 3:1), the serpent represents the seductive power of nature, the plurality of context. And again, the threat here lies in language: Eve claims that the serpent 'beguiled' her, causing her to eat the fruit (Genesis 3:13).[33] Even in paradise the traces of language are uncontrollable.

Indeed, here we see the connection between law and accident, for the misrepresentations that produce the Fall become the very structure upon which the whole of salvational law is founded. Mary as the turning of Eve and product of the law is the result of this accident. The Holy Virgin comes to represent lack, desire and the basis of uncontrollability out of which ostensibly positive concepts, like God's grace, power and love for humanity, grew. We begin to see that the opposition between Mary and Eve, good and evil, text and body, is more appositional and interdependent than the Christian ethic of transcendence suggests.

The conjunction of the Annunciation and the Incarnation is one place where the confusion that still persists in Mary's restoration of Eve becomes apparent. Countless images in the early church reflect the belief that these two events happened simultaneously,[34] and by the time of Chaucer's early translation of Guillaume de Deguilleville's 'La Priere de Nostre Dame', it had found its way into popular literature. Chaucer writes in praise of the Virgin in his abecedarius that 'the Holi Gost thee soughte / Whan Gabrielles vois cam to thin ere' (ll. 114–15). Additionally, Hirn cites several poems that refer to Gabriel as 'seminiverbius'. St Bernard's (1090–1153) *Sermo II in festo Pentecostes* provides yet another example:

> missus est interim Gabriel angelus a Deo, ut verbum patris per aurem virginis in ventrem et mentem ipsius eructaret, ut eadem via intraret antidotum, qua venenum intraverat.

> (In the mean time, the angel Gabriel was sent by God that he, himself, might emit the word of the father through the virgin's ear into her womb and mind, so that by that way by which the poison had entered, the antidote might enter.)

This passage uses the typological connection between Eve and Mary in order to institute again the divine symmetry of Mary's turning the name of Eve. But as Genesis suggests its own narrative-dependent status, the passage indicates that it is the word itself that is dangerous, that has in it the power to kill and heal. The danger of the word is simultaneously its potential, as *venenum* and *antidotum* enter in the same way;[35] and this figuring of language is at once supplemented and supplanted by the female figures in the narrative. Eve is written as body in the creation myth and this begins the narrative of salvational law; Mary's body is written as prophecy, stemming from Eve's sin and is the outcome and fulfilment of law; and so in the narrative design that conjoins these figures, the body of each figure must be divided by the other and made subject to linguistic and exemplary confusion. Assigned the place of accident, mistake, defect, Eve is the predication of law, while Mary is the figure whom divine law has created but human law as iteration of divine cannot control. The inverted double of Eve's, Mary's body is figuratively the result of accident, of the misinterpretation of words, even as its unique status is paradoxically created by standard repetitions of words. The Annunciation repeats the beguiling of Eve in Eden and the word changes from evil to divine and yet, in this very repetition, we can begin to see a divisiveness in words, texts, bodies and cultural histories that must vex all tellings of this narrative.

These confounding narrative complexities, which point to the limits of any narrative construction of character, can be understood still more fully by turning to the example of Chaucer's Constance, who is so crucially concerned with the question of law. Explicitly and implicitly, Constance shares with her mothers-in-law, the Sultaness and Donegild, a relationship similar to that which Mary shares with Eve, that of the inverted double. Constance prays to Mary (2. 841–54) and to the cross (2. 451–62) and the text also represents her with imagery familiar to Marian devotion.[36] The Man of Law's tale invokes other similarities: he narrates Constance's death over and over as he attempts to substantiate the virtues he holds dear. As Carolyn Dinshaw very aptly points out, Constance is first introduced into the tale as narrative: 'She exists as a tale of a virgin'[37] circulated by the 'commune voys' (2. 155), constructed via discourse very much as Mary had been. As with the story of Mary, this drama's main character is made what she needs to be:

> In hire is heigh beautee, withoute pride,
> Yowthe, withoute grenehede or folye;
> To alle hire werkes vertu is hir gyde;
> Humblesse hath slayn in hire al tirannye.
> She is mirour of alle curteisye;
> Hir herte is verray chambre of hoolynesse,
> Hir hand, ministre of fredam for almesse [generosity in giving].
>
> (2. 162–8)

These lines could easily be about the Holy Virgin, who is variously described as the most spacious chamber that could hold the unholdable God, as a mirror of virtue (by Ambrosius) and as the prettiest but most humble maiden in any context.[38] Such orthodoxy has led many scholars to assume Constance's passivity. Modern readers tend to view Mary as passive.[39] Similarly Carolyn Dinshaw calls Constance, via Lévi-Strauss, a commodity passed around among men, a blank page waiting for signification.[40] In a Bakhtinian reading, Juliette Dor describes Constance as 'single-voiced', repeating 'monological discourses without ever expecting a reply', and as obedient to the omniscient voice of God, represented on earth by her father and others who control her life, in the same way that Mary was controlled by earthly parents and God.[41] Dor's intention in drawing this comparison between Constance and the Holy Virgin is to illustrate just how traditional and passive Constance is. By recalling these likenesses, the Man of Law invokes the propriety of the law in its relation to storytelling in an attempt to establish firm categories of good and evil, categories that cannot be 'pynche[d]' (1. 326).

On the evil side, the Man of Law indicts the Sultaness and Donegild in typically misogynistic terms, connecting them with their originally sinful ancestor. The Sultaness has her own son and everyone in his wedding party, except Constance, killed on the wedding night. For this crime, the Man of Law disparages the Sultaness in two ways: by saying she is a 'feyned womman' (2. 362) and by saying she is just like a woman. He calls her a 'serpent under femynynytee' (2. 360) or a snake in women's clothes and 'Eva' the 'instrument' of 'Sathan' (2. 368, 370, 365). These metaphors recall the orthodox medieval misogynistic reading of the fall. The woman is associated with the costume and tool of evil. She is associated with secondary nature; here she is even secondary to evil. In effect, she is metaphor itself and as such she recalls the fallibility of the human flesh, that tissue of flesh, the 'robe' and 'wede'[42] that Mary gave to Jesus in order to make manifest the Trinity. Even Mary's long-lasting procreative effects are mirrored in this curse's 'al that may confounde / Vertue and innocence . . . / Is bred in thee' (2. 362–4). And this breeding is why humanity has been 'chaced from [its] heritage' (2. 366).

The use of 'confounde' is pointed here: meaning to mix or pour together, it describes a process in which discrete elements are combined to become something different. From this sense arises the more metaphorical one of 'confused' or 'confusing'. And what is confounding in this sense is that the passage reminds us of its own metaphoricity even as it demonizes figuration. Thus, the contradiction of the Sultaness being both a feigned woman *and* a woman just like Eve evidences the structure and the structural limits of this system of making meaning; the curse brings into relief the confounding limits of narrative construction that were made evident in arguments over Mary's conception and the Incarnation. The emphasis on procreation, heritage and marriage (2. 369) – in Chaucer's understanding of their use and misuse – underscores the many overdetermined elements of cultural heritage caught up in this narrative and the tenuous nature of the exemplary outcome that Constance represents. The foregoing passage attempts to assert logical control over its figurative terms in order to apply them to its purpose – the curse of the Sultaness. Yet it points to its own failure by calling up the name of Eve and her connection to metaphor.

Similarly, the Man of Law curses Donegild. Donegild's jealousy over her son's marriage to Constance leads the older woman to counterfeit letters about the birth of the couple's child. Upon receiving these letters saying that his wife – described as 'an elf' – has given birth to 'a feendly creature' (2. 754 and 751), Alla writes back to Constance saying that he loves her and the child and that he will 'Welcome the sonde [dispensation] of Crist for everemoore' since he is 'now lerned in [Christ's] loore' (2. 760 and 761). But Donegild intercepts this letter as well and counterfeits another one in Alla's name, indicating that Constance and her son should be exiled on the same ship in which she arrived. In his curse of this woman, the Man of Law claims to have no 'Englissh digne' ('English appropriate'; 2. 778), to speak of her sin; only the 'feend' can 'enditen' her (2. 780 and 781). The verb 'endite' here has specific legal connotations but also suggests the process of storytelling.[43] In the *Monk's Tale* (l. 3858, group B numbering) it carries the weight of 'accuse', as it does here; but in other usages in Chaucer, 'to endite' is to compose, transitively or intransitively. It is a verb that suggests writing, describing, relating, drafting, telling. Indeed, an 'inditing' is a composition or the style of a composition.[44] Given this, the use of 'enditen' here illustrates a particular crossing of the boundary lines between law and literature, a legal 'caas' and a poem. The Man of Law, however, seems unaware of such similarities since he claims he has no tale to tell, as if every case he knows since the time of William the Conqueror (1. 323–4) is not also a story. As the verb 'endite' suggests here, exemplarity is a strategy law shares with poetry. The Man of Law's own prefatory remarks are evidence of this connection as he serves as Chaucer's own copyright representative, listing works of the poet and providing synopses of some.[45] His tale itself is a repetition of one he heard from others (2. 132) and yet with the context of the word that can be both poison and remedy – which is the Eve/Mary binary – brought to bear upon this story and its telling, even the most standard repetition of law and the notion of transcendence upon which it operates cannot remain untouched.

The Man of Law's curse of Donegild also suggests something more, something revealing about the function of law as the teller of this tale understands it. The narrator claims to have no language to match the crime he sees before him. Because Donegild's sin mirrors Eve's in many ways, he does not want to own her as a character in his tale; his language cannot even speak of her. Only the devil seems to have the words and the laws to fit the crime. Though the fiend, ruler of what is evil, was understood in the period to be ruler of nothing, a negative, non-productive deficiency,[46] he still has the potential to make law. Indeed, Satan has the power to indict Donegild, to make her into a criminal; that is, to write her character as a traitor (2. 781). In the figurations of his curse, the Man of Law gives over the power of creation to that which he would damn.

Donegild's sin is that her hand wrote the letter that caused her daughter-in-law and grandchild to be exiled. Thus, she disseminated 'al the venym of this cursed dede' (2. 890 and 891), recalling the association of this imagery with Eve's sin. Furthermore, the insinuation of a character from outside the narrator's frame of reference – that is, escaping his ability to recount – reminds us of the confounding unreliability of that frame. But the Man of Law makes her fit into his story; that is, he finds English to talk about her and his sentence for her is death. But in sentencing her he cannot help but show the disturbing traces of other stories, their threat and potential. The fact that Donegild is, herself, a creative writer of sorts similarly illustrates this principle.

In such resolutions we witness the normalizing and naturalizing functions of narrative. The Man of Law uses Constance's reactions to these various situations to reinstitute Christian laws and mores and to provide the 'mirour' (2. 166) of Christianity to extra-narrative threats. For instance, early in the story the Sultaness defends her own religion, saying,

> But oon avow to grete God I heete,
> The lyf shal rather out of my body sterte
> Or Makometes lawe out of myn herte!
>
> What sholde us tyden of this newe lawe
> But thraldom to oure bodies and penance,
> And afterward in helle to be drawe,
> For we reneyed Mahoun oure creance? (2. 334–40)

With its emphasis on religion as law, this passage echoes an earlier one in which the Sultan discusses with his lords how best to obtain Constance as his bride. The Muslim fellowship recognizes the

'diversitee / Bitwene [the] lawes' (2. 220–1) of their faith and the
Christian one. But by the time that the Sultaness has been cursed and
Constance begins to pray[47] to the cross, the narrative claims that there
is 'No wight but God' and 'No wight but Crist, sanz faille' (2. 476 and
501) who can know the secrets of the universe. All the other 'laws' are
erased and subsumed. The Muslim laws and believers become the
vehicle of legitimization for the Christian ethic. The lines that present
the story of Constance's time among the Muslims (2. 211–504) recreate
the misogyny and the racial, or 'heritage-centred', anti-sociality of the
creation myth. In this way, these lines pose a threat to the narratively
established boundaries of Christianity, even as the narrative and
heroine remain examples of the Man of Law's faith.

Similarly, as the tale describes Constance's dealings with Donegild,
the Man of Law's narrative concerns make apparent the self-contradictory construction of the exemplary Christian figure of Constance.
On her way to Alla's kingdom, Constance launches into a prayer to the
Holy Virgin as her rudderless ship is launched to sea:

> 'Mooder,' quod she, 'and mayde bright, Marie,
> Sooth is that thrugh wommanes eggement
> Mankynde was lorn and damned ay to dye,
> For which thy child was on a croys yrent.' (2. 841–4)

Like many commonplace prayers to the Virgin, this one calls on
the paradox of Mary's being both 'mooder' and 'mayde'. With her
repetition of this prayer, Constance is once again allied with Mary and
seemingly set apart from Eve, the woman through whom 'Mankynde
was lorn'. Yet the Man of Law's concern earlier in the text over how
'ful hooly' wives (2. 709) are required to lay a little of their 'hoolynesse
aside' (2. 713) in the marriage bed recalls and rewrites Donegild's
earlier concern over her son taking 'So strange a creature' as his mate
(2.700). The full passage reads as follows:

> They goon to bedde, as it was skile and right;
> For thogh that wyves be ful hooly thynges,
> They moste take in pacience at nyght
> Swiche manere necessaries as been plesynges
> To folk that han ywedded hem with rynges,
> And leye a lite hir hoolynesse aside,
> As for the tyme – it may no bet bitide. (2. 708–14)

The passage intimates a network of different and contradictory discourses which the Man of Law tries to negotiate. The impetus behind this desire for normalization is matched by that over the nature of Joseph and Mary's marriage.[48]

Even though the belief in Mary as eternally spotless never wavered,[49] her sexuality was incorporated into canon-law disputes over marriage in the twelfth and thirteenth centuries. Since Mary was both the perpetually virginal mother of God and a human wife, consequently she became the centre of debates over what constitutes a valid marital bond and came to exemplify a definition of marriage based largely on legalities of consent and not copulation. In the same way the Man of Law attempts to harmonize sexuality and spirituality, many medieval definitions of marriage attempted to develop definitions of marriage that would allow for valorization of both human sexuality and spiritual union. Penny S. Gold and Dyan Elliott collect and explore several of the most influential arguments concerning Mary and Joseph's marriage which, despite their many differences, illustrate the normalizing influence of Christian rhetoric. Such a rhetoric uses as its supports legal, philosophical and scientific discourses. The information that Gold and Elliott collect illustrates the difficulties in, and various results of, trying to find a definition of marriage for the holy couple.

Augustine took a secular approach based on Roman free marriage, a private agreement between individuals in which consummation was not even necessary: 'In line with this secular framework, Augustine distinguished between the end of marriage (which is procreation) and the essence of marriage, which is the agreement between the spouses.'[50] He argued further that the bond between husband and wife in a marriage that is chaste is stronger because the partners are connected by affection and agreement, not carnality.[51] Ultimately he argued that Joseph and Mary were the prime example of spiritual marriage because they had all three of the 'goods' of marriage: harnessing of post-lapsarian concupiscence; faith, or sexual fidelity; and indissolubility.[52]

Gratian, in his *Concordia discordantium canonum* (*c*.1140), and Hugh of St Victor (1097–1141) attempt reconciliations of the apparent contradiction of a sexless marriage. Gratian revises the system of the three 'goods' of marriage – naming them as fidelity, offspring and the sacrament – of which Mary and Joseph had all three, but only in name. Thus, Gratian adds that a marriage in name is different from but just as valid as one that also has the substance (*res*) or effect (*effectus*) of physical union. In *De beatae Mariae virginitate*, Hugh of St Victor lays

out a twofold plan of marriage in which there is the marriage which
is consent, and the office of marriage, which is copulation, each of
which is a sacrament. Thus, for Hugh there can be true marriage before
sex, and marriage can be holy without sex, because without sex the
union is a spiritual one like that between God and the human soul.
Even so Hugh also valorizes the union of the flesh in marriage. Gold
characterizes Hugh's position as follows: 'the intercourse of the flesh
(the office of marriage) typifies that union made between Christ and
the church through Christ's assumption of the flesh; thus there could
be no sacrament of Christ and the church where there was no carnal
mixing'.[53]

Peter Lombard followed in the same tradition, although he was
more interested, like Gratian, in finding ways to make sense of contradictory opinions passed down in the Christian tradition. In the next
century, Thomas Aquinas and Albertus Magnus were to be more
tolerant of the human, physiological aspects of marriage and define it
as 'an institution of nature'[54] and not an act of spiritual character; yet
Thomas remained firm in the belief that Mary was perpetually virginal.
These Dominicans 'attempted to vindicate the good of matrimonial sex
by restoring it to its rightful place in the order of nature'.[55] As they
codify marriage law, these thinkers only reinstate the dichotomous
categories of the Neoplatonic system they inherit and inhabit. Indeed,
the period's fascination with the paradoxes that Mary represents grows
out of this valorization of duality. The confounding problem here,
then, is that this process of harmonization paradoxically serves to
reinscribe the terms of the binary opposition that it is meant to
overcome. Mary is the spiritual body from whom 'he tok fleysh & blod,
/ ihesus, heuene kynge'.[56] Chaucer, repeating church liturgy and
imagery, has the Prioress call to the Holy Virgin, 'O mooder Mayde, O
mayde Mooder free! / O bussh unbrent, brennynge in Moyses sighte'
(7. 467–8). These are only a few examples from the English tradition of
countless such paradoxes. An 'Orison to the Blessed Virgin' dating
from 1333 foregrounds the familial and social ideologies that bound
and confound this symbolic system:

> Þou wommon . . .
> Þyn oune uader bere.
> Þat on wommon was moder
> To uader and hyre broþer –
> So neuer oþer nas.

>   Þou my suster and moder
>   And þy sone my broþer –
>   Who shoulde þeonne drede?
>   Who-so hauet þe kyng to broder
>   And ek þe quene to moder
>   Wel auhte uor to spede.[57]

(Thou, woman, who bore your own father. That one woman was mother to father and her brother. Never another one was like this. Thou are my sister and mother and your son my brother. Who should be afraid of you? Whoever has the king as brother and also the queen as mother, you certainly ought to prosper.)

Within such a pervasive system of imagery, Mary becomes exemplary for behaviour in Christian marriage even as the resulting system of rhetoric, in which soul and body are categorically opposed, produces the ideological context in which the Man of Law must seemingly compromise Christian precepts in bringing Constance to bed on her wedding night. It also allows him an apparent ease with which to moralize on the institution of marriage: 'Housbondes been alle goode and han ben yoore; / That knowen wyves; I dar sey yow na moore' (2. 772–3).

Given these complexities in narrative strategy and their bedevilling consequences for the operation of exemplarity, we begin to see how and around what terms this teller stops the slippages of the discrete elements of his rhetoric. We see what he takes as, and makes into, foundational components. In the Man of Law's curse of the Sultaness, the Muslim law becomes a set of terms that supplement and mediate Christian laws. His opinion takes its shape from the very thing that it curses. As such a medium, these terms remind us of the intersections of substitutions and traces that produce the 'law'. These intersections are most apparent in the tale's anxiety over the 'feyned womman', the Sultaness (2. 362). Similarly, Donegild, neither true nor false, marks the status of the break that establishes the truth of the tale. These characters are explicitly both inside the tale and on its borders and as such make us rethink the status of other ostensibly more exemplary characters. The Man of Law's logic becomes a shadow that is everpresent, reasserting its self-identity at the same time that this reassertion points to the umbrageous nature of this identity. Tensions surround these characters; these tensions bleed on to Constance's narrative existence and point to the Man of

Law's pervasive desire to keep his world from falling apart by trying to control each of its constituents. These stoppages become the foundation for monuments to a certain type of logic. Here, they monumentalize Christianity, Constance and the Man of Law himself. By invoking exemplarity as a mode of storytelling, the tale points to the spectre that animates this monumental logic, a spectre that 'can no longer be distinguished, with the same assurance, from truth, reality, living flesh'.[58] Subsequently it is no wonder that Constance cannot assuredly be distinguished from her ghost, a characteristic she shares with the Sultaness and Donegild.[59]

The first picture provided of Constance as a living ghost is on the day she is to be sent off to marry the Sultan, a day described as 'fatal' (2. 261). Lines 190–203 discuss the laws of fate, the 'large book' that is in 'hevene ywriten' (2. 190, 200). Though not Constance's death but the Sultan's is predicted in these lines, Constance is the ghost, who 'with sorwe al overcome / Ful pale' goes to meet her fate (2. 264–5), the possibility that she might 'spille' or die ever present (2. 285). As she floats on the sea after the Sultaness – that 'wikked goost' (2. 404) – has set her out in a rudderless ship, Constance waits 'After hir deeth ful often' (2. 467). When she finally lands, 'In hir langage mercy she bisoghte, / The lyf out of hir body for to twynne, / Hire to delivere of wo that she was inne' (2. 516–18). A young knight falls in love with Constance and loves her so much 'That verraily hym thoughte he sholde spille' unless he has his way with the foundling (2. 587). When Constance refuses his advances, he kills her benefactress in retaliation and she is blamed for the murder. The narrator describes her at her trial: 'For as the lomb toward his deeth is broght, / So stant this innocent bifore the kyng' (2. 617–618). As she stands accused, the narrator again describes her with the pallor of death:

> Have ye nat seyn somtyme a pale face,
> Among a prees, of hym that hath be lad
> Toward his deeth, where as hym gat no grace,
> And swich a colour in his face hath had
> Men myghte knowe his face that was bistad
> Amonges alle the faces in that route?
> So stant Custance and looketh hire aboute. (2. 645–51)

After having Alla's child and being sent away, she again appears as a shadow of the grave, 'with a deedly pale face' (2. 822).

The story of Constance's (potential for) death is told again and again as the tale reinscribes its terms. Certainly, such references to a sacrifice being led to death remind readers of Christ; in 2. 631–7, Christ is explicitly mentioned. And yet these lines also remind us of another way in which Constance is like the Blessed Virgin, whose death was also foretold and made an adumbration of Jesus's. Luke tells the story of the Purification. Mary and Joseph take the infant to the temple 'according to the law' (2:22, 24) and present him to the priest, Simeon. Simeon's blessing includes a prophecy for mother and child:

> And Simeon blessed them, and said unto Mary his mother, Behold, this child is set for the fall and rising again of many in Israel; and for a sign which shall be spoken against; (Yea, a sword shall pierce through thy own soul also,) that the thoughts of many hearts may be revealed. (2:34–5)

During the Middle Ages, this sword was paralleled to the lance that pierced Jesus's body on the cross, a reading which recalls the *mater dolorosa*.[60] Again, damnation, salvation and redemption are blended through the medium of the prophetic metaphor that is Mary. The prophecy of Mary's death allows her death to become exemplary of narrative design, an element in a plot moving towards a teleological, indeed eschatological, ending.[61] Like Constance's, Mary's own death story is one that grows with time. From the early centuries of Christianity to the Middle Ages, Mary's story grew from being merely a fact of history to a topic of disputation and literary investigation, and even though the stories about her may have been different, the eschatology remained essentially the same.[62] Ultimately, through many retellings of her death, Mary lives on through the stories of the Assumption of her body or her Dormition at the time of her leaving earth. Similarly, Constance's death is prophesied and even shown time after time. In an almost exact parallel to the prophecy about Mary's death, the Man of Law creates the potential for Constance's death as an example of his moral system:

> So vertuous a lyvere in my lyf
> Ne saugh I nevere as she, ne herde of mo,
> Of worldly wommen, mayde, ne of wyf.
> I dar wel seyn hir hadde levere a knyf
> Thurghout hir brest, than ben a womman wikke;
> There is no man koude brynge hire to that prikke. (2. 1024–9)

The narrator tells the tale of Constance's death over and over again, yet the tale ends with Constance's living on in the present tense.

Again, however, the exemplarity here must prove confounding. Thus, the issue of death in the *Man of Law's Tale* initiates the question 'Where is the law?' It seems to be written on the pale faces of the dead women who figure as examples in this tale[63] and therein lies the problem. Recalling the example of Mary, Constance's ghosts reflect the teleological urge of the law and are its manifestations and yet these very manifestations – repeated and varied endlessly[64] – also illustrate the errancy of metaphor and the way that anything can be repeated infinitely.[65]

The tension between the theology of the system and the mimetic status of the system becomes most apparent in the structure of exemplarity on which the tale and the narrator's profession itself operate. Mary and Constance are examples of a system that makes itself through its examples. Whether she is read as a model of being a true daughter, wife, mother, Christian, or saint, Constance's status as example marks both the problematic iterability of exemplarity and the desire to stop it, to halt iteration by walling it up.[66] Two times in his tale, the Man of Law brings lists of examples to bear upon the life of Constance. In both of these instances – ll. 470–504 and 932–45 – the narrator uses examples from the Bible and apocryphal and hagiographical writings to explain why Constance was not killed by her adventures at sea. In the first passage he alludes to the stories of Daniel in the lions' den, Jonah and the whale, the Hebrew people's escape from captivity, Saint Mary of Egypt's life in the wilderness and the feeding of the 5,000 with five loaves and two fishes. The second passage calls up the examples of David and Goliath and of Judith and Holofernes. Used to build a case, that is, to provide precedents for fictional events, these examples suggest the potential to call up other contexts infinitely. The examples are about death and overcoming it,[67] yet they indicate a complex relation to death when viewed as monuments created to wall in the traces of language. The Man of Law's intention in invoking these examples is to illustrate God's grace and transcendent presence, yet he constantly relies on the traces of other narratives in this process of signification. In a tale that focuses so heavily on astrological fate[68] and divine justice – or God's 'sonde' (2. 523, 760, 826, 902) – the tale points to the anagogical differences of perspective upon which it operates, as most hagiographies do.[69] Yet the tale's focus on how law is constructed – which is how it is put to use –

emphasizes the limits of law, narrative and language. From the perspective we have been establishing here, we see that ghosts, umbras and phantoms of other contexts are invoked in each exemplary repetition, even as examples do indeed reify concepts. Each example contains not only the use the Man of Law wishes it to hold and to which he tries to hold it, but also the potential for figurative errancy, contradiction, otherness or 'sin'.[70]

Exemplary of the Man of Law's system of values, Constance represents the narrator's idea of law and propriety and yet this very act of representation divides his notion of transcendence. From this perspective, Constance can be understood to supplement and re-animate the Man of Law's books and also to expedite and inspire further writings,[71] which in turn will substitute for her. While supplementing previous texts – the 'caas and doomes alle' (1. 323) the Man of Law has in his memory – Constance's story will also authenticate these same texts, because the legalistic mode of discourse, which we have seen maintaining and being maintained by theology and philosophy, uses and recreates the opposition between text and body to ascribe and maintain authority. Constance becomes a shadowy point of mediation between reception and exemplary reproduction. As such, she is made to function as a site where one realm of knowledge is transformed into another with a different author. She begins to signify the Man of Law but only in a sense that diffuses that very proper and proprietary name into a shadow.[72]

Near the end of the tale, as he is about to be reunited with Constance, Alla, her second husband, ponders the mystery of this event:

> 'Parfay,' thoghte he, 'fantome is in myn heed!
> I oghte deme, of skilful juggement,
> That in the salte see my wyf is deed.'
> And afterward he made his argument:
> 'What woot I if that Crist have hyder ysent
> My wyf by see, as wel as he hire sente
> To my contree fro thennes that she wente?' (2. 1037–42)

The passage confronts the notion of death as an absolute limit along traditional Christian lines of argument. Yet it also indicates how Christianity articulates its own ethic of death through the 'fantome'. We can now see that the phantom in his head is not merely the vision he has had of the woman he thought was dead, but also the 'argument' that his new-found Christian faith instigates[73] through the twists, turns and tropes that make its narrative into theology. In this tale, the ghost that Constance must always exemplify is the ghost of logic, the ghost of the Eve/Mary binary, that allows the Man of Law to repeat his tale while denying the disturbing implications of such repetition.

2

Shadowy Differences:
Marian Tales of Gender in
The Wife of Bath's Prologue and *Tale*

> Between the pre-text and the text falls the shadow of narrative indeterminacy.
>
> (Ruth Morse, *Truth and Convention in the Middle Ages*)

In the Ellesmere manuscript tradition, *The Wife of Bath's Prologue* and *Tale* follow the Man of Law's tale of Constance. Those reading in this tradition move from a teller invested in the authority of example and tightly structured stories to a teller who questions the power of narration and written 'auctoritee' (fragment 3, l. 1).[1] Alisoun of Bath begins her prologue by seeming to rely on a binary opposition between experience and authority, but as her personal history progresses, such neat binaries are broken down. As it reveals the secrets and strategies of being a wife, her autobiography uses and abuses words of clerk and church, inflecting them with bodily appetites and personal desires. In this way her often self-contradictory, self-revelatory prologue, set in counterpoint to the romance of her tale, calls readers' attentions to the conflicted arena of sexuality.[2] Alisoun takes the Man of Law's clerkly strategy of exemplarity and uses it for her own purposes. The resulting tale foregrounds the textuality of authorities and of bodies. In effect, she takes the traditional identification of women with linguistic errancy and shows this rhetorically culpable condition to be necessary to the engendering of meaning in narratives, including the most sacred stories of Christian tradition. In this way, her errant narrative – and errancy in general – may appear revelatory and the character of the woman may upset spiritual tradition not (as tradition would have it) by violating it, but by faithfully observing the confused conceptions of corporeality on which it is based. The way Alisoun faithfully mimes exemplarity, then, has consequences for the general understanding of sexual difference in Christian tradition, its representational binaries and founding indeterminacy.

Though nominally absent from Alisoun's tale – conspicuously so – Mary is very much a part of it, for hers was the authority of the image of essential femininity, a lens through which any other female literary character must be viewed. Therefore, to understand what is at stake in the way Alisoun tells her tale, we first have to be familiar with some of the key elements in Mary's narrative, such as her association with literature, the Annunciation and Incarnation and the auricular insemination. Most important, though, is her association with Eve, for such a yoking – defining one extreme by the other – has always within it the means to undo opposition. Thus, the same Mary that has served as a founding figure of Christian tradition has also proved troubling to that tradition, raising questions about its ability to represent coherent standards of 'sameness' and 'difference', especially when it comes to questions of corporeality and sexuality; and it is because Mary has proved so troubling that Alisoun can be even more so.

The Trouble with Mary

How do stories about Mary reveal Christianity's – indeed, Western culture's – urge to monumentalize binary gender differences? The concern over Mary's body within the Christian narrative of transcendence provides us our first clue. Additionally, we will see how, more and more, Mary came to be represented as reading and learning about the prophecies that augured her existence.[3] Texts with which the Virgin is shown to be familiar define her body in no impure terms and yet she must still suffer under the inheritance of original sin. Part of this inheritance is the need for salvation itself, a need tied to the inferior status of the flesh, that part that drags the eternal soul down, that part so long associated with those dangerously fruitful, forbidden-fruit-eaters – women.

The earliest apocryphal stories of Mary call her one of the 'pure virgins of the tribe of David' asked to weave 'the scarlet and the purple'.[4] But like the other virgins of the temple, she was asked to leave when she became a woman, that is, when she began menstruating. Her body becomes an issue in her community again when she is pregnant. As Theresa Coletti points out, in writing about the English mystery-cycle dramas, these plays often present a Mary who has a life that is not so different from that of some of the women in the audience who may have been scorned merely for being women.[5] Though she is the mother of God, Mary is blamed by her husband for being such a foolish young woman as to be tricked by a young handsome man calling himself an angel. Further, Joseph's reaction to seeing his wife pregnant is merely typical of community standards. Despite its prophesied doctrinal existence, the idea that God would have con-descended to be embodied through the medium of a woman's body, especially one that lactated and menstruated,[6] remained a prevalent topic of disputation in the period. In the cycle dramas, for instance, Mary is simultaneously the queen of heaven, medium of salvation for mankind, and its inverse – a woman, carnal and desiring. For instance, the *York* cycle play 'Joseph's Trouble about Mary' concentrates on the relationship between husband and wife. This play begins with the 'elde, / Wayke and al vnwelde'[7] Joseph lamenting at length about how un-lucky he is to have been wed to a young wife, a complaint that Alisoun of Bath will inflect in some revealing ways in her *Prologue* and *Tale*. His complaints grow from his knowledge that Mary is pregnant and became so while he was away. His main concern is over the 'shame' and 'blame' (ll. 54 and 60) that will fall on him when her pregnancy is discovered. The *N-Town* expands on this fear of communal retribution with its 'Trial of Mary and Joseph'. Both Joseph and Mary, revered as the holy parents by the play's audience even as the two are denigrated during the drama, are blamed for their sexual appetites. Detractors call Joseph an 'olde shrewe' who is so 'anameryd' with Mary that he must have her.[8] Similarly, Mary is 'a ʒonge damesel of bewté bryght' who is so 'fresch and fayr' that she would cause even 'A ʒonge man to haue delyght' (94, 91 and 93). Once Joseph has proved his innocence by passing a test of drinking a holy potion (230–57), the detractors and judges turn their attention to Mary. She must ask twice before being allowed to prove her innocence in the same way as Joseph (294 and 333). In between her requests, one of her detractors makes jokes about how she might have become pregnant, while one of the lawyers brings her own body as evidence against her (302–5):

> Þu art with chylde we se in syght;
> To us þi wombe þe doth accuse!
> Þer was nevyr woman citt in such plyght
> Þat from mankynde hyre kowde excuse.

Such a focus on Mary's physiological existence and the implication that her body speaks against her illustrates the medieval Christian conviction that female flesh was essentially suspect. Even the flesh of the mother of God could carry with it an inappropriate potential.

Yet the texts that were maintained to presage the Virgin's existence defined her body in entirely different terms. Mary herself was often depicted as intimately connected with literature, especially the act of reading, and particularly during representations of the Annunciation. By the fourteenth century, the image of Mary as a reader was common in iconography of the Annunciation.[9] Textually Mary's education begins quite early in her life. In return for being granted the blessing of conceiving, Anna and Joachim promised their child to the temple where Mary remained from the age of 3 until she was 12. The Gospel of Pseudo-Matthew reveals that Mary was instructed there in the law of God. The *N-Town*'s 'The Presentation of Mary in the Temple' takes up this theme and develops it. Mary earns her place in the temple by being able to recite at the age of 3 (l. 164) 'þe fyftene grees' by which believers may ascend to be with God (ll. 97 and 102–61). Then the priest instructs her in proper Trinitarian devotion (178–85) and the act of contrition (198–201) among other things, ending by telling her that she is there 'to lerne þe goddys lawys and scrypture to rede' (209).[10] By the fourteenth century, she was also believed to have been schooled in the prophecies of the Old Testament and even in the seven liberal arts.[11] Even by the thirteenth century, representations occur in which Mary is shown reading Isaiah 7:14, which prophesies the virgin birth of Immanuel, enmeshing her sexuality in the necessities of Christian history. Remarkably, then, Mary is represented as being familiar with the texts in which her holiness and purity seem without question and thus becomes a body of text, brought about by that literature that would make her part of a larger narrative.

So there are the two strains in which the story of Mary is enmeshed: the tale of the dangerous quality of women and that of a pure woman who will be the mother of God. Of course, then, she is one version of the foundational paradox of Christianity itself: that in taking on the fallen flesh, God would become human. And yet the model of the

Christian narrative that surrounds Mary reveals a profound indebted-
ness to preconceptions of binary gender difference. Indeed, in being
established, the story of the Incarnation, among other incidents of
Mary's life, must reify the differences between the sexes as a way to
express the differences between the mundane and the divine. So in
understanding the ways in which Mary's sexuality was entangled
within the necessities of salvation we can also understand how convictions about gender differences turned pretexts into the truth.

Such necessities can be understood more fully by turning to
medieval representations of the Annunciation and Incarnation, for
within them we can begin to see the ways in which salvation is yoked to
damnation and tethered to foundational fabrications about gender
difference. The Annunciation and the Incarnation were believed to be
simultaneous events, as the Word of God was immediately translated
into the body of Jesus.[12] However, Mary's body cannot be elided from
the process if Jesus is to be completely human. As we will see,
presumptions about sexual difference mark the narrative in revealing
ways. In *Christian Iconography: A Study of its Origins*, André Grabar
describes a common representation of the Annunciation in which the
child is already present even as Gabriel speaks to Mary. Grabar finds
the earliest evidence of this representation in the eastern church in the
ninth century and claims that it was prevalent in the western church by
the thirteenth century. This representation is striking because it
contains the image of the Holy Ghost, in the form of a bird or waves of
light or both, coming down to the praying Virgin within whose breast
the child already resides.[13] Such conventional representation dem-
onstrates the common belief that the Incarnation begins at the moment
of the Annunciation. A twelfth-century eastern icon and the liturgy
upon which it was based illustrate this tradition, which the western
church was to take up little more than a hundred years later. The
liturgy reads, 'As she heard the words of the archangel so she received
in a supernatural manner in her undefiled womb the Son and the Word
of God, his wisdom.'[14] The icon represents this idea by having Mary
listen intently to Gabriel and, as she does so, point to the child inside
her, visible through her garments.

In addition to the visual images, the literature of the period also
reflects this understanding of the Incarnation as simultaneous with the
Annunciation. For example, a religious lyric dating from the first half
of the fourteenth century and occurring in at least four manuscript
versions speaks of Mary's joy upon learning from the angel that

'crist'[15] has said that the 'holi gost scholde in [her] bodi wende' (26:7). Here, Christ pre-exists the Annunciation and is, in fact, part of its cause and yet he is also intimately tied to the changeable, permeable body of Mary. Indeed Gail McMurry Gibson suggests that the almost overwhelming focus on the Incarnation as a devotional item tended to 'make the Virgin Mary – perhaps even more than Christ himself – the very emblem of Christian mystery'.[16] Such visual and verbal portrayals reinforce the idea of the textual nature of Mary's body in the way that words alter it so immediately. But in what ways does this most perfect of women remain a palimpsest on which the marks of original sin are discernible even after she has been so throughly revised by the Word?

One motif of representation will provide some insight to begin answering this question. Schiller describes an image from one twelfth-century missal in which 'Mary of the Annunciation stand[s] on the snake . . . Below the Virgin and Gabriel, King Solomon appears, holding a scroll with the text of Proverbs 9:1: "Wisdom hath builded her house, she hath hewn out her seven pillars."'[17] These seven pillars foreshadow the fourteenth-century belief in Mary's instruction in the seven liberal arts and their architectural resonance suggests that Mary is, herself, the house of Wisdom, the site of Jesus's residence on earth even at the moment of Annunciation. Most striking, however, is the way in which this image ties Old Testament to New, Mary with the snake of Genesis, salvation with damnation. Once again we are made aware of the textual existence of Mary, how she is circumscribed by words, by what has (believed to have) been said about her. Similarly, an 'Ave Maris Stella' dating from the first half of the fourteenth century speaks of the 'gretyn uncowþe / þat [to Mary] was sayd of Gabriel mowthe' (41:5–6) as the precipitating factor behind humanity being returned to 'pes' (41:7) and righting 'þe name of heue a-gayne' (41:8). A mid-century 'Ave Maris Stella' repeats a similar sentiment (45:6–8):

> Thurght gabrols mough and mainc;
> In pais þou put vs out paine,
> Turnand þe name of eue againe.

Both of these lyrics refer to the typological connections between Eve and Mary. Typological readings produced a trope in which the Virgin was understood to be the inversion of Eve, or her positive double. Mary turned the (original) sin of the world into salvation, turning 'Eva' into the 'Ave' of blessing with which Gabriel accosted Mary when he announced that she was God's chosen one.[18] This word play was common in the period and expressed a belief in divine symmetry. Through it we can see how Eve's actions in the garden have precipitated every essential quality of Mary's existence; purity itself, as exemplified by Mary, has meaning only within the frame of reference that is the text of the fall of humanity in the garden. These examples illustrate the complex systems of stories and meanings that produce salvation, a process in which Eva can never entirely be tamed.

Such popular representations grew out of readings of the gospels, canonical and apocryphal, in which the Incarnation is assumed and that, again, illustrate the way in which salvation and the narrative of transcendence upon which it is built are dependent upon an idea of sexual difference that makes of women inferior beings, with bodies subject to outside influences. These readings trace some of their origins back to interpretations of Psalms 45:10: 'Hear, O daughter, consider and incline your ear.' This psalm was interpreted as anticipating Mary's humility as well as the physiology of her immediate auricular insemination with the Word. Verses in Luke were typologically connected to this Old Testament command. In Luke, the angel of the Annunciation, Gabriel, makes the assumption that Mary is with child immediately after speaking with her. He moves from the future tense of 'The Holy Spirit will come upon you and the power of the Most High will overshadow you' (1:35) to the past tense of 'your kinswoman Elisabeth . . . has also conceived a son' (1:36). The Incarnation is a *fait accompli* once it has been announced to Mary and matched by her own words: 'Behold, I am the handmaid of the Lord; let it be to me according to your word' (Luke 1:38). In the *Protevangelium*, Mary goes to visit her cousin Elizabeth soon after the Annunciation and Elisabeth at once recognizes the miraculous state of Mary's body, calling her 'the mother of my Lord' (12:2). In the early fifth century, in his *Confessions*, Augustine was to write of the Annunciation that through it the 'Word, the Beginning, made himself audible to the bodily ears of [humanity], so that they should believe in him and, by looking for him within themselves, should find him'.[19] By the fourteenth century the insistence on the *conceptio per aurem* and its concomitant affective devotional practice was strong.[20]

However, the auricular insemination also recalls original sin. From the perspective of Eve and the Fall in the garden, medieval semiotics paired women's sexuality with language, particularly its more errant operations. Mary's *conceptio per aurem* is another component of this system of making meaning. In it the Annunciation/Incarnation becomes an attempt at a systemic recuperation of female sexuality and errant language; it provides the *antidotum* to the *venenum* permeating humanity ever since Eve's conversation with the serpent.[21] The only way humanity may be saved from the concupiscence and mortality that arose from original sin is to be bought back by the singular body capable of making such a purchase. Or as Albertus Magnus (1206?–1280) wrote in his tractatus on the Incarnation:

> All men were living under sin; although man was in debt, man nevertheless was not able to buy [himself] back; therefore it was necessary that there be someone more than man who could buy [him] back. But below, it is proved that the angel was not capable of being united [to the flesh of man]; therefore, it was necessary that it be God and man; so, it was inevitable for God to be incarnated.[22]

Albertus's voice is a typical one among many in a long tradition of reasoning about God's human existence. Some 800 years earlier, in the *Confessions*, Augustine wrote of humanity's inability to access God in any way 'but dimly, through the clouds', making God's bodily existence necessary for human understanding.[23]

The sublative urge in these examples is evident. The argument is that God descended to the earth and condescended to take on the robe of flesh, 'the pollution of the body'.[24] The idea of condescension suggested in this logic illustrates the Christian inflection of the classic Platonic hierarchical dichotomy of mind over body and the Aristotelian notion of form over matter. In the Christian tradition this hierarchy was translated into sexual difference as Adam, made first and 'in [God's] own image' (Genesis 1:27), carried the divine form, while Eve, who was 'taken out of Man' (Genesis 2:23), was associated with the flesh. The female's association with body and excess led Paul to caution Timothy about the dangers of the way women dress and of their speech (1 Timothy 2:9–15). With Paul's admonition that 'a woman [should] learn in silence' matched by Augustine's later claim that 'truth [is] something incorporeal',[25] we can imagine some of the cultural constraints placed on the woman as the silent body – or recklessly obstreperous one – and the figurations that arise from this ethic.

The medieval concept of Mary, in her humility and servitude to God, is one such figuration, while anti-feminist tropes represent the non-exemplary outcome. The interrelatedness of these discourses will be made clearer by understanding Mary's role in the Annunciation, particularly her vocation as a weaver, for in understanding the metaphor which ties clothing to maternal flesh we can begin to see some of the predicates of sexual difference that are transferred into the self-contradictory narrative of Alisoun of Bath.

As Caroline Walker Bynum points out in her writing,[26] as much as dichotomies like mind/body, divine/human and masculine/feminine were present and effective during the period, so were crossings of the lines that created them:

> Not only did theology, natural philosophy and folk tradition mingle male and female in their understanding of human character and human physiology, theological and psychological discussion also sometimes mingled body and soul. . . . [B]y the thirteenth century the prevalent concept of person was of a psychosomatic unity.[27]

Using such metaphors as Jesus as mother or the female holy person as knight, religious practice and imagination in the Middle Ages often operated by invoking certain categories only so that those categories could be crossed, again reflecting one of the central paradoxes of Christianity in which God is without boundaries. Yet, concurrent with this practice are the many instances in which the dichotomies of soul/body, man/woman and authority/experience, among others, remain as the defining controlling categories. Indeed, it is possible to be innovative by crossing categories only when such categories are firmly in place, because crossing categorical boundaries invokes those boundaries and reinscribes them.

Mary is a prime example of how these categories were activated. As indicated by her education in Old Testament lore, Mary was the product and producer of prophecy, subject to but definitive of Judaic law. More specifically, Mary was one of the pure women asked to produce the scarlet and purple of the temple veil (*Protevangelium*, 10:1). The *Protevangelium* explicitly connects Mary's weaving functions in the temple with the Annunciation. After beginning to spin the scarlet, one day Mary ventures out for some water:

> And she took the pitcher and went forth to fill it with water: and lo a voice saying: Hail, thou that art highly favoured; the Lord is with thee: blessed art thou among women.

> And she looked about her upon the right hand and upon the left to see
> whence this voice should be: and being filled with trembling she went to
> her house and set down the pitcher and took the purple and sat down
> upon her seat and drew out the thread.
> And behold an angel of the Lord stood before her saying, Fear not,
> Mary, for thou hast found grace before the Lord of all things and thou
> shalt conceive of his word. (11:1–2)

Mary then asks the angel if she will conceive like other women to which
the angel responds that she will not but instead will be 'overshadowed'
by the Lord (11:2). Then follows, as in Luke, her acceptance of her
role.

In this second-century account of the Annunciation/Incarnation, we
can see that the story has grown in scope. Instead of sitting somewhere
out of context as in Luke, Mary now is in specific places performing
specific tasks. Mary's biography has moved into the realm of storytelling; she is now presented as a character of sorts with motivations
for her actions explicitly stated. This retelling is most striking, however,
for the way in which it so effortlessly interchanges bodies and words.
Luke makes clear the physiological aspects of the Incarnation saying
that Mary 'will conceive in [her] womb and bear a son' (1:31). But the
Protevangelium passage uses a much more ambiguous description of
what will happen in saying that Mary will 'conceive of [God's] word'.
'Conceive' is from the Latin *concipio*.[28] A derivative, *conceptio*, means
'becoming pregnant', but noticeably most of the definitions for
concipio refer to acts of expression and understanding.[29] Mary makes
the assumption about the physicality of what will happen to her
when she asks how she will conceive and give birth. Mary's becoming
pregnant is, then, something else as well: it captures for us the textual
existence of bodies and the bodily existence of even the most profound
of all texts according to medieval Christianity. In *Stabat Mater*, her
investigation of the semiosis of the *conceptio per aurem* and its extra-
polations, Julia Kristeva reads this capture as a type of bypass of the
female body, saying that thus female 'sexuality is brought down to the
level of innuendo'.[30] Nevertheless, I suggest that Mary's body is never
bypassed completely – can never be – however strongly the urge toward
its sublation may be represented. For what begins to become clear in
the story of the Annunciation/Incarnation is that the word of God is
now profoundly sensible to the fallen ears of humanity; and such
sensual hearing is an integral part of the narrative of salvation. The

emphasis on Mary's body in the dramas and the connection between
Mary's role as the Mother of God and her weaving, then, make explicit
the interdependence of texts and bodies in producing the rhetorical
authority of the church.[31]

In the *N-Town*'s 'The Salutation and Conception' and *York*'s 'The
Annunciation and Visit of Elisabeth to Mary', the state of Mary's
body continues to be of great concern. In the *N-Town* play, Mary is
astounded at Gabriel's words that she 'xal conceyve in [her] wombe
indede / A childe, þe sone of þe Trynyté' (ll. 239–40). She responds:

> In what manere of wyse xal þis be?
> For knowyng of man I haue non now:
> I haue evyrmore kept and xal my virginyté.
> I dowte not þe wordys ʒe han seyd to me,
> But I aske how it xal be do. (ll. 246–50)[32]

The *York* play follows suit, both in Gabriel's announcement and in
Mary's response. Mary does add an emphasis on knowing and
speaking the truth, 'the sothe to saye', about her 'maydenhode' (174)
and on the spectre of Eve when she claims not to be 'fyled' by 'werkis
wilde' (173 and 175). Both plays end the scene with a focus on the
words of the angel and Mary's acceptance of them. In the *N-Town*
Mary says 'Aftyr þi worde be it don to me' (288). In *York*, she says 'Be
done to me of all manere,/ Thurgh thy worde als þou hast saide'
(191–2). In such scenes, that figuratively tie Eve's errancy to Mary's
perfection, we are brought to recognize the relationship between words
and bodies. In this instance it would seem that the liability of female
flesh to err has been recuperated by the Word of God.

Similarly, Mary's weaving seems to be another way by which female
flesh is brought back into the heavenly fold. Schiller collects many
images based upon the *Protevangelium*'s articulation (or jointing
together) of the vocation of spinning and weaving with the Incarnation
itself. Many of these images show Mary holding the spindle.[33] Also,
medieval lyrics illustrate ways in which the period figured Mary's
weaving of Jesus. In Brown's fourteenth-century collection, the
Incarnation is presented through a clothing metaphor in two poems. An
'Orison to the Blessed Virgin' attempts to represent the mysteries of
salvation by claiming that Jesus took on the 'robe' of human flesh (16:19
and 48) and that Mary 'ʒeue hym my wede', the clothing of humanity
(16:31). The narrator of a short poem from later in the century (1372)

wishes to be 'clad in cristes skyn' (71:3) in order better to understand Christ's suffering on the cross. These examples illustrate that, although 'Wearing the tissue of . . . flesh'[34] was not the primary figure for speaking of the Incarnation, it was one with some currency.

This clothing metaphor suggests an incidental quality to the flesh of God: as that which is mutable, it cannot also be intrinsic to the transcendent Godhead. Flesh can – and must – be shed at the time of death if a soul is to be perfect and able to enter into God's presence. Yet the fallibility of the flesh, originating with Eve, instigated the need for salvation and therefore instigated the salvational narrative itself, making necessary a fleshly version of God. Mary represents a sublated version of this flesh; merely mutable and not fallible, she enacts bodily not only salvation but also the narrative desire for it in her conjunction with Eve.

The story of Mary must grapple with this cultural inheritance at every turn and trope, a struggle that leads us back to the focus on Mary's body in all this literature. Chaucer's *Tale of Melibee* renders this idea of female physiology just barely under control as Dame Prudence addresses her husband saying, 'For certes, sire, oure Lord Jhesu Crist wolde nevere have descended to be born of a womman, if all wommen hadden been wikke' (fragment 7, l. 1073). Even as scenes such as those from the cycle dramas or images like those from the lyrics recuperate the dangerous qualities of female flesh, they also serve to establish its errancy or indeterminacy as the foundation of salvation. Given that the displacement of this errancy on to the flesh, and more specifically on to female flesh, can be understood as a defining moment of sexual difference, Mary's corporeality remains troubling. In 'Purity and danger: the paradox of Mary's body and the en-gendering of the infancy narrative in the English mystery cycles', Theresa Coletti argues on the general level that 'Mary emerges as a sign of difference, of the irreconcilability of matter and spirit, the human and the divine.'[35] And what our view has shown us is that one way such ostensibly transcendental differences are embodied is in the realm of sexual difference. For we must remember that Eve came from the prelapsarian Adam, the supposed unsullied human original from which all humans derive as copies. Yet Eve predicated accident, otherness and sin. When viewing the story of the Fall from this perspective, what we are obliged to acknowledge is that the potential for accident lay originally in Adam, the male, and yet the Christian narrative displaces this dangerous potential on to the female. What we can now conceive, however, is that this risk seems always to have been possible and is in some sense a necessary possibility if the substance, or what Christian doctrine would understand as non-accidental occurrences like Mary's story, is to be significant. This complex narrative strategy reveals why Christianity is compelled constantly to reaffirm binary gender differences: the powerful image of the sinful, fleshy Eve/woman (or as a sublated version of this tale, as in Mary's story) allows Christianity to figure evil itself. In other words, the hierarchical, oppositional view of sexual difference provides this overdetermined narrative with a crucial – if not a constitutive – mode for conceiving of some of Christianity's central beliefs and conventions. 'Woman' and/or the related concept 'flesh' becomes shorthand for a variety of concepts that signify a moving away from the one true good, concepts like difference, uncontrollability, sin and evil.

So the transcendent concepts of good and evil, salvation and damnation, divine and human, are embodied, yoked tightly to a discursive understanding of sexual difference. The yoking of Eve and Mary indicates a powerful relationship among figuration, bodies and faith, a relationship that forces us to acknowledge that the basic concept of the binary as timeless – the 'this or that', the 'inside or outside' – is itself a discursive product. For what we can now perceive is the way in which the *this* is related to the *that*, is indeed coterminous with it, produced as different within complex and often contradictory systems of meaning. Our view of this process allows us to see the underlying fluidity that serves as the foundation for neat dichotomous categories. Seeing the formulation of these ideas, we can also recognize the ways in which such ideas, such binaries, were made to seem original and teleological.

In the same way that Mary's story has shown us the process, Alisoun of Bath's *Prologue* and *Tale* similarly investigate how things are made to signify. Most specifically, as she tries to articulate what being the woman she is, is like, Alisoun's errant words are reflective of the underlying indeterminacy of sexual difference in association with the power this concept has to define people's lives and bodies.

In the introduction to her book *Chaucer's Sexual Poetics*, Carolyn Dinshaw takes a look at the intersection of some prescribed gender roles and their relation to language itself. She traces the thoughts of several medieval writers on the dangers of the body, particularly the female body and its relationship to ways of reading. She highlights 'the patristic association of the surface of the text (the letter) with carnality (the flesh, the body) and carnality with woman'.[36] While my reading certainly does not deny the potency of such anti-feminist constructions, examining the ways in which they have been articulated and solidified can provide another mode of understanding what is at stake in their formation. Reading the texts produced by these discourses through the lens of Marian figuration can provide a frame through which to see the materiality of texts and of their rhetorical authority to establish truth and to see that, like the vagrancy of female flesh, authority's possibilities lie in its dangers. So what Dinshaw says may be true:

> literary activity has a gendered structure, a structure that associates acts of writing and related acts of signifying – allegorizing, interpreting, glossing, translating[37] – with the masculine and that identifies the surfaces on which these acts are performed, or from which these acts depart, or which these acts reveal – the page, the text, the literal sense, or even the hidden meaning – with the feminine.[38]

Nevertheless, the polyvalent and juxtapositional functions of Mary's body as a signifier can offer a somewhat different perspective from which to view the congruence of texts and bodies. The necessities of Mary's physiology affect her story and therefore highlight not just the process of signification being performed on bodies but also the potential of those bodies to signify and to recirculate meanings. In effect, the representations surrounding Mary's body foreground that what Dinshaw calls the 'hidden meaning' and the 'literal sense' are coterminous. In other words, the act of making something signify is also the act of being signified. Neither the idea of a prediscursive body and its gender nor of an all-inclusive language remains untouched once all are perceived as series of junctures, articulated or jointed together. An investigation of ways in which Alisoun of Bath's story seems to double Mary's will reveal similar and similarly revealing junctures.

The Trouble with Alisoun

How big is the step from the Holy Virgin Mary to Alisoun of Bath's inquiry into 'virginitee'? Mary seems conspicuously absent from the Wife's 162-line investigation that mentions virginity six times (fragment 3, ll. 62, 72, 82, 91, 105, 142) and Jesus four times (3. 10, 15, 107, 139, 146), even remarking on his being 'a mayde' (139).[39] Additionally, later in her prologue (715–18), she speaks of

> . . . Eva first, that for hir wikkednesse
> Was al mankynde broght to wrecchednesse,
> For which that Jhesu Crist hymself was slayn,
> That boghte us with his herte blood agayn.

Pairing Eve and Jesus in this way seems odd in light of the many examples we have perused so far. Jesus is usually figured as Adam's inverse. Why, then, is Eve not paired with Mary? Adam himself even shows up later in the Wife's discussion when she discusses the 'mark of Adam' (3. 96). Virginity, Jesus, Adam, Eve and sin – the text leaves out Mary, the term between human and divine in the Christian narrative. Even in this early part of her confessional *Prologue*, the Wife's words begin to disperse accepted and expected rhetorical modes. In so doing, this *Prologue* begins, too, to disperse the ideas usually represented by certain ways of talking about things. This example, not so important in many ways, will nevertheless serve as the example that will begin our investigation of how the *Wife of Bath's Prologue* and *Tale* reveal at every level the figurative existence of the truths about sexual difference that the anti-feminist tradition holds to be self-evident.[40] What the Wife's *Prologue* does is to illuminate how living up to such prescribed roles, fulfilling them to such a degree so as to be blatantly *performing* or *miming* them, can prove to reveal the limiting absurdity of a notion of sexual difference that subjugates one sex simply because its members have a '*bele chose*' (3. 447) instead of an 'olde sho' (3. 707).[41] The Wife of Bath questions and uses – questions by using – society's interpretation of bodies. She uses the clerks' technique of exemplarity to perfection, matching her detractors point by point, piece of evidence by piece of evidence, and yet produces a vision of being a woman that, though strikingly similar to the notion of woman posited by anti-feminist rhetoric, nevertheless serves to break apart many of the joints of this rhetoric.

That we believe that Alisoun has beaten her male foes at their own game is not the main point here. We can sit and disagree with this woman's interpretations of doctrine, morality, astrology and medicine all day, as many scholars have done, by interpreting her words in comparison to theological texts of the time. For instance, she reinterprets the story of the Samaritan woman at the well (3. 14–25) and Paul's notion of the marriage debt (3. 115–34, 152–62), and uses Jerome against misogyny (e.g. 3. 51–61, 71–2, 135–42). Her different, heterodox interpretations, however, do not constitute her main accomplishment.

Instead, the success in her miming of dominant discourse is that she foregrounds *method*. By highlighting *how* ideas came to seem logical, Alisoun creates an overt relationship between *what* she speaks about and *how* it is represented. We are pressed to recognize the similarity between how the Wife speaks and the contradictory, sanctimonious doctrines of the church and its male advocates. What the Wife's *Prologue* will evidence is that we can no longer view as separable the 'how' and the 'what' of any utterance, and so the notions about gender that are supposed to be revealed may be seen, instead, as at least partially constructed within and by the very language and conventions used to express them. Looking at such concepts in this way undermines any sense of closure or the rhetorical authority of any utterance. It would seem that one of Alisoun's primary goals in her *Prologue* is to undermine the concept of static, binary sexual difference. What we will see is that in dealing with the discursive reality of gendered roles, the Wife uncovers the multiplicity of gendered experience.

The parallels between Mary and Alisoun exist in that space where bodies and texts overlap, a perspective that allows us to see the process by which certain human characteristics were made to seem like natural, timeless effects of physiological difference. The act of story-telling is also a central factor of similarity between the two. Whereas Mary has stories told about her – stories that form who she is, who she can be – Alisoun tells stories about herself, but stories that reveal how the discourses of her culture have shaped her, just as those about Mary shaped her. We will see that Alisoun's *Prologue* uses many of the same narrative techniques and motifs that were used in stories about Mary. She emphasizes gendered bodily existence in a world of discourses, a world that relies on things like secrets and common sense to create and validate its ideological biases.

Basic textual parallels between the two women also exist. In two essays Melvin Storm has investigated some convincing textual connections between Alisoun and Mary. In 'Alisoun's ear' Storm argues that the Wife's deafness is a sign of her unregenerate spiritual state and faulty intellectual capabilities. By tracing out a long line of patristic thinking that equates good 'hearing with the apprehension of truth',[42] Storm's conclusion is that the Wife, hearing in only one ear, is deaf to the salvational new law.[43] In contrast, of course, Mary's ear was most profoundly open to receive the Word of God. This acceptance implies her wholly regenerative nature and her recursively established ability to learn and live by the law.

In 'The miller, the virgin and the Wife of Bath', Storm analyses parallels between Alison of the *Miller's Tale* and Alisoun of Bath to support his conclusion that 'the Wife of Bath is the true inversion of Mary'.[44] He cites several previous studies on parallels between the Miller's Alison and Mary[45] and then develops further parallels between the two characters of the *Canterbury Tales*. Again, the issue of the Wife's hearing is the focus. Among other likenesses she shares with the Holy Virgin, the Miller's Alison is compared to a 'wezele' (1. 3234), an animal that was believed to conceive through the ear and give birth through the mouth 'just as the Virgin was envisioned as conceiving through the whispering of an angel or dove representing the Holy Ghost and, in turn, giving birth to the Word Incarnate'.[46] The likenesses Alison shares with Alisoun of Bath are numerous and include 'details of character, of appearance, . . . of speech and . . . shared social circumstance'.[47] Storm concludes that with the 'intermediate parody'[48] of the Miller's Alison, the Wife of Bath is brought into stark contrast with Mary. Her 'deafness, her evident barrenness and her unregenerate nature'[49] all recall the Annunciation and her distance from salvation.

While the thematic and patristic evidence that Storm compiles provides a convincing picture of the connections between Mary and Alisoun, its focus on how the context of Marian imagery provides Alisoun of Bath's story with a frame of reference is troubling. Storm tends to treat the Wife as a purely textual creation and the Virgin as purely contextual, not a product of cultural and rhetorical convention, whereas we have seen that the Virgin's life is a story, too. With this caveat in mind, however, Storm's insight – if not his conclusions – provides us with a basis for exploring Mary and Alisoun as allied characters.[50]

As Storm's articles suggest, the Wife's unregenerate characteristics recall the original sin of Eve, but after our investigation into how Mary's story relates the creation of discursive sexual difference, we must now acknowledge that the relationship between an exemplary maiden and a sinful wife is more complex than that of a simple hierarchical binary. For what we have discovered is the mutual dependence between that which is exemplary and that which is anything but. The textual and thematic parallels between these two characters will serve to illustrate this point further and indicate ways in which it is tied to embodiment. Alisoun, like Mary, is a weaver of fine cloth (1. 447), but more telling than this and the other textual similarities previously indicated is the similar way that the bodies of both women represent but also refashion the changing textures of their cultures. Where Mary is the juxtaposition of 'Glorious mayde and mooder' ('An ABC', l. 49), 'doghter of [her] Sone' (*Second Nun's Prologue*, 8. 36), Alisoun embodies another paradox, that of exemplifying some of the same anti-feminist tropes against which she argues. The stories of both women revolve around secrets – how and how well they are kept. Mary may wish to keep 'all . . . things, pondering them in her heart' (Luke 2:19), but her pregnant body reveals her inner secrets to a suspicious husband and a legislative community. Alisoun reveals truths about her body – where she has the marks of Venus and Mars and their significance (ll. 604–26) – but only under the guise of 'pleye' and only after warning that 'For half so boldely kan ther no man / Swere and lyen, as a womman kan' (3. 227–8), emphasizing the intertextual and perspectival nature of her utterances.[51] Both women are readers and are read to; both have divinely ordained bodies; both share a bodily and revelatory relationship to statements of truth. In a rewriting of the way in which Mary's story produces normative discourses from a basis of indeterminacy, Alisoun's *Prologue* takes normative discourse and reverses it to its underlying indeterminacy. What her words reveal is the plethora of ways of being gendered in contrast to the phallocentric discourse of binaries.[52]

The Wife of Bath's autobiography and the tale she tells as her offering to the game that comprises the frame of the *Canterbury Tales* initiate the question of gender by highlighting the culturally constructed character of gender. Her discussion of the debate over why 'membres . . . of generacion' (116) were created implies an understanding that bodies cannot be said to have a signifiable existence prior to their being inserted into a recognizable set of discourses (119–28):

> Glose whoso wole and seye bothe up and doun,
> That they were maked for purgacioun
> Of uryne and oure bothe thynges smale
> Were eek to knowe a femele from a male,
> And for noon oother cause, – say ye no?
> The experience woot wel it is noght so.
> So that the clerkes be nat with me wrothe,
> I sey this, that they maked ben for bothe,
> This is to seye, for office and for ese
> Of engendrure, ther we nat God displese.

The rather technical use of 'purgacioun' (3. 120), 'uryne' (3. 121), 'femele' and 'male' (3. 122), even when mixed with colloquialisms like 'thynges smale' (3. 121), intimates the way in which different discourses and rhetorical modes affect perception of basic differences between men and women. For instance, medieval physiological research focused on discovering the essential function of any organ. Organs functioned less as a part of an individual body and more as manifestations of eternal forms.[53] The Wife's attention to organ purpose recalls this scientific and etymological system of ordering the world. Invoking the name of God, mixing this theology with science and adding her own colloquial perspective on sex, she reminds her audience of the interdependence between modes of discourse and human desires.

Her euphemism in these lines will be matched later in her *Prologue* by her reference to her own 'thynge' with the euphemisms *'bele chose'* and *'quoniam'* (3. 510 and 608). Such usages, coupled with scientific and theological terminology, bring to the fore the many complex ways in which the body was named and made into a kind of text to be read in different languages. Her investigation into why men and women have different 'thynges' illustrates that the physiology itself is another term in a culturally determined, not solely physiologically based, set of differences. The 'membres' have similar functions in excretion and similar goals in sex but are different in form. From the perspective offered in this passage, sexual organs do not carry significance outside a dualistic referential framework. Alisoun had begun her analysis with a phrase – 'Glose whoso wole' – that indicates the way in which the glossator or reader's perspective affects what the body parts signify. She concludes her discussion with a passage that clearly illustrates an understanding of the interdependence between semiotic systems, their figurations and the bodies that manifest them (129–32):

> Why sholde men . . . in hir bookes sette
> That man shal yelde to his wyf hire dette?
> Now wherwith sholde he make his paiement,
> If he ne used his sely instrument?

This passage references 1 Corinthians 7:3–4:

Let the husband render unto the wife due benevolence: and likewise also the wife unto the husband. The wife hath not power of her own body, but the husband: and likewise also the husband hath not power of his own body, but the wife.

Once again, whether or not Alisoun has correctly read the doctrine of the marriage debt is not my interest here.[54] Instead, what seems remarkable about both passages is the way in which texts become contexts that make sense of body parts, suggesting that those parts have no significance without the supporting bulwark of contexts. In this particular passage, the body, specifically the sexual body, seems to hold no value until entered in the ledger book and brought into a bargain with another body. What holds the ideas about gender in place in this passage is not a belief in sexually differentiated behaviour as naturally mandated. Instead, diffused across several culturally constructed spectrums, bodies begin to signify. 'Bookes', whoever will 'Glose' them and the bodies set in them, become the contextual anchors of what is signified by the words 'man' and 'woman'.[55] As we continue our investigation of what Alisoun says and how she says it, we will continue to see that she repeats and parodies the words of authority – in the realms of science, theology, economics – while at the same time parodying her own experience. Indeed, Mary Carruthers calls her a 'master of parody' who 'teaches that the "truth" of any picture often has more to do with the prejudices and predilections' of those who produce it than it does with the subject.[56] In so doing, she reveals that both are merely representations of the idea of the natural, the original, or what is 'right ynogh' (l. 2), neither with a greater claim to veracity than the other.

What does it mean to have a certain set of instruments if they make sense only in relation to another set? The discourses of medieval science relied upon such relational definitions in describing the functions of the human body. Most revealing is the general medical understanding of why men and women have different body parts. Galen (130?–201?) provides a foundation for later physiological analyses, saying, 'in women the parts are within [the body], whereas in men they are outside'.[57] In the fourteenth century surgeon Guy de Chauliac (c.1300?–68) wrote in the *Chirurgia magna* (1363) 'The apparatus of generation in women is like the apparatus of generation in men, except that it is reversed' and 'the womb is like a penis reversed or put inside'.[58] In general, medieval scientific views, based on Aristotelian and Christian presuppositions, held the male body to be paradigmatic since it was believed that the semen carried in it perfect form, sent directly from God. Yet, this paradigmatic form is also the body that in Eden had the potential to produce the inexact copy of Eve and that each day continues to have the potential to produce the 'imperfect[ion]' and 'mutilat[ion]'[59] of the female body. We can see that, according to this theory of gender differentiation, the male body and the female body were versions of the same thing. And yet in the Wife's *Prologue*, and in the anti-feminist texts that it incorporates, we can see a belief in the profound difference between the sexes. If the difference was not necessarily in the body, according to medieval science – and the many discourses of theology and philosophy that served as its bulwark – then we must again recognize that what holds in place the idea of a binary, oppositional difference between the sexes is the very thing that also can undo such opposition: the way people talk about it.

And the Wife of Bath is certainly a talker. Alisoun's discussion of virginity, which is mixed in with her discussion of multiple marriages (3. 1–118), reveals the limiting absurdities of binary oppositions, unmasking some of the insecurities of the dominant culture, and thus begins to break down some ideas about gender. Specifically, she takes the strategy of the clerks – that is, the use of examples from the Bible, glossed 'up and doun' (3. 26 and 119) – and makes it into a strategy of her own, turning the meanings of verses to her own purposes and citing verses that might usually not have been glossed quite so often, like the story of 'Lameth' (3. 54) for instance. In her faithful miming of this strategy, we can see the parody in the *Prologue*. For in her exaggeration and miming of this clerkly strategy, we are left to wonder how accurate any gloss can be. Even the simple, glossy logic of her argument explaining why everyone cannot be a virgin serves to illustrate how her rhetorical mode parodies – and thus calls attention to the limits of – normative binary, oppositional discourse generally.[60] She asks: 'And certain, if there were no seed ysowe, / Virginitee wherof thanne sholde it growe?' (3. 71–2). Such a sex-positive statement is not surprising from the Wife and, combined with all the other indecent details of her *Prologue*, serves to exaggerate her already excessive sexual character. Additionally, her statement reveals the connection between sexual intercourse and virgins, a connection that may leave the ideal of virginity intact but shows its relation to much more carnal endeavours.

As the Wife proudly tells of the way she controlled her first three husbands, older men all, she repeats typical lines from anti-feminist discourses, illustrating the ostensibly mutually exclusive categories to which women are subject. She complains about the strictly negative view of women. If a woman is 'povre' then she will be expensive to keep (l. 249); if she is 'riche' then the man must 'soffre hire pride and hire malencolie' (ll. 250–2); if fair, then unchaste because all the bachelors will chase after her; if foul, then also unchaste because like 'a spanyel' (l. 267) she will leap on any man who presents himself. These few examples are indicative of the compendium of anti-feminism that the Wife collects. But the Wife is also astute enough to question the source of these examples. She asks

> Who peyntede the leon, tel me who?
> By God, if wommen hadde writen stories,
> As clerkes han withinne hire oratories,
> They wolde han writen of men moore wikkednesse
> Than al the mark of Adam may redresse. (3. 692–6)

Her question and conclusion contest the singular authority of 'auctoritee'. This passage reminds us that authority cannot be conclusively attributed solely to a divine origin but is dispersed across a range of specifics including those of class – 'clerkes' – and place – 'oratories' – as well as those of gender.

In the Wife's recounting of her constant struggles with her fifth husband, Jankyn, who insists upon reading exemplary stories of detestable women to his wife, we are provided with another example of the clerkly strategy of glossing the world 'up and doun'. Alisoun mentions some of her husband's favorites: Eve, 'Dianyre' (3. 725), 'Xantippa' and her 'pisse' pot (3. 729), 'Phasipha' and her sexual abominations (3. 733) and 'Clitermystra' (3. 737). She complains how he would read his book 'with ful good devocioun' (3. 739) and was full of 'mo proverbes / Than in this world ther growen gras or herbes' (3. 773–4). Jankyn's reliance on examples and proverbs seems very much like Joseph's and the judges' reliance on empirical evidence and the words of law as they try to determine the pregnant Mary's fate. Like stories about the Incarnation, Jankyn's book and his recital from it reify a concept of binary gender difference that, not surprisingly, allies women with evil. Returning to a passage touched upon earlier will help me to clarify this point further. The first evil woman that the Wife says Jankyn read to her about was 'Eva' whose 'wikkednesse' brought 'al mankynde to wrecchedness' (3. 715 and 716). Clearly, mankind is threatened by this evil woman, who is contrasted not with Mary but with 'Jhesu Crist' (3. 717). The elision of Mary from the equation emphasizes the way in which woman is allied with evil and man with good.

However, we must wonder how different the Wife is from her fifth husband when it comes to anti-feminist rhetoric. After all, we recognize

that the Wife is a consummate story-teller and, as H. Marshall
Leicester puts it in *The Disenchanted Self*, this tale is striking for
making explicit 'the way language creates people'.[61] Surely the wife
that the Wife was to her first three husbands is a creation on the textual
level, manifesting every anti-feminist stereotype from her over-
abundant sexual desire to her greed for money and power; from
her tendency to gossip to her tendency to wear her husbands out
with talking and sex. Jankyn's book serves as yet another textual
version of femininity in *The Wife of Bath's Prologue*. We must wonder
why Alisoun protests his version of things so vehemently, given that
she seems very similar to one of Jankyn's examples, 'Eriphilem' who
betrayed her husband for a brooch of gold (3. 743–46). Certainly, she
says that she hates 'hym that [her] vices telleth' her (3. 662) and this
explanation is satisfactory on the level of psychological motivation.
Yet Alisoun is something other than a talking head to be psycho-
analysed because, within her own story of herself and within the
exemplary stories of the old clerks and the young one who can 'glose'
her so well (3. 509), she *is* the example. And what happens when, to
paraphrase Luce Irigaray, the examples speak?[62]

The example becomes something else. Alisoun is more than just an
anti-feminist stereotype, for by telling a life story, the *Wife of Bath's
Prologue* takes away Alisoun's exemplary status. She exists somewhere
else apart from as an example of errant, Eve-like corporeality and
loquacity; she is more than just an example of what happens to someone gap-toothed with the marks of Mars and Venus; she is something
else besides a girl who uses her sexuality to gain material wealth.
Indeed, all the aspects of her life that she reveals to listeners and
readers alike illustrate that there is something always spilling over the
edges of any category into which she might be forced or might force
herself. She is exemplary of no one concept and, in the confusion of
all the things of which she might be held accountable as an example,
her existence in text points to the similarly textual existence of all
concepts held to be exemplary, or worthy of imitation, like that
emblem of femininity, Mary.

By miming the strategies of 'auctoritee' in her opening sermon on
virginity (3. 1–183) and by showing herself to be exemplary of so many
things, the Wife is not violating the rules of the church's rhetorical
authority but is observing them faithfully in all their convolutions. Her
prologue may seem confused, contradictory and overly anxious, but in
being so it reveals – by bringing to the surface – the same confused,

contradictory and overly anxious aspects of the 'auctoritee' that she mimes. She also reveals herself not as some force diametrically opposed to traditional authority but as simply another player within the rules authority establishes. This aspect of the Wife's rhetorical strategy is yet another way in which the *Prologue* breaks down the power of the representational binaries of the Christian tradition, 'auctoritee' and 'experience' (3. 1) composing only one of them.

This very strategy of miming, or playing by the rules, then, proves to be Alisoun's most powerful gambit, for in illustrating the rules of exemplarity in her way, indeed by embodying them, Alisoun reveals that they are just rules. Alisoun's question 'Who peyntede the leon?' indicates on the dramatic level that she realizes the slippery nature of exemplarity as a strategy of world-building. Indeed, her whole prologue, with its incorrect citations, misquotations and mistranslations, relies on using the strategy of exemplarity and the words of the clerks, but her appropriation and misuse (from the clerks' perspective) of this strategy indicate the limits of this discourse and its mores. As she faithfully mimes this strategy, transforming it into something to serve her purposes, her 'ensamples mo than ten' (3. 179) serve to pluralize exemplarity and unfold the ostensibly unified discourse of gender. Her experience inflects her use of 'auctoritee' and, thus, breaks the authority of 'auctoritee' apart. She points out that the beliefs of the church belong to someone's narrative, 'thy tale' (3. 262), and so may be seen as just as opinionated as her own convictions.

Alisoun, then, may understand the 'mark of Adam' (3. 696) better than Adam's own descendants, those men who continue to try to write the world from their own perspective alone. In the Wife's narrative, as in the culture out of which it grew, men are the ones writing, glossing and painting rubrics – in other words, they are the ones trying to take different texts and different experiences and shrink them down into one meaning that can be written in big letters and big words for all time. According to medieval thinkers who considered writing and its relation to humans – like Augustine in *On Christian Doctrine*, 2. 2, and Alan of Lille in *Plaint of Nature*, prose 2 – the 'mark of Adam' was considered primarily to be transient. Augustine claims that even the words of the Bible signify only conventionally since they are words used by men for men. What the anti-feminists and the glossators seem to misunderstand, then, is the conventional sets of values that go along with – indeed are created by – conventional uses of language.[63]

The Wife's strategy of exemplarity must have consequences for our understanding of the rhetorical force of the church's anti-feminist dogma and its inverse, the valorization of the sealed-up virginal female body. Alisoun says that she 'quitte [her husbands] word for word' (3. 422) and she describes her fist-fight with Jankyn in which she 'quittes', or repays, or requites, her husband mark for mark, blow for blow (3. 788–808). She matches the 'mark of Adam' with 'Martes [Mars'] mark upon [her] face, / And also in another privee place' (3. 619–20) and 'the prente of seinte Venus seel' (3. 604); in so doing, though she interprets her body using the discourses given her by her culture, she also remarks those discourses with her body.

Yet she does not simply argue in favour of experience over authority; more explicitly, what her prologue does is illustrate the overdetermined nature of the relationship between bodies and words. Whereas Marian figuration works by sublating its reliance on Eve's errant body – that is, hiding the indispensable status of bodies and words in the formulation of transcendence – the *Wife of Bath's Prologue* and *Tale* emphasize this relationship and so transform its status. Alisoun's similarity to the period's image of Eve calls attention to the semiotic networks that produce not only binary gender formations but also the moral distinctions within them. Like Eve, Alisoun is a supplement of Mary, a representative of the transgressive potential of female flesh that makes Mary's virginity valuable. Alisoun, in the tradition of Eve, provides a counterpoint – or part of the recognizable set of discourses – that can make the paradox of virginally maternal Mary's body mean something.

The figurative status of such moral distinctions can be further clarified by an investigation of the use of substitutes or doubles in the stories of both Mary and Alisoun. Most importantly, each has an older confidante who advises her younger counterpart and acts as a sounding board for their revelations of secrets, 'mysteries' (*Protevangelium*, 12:2) and 'privetee' (*Wife of Bath's Prologue*, 3. 531). Before we can understand the way in which 'doubling' covers over an overdetermined discursive network, we need to consider the details of this doubling strategy and the narrative inevitability it helps to produce and yet jeopardizes.

Elisabeth serves as Mary's mirror. Like Mary, her old friend was known as a weaver of scarlet cloth (*Protevangelium*, 12:2). Like her younger counterpart, Elisabeth becomes pregnant miraculously, but in contrast to Mary the miracle of her pregnancy is that it occurs 'in her old age' (Luke 1:36). Each woman's son has a unique but interrelated function in the world: John was the singular prophet for the only son of God. Elisabeth is the first, besides Mary and Gabriel, to proclaim that the child Mary will bear will be divine, a proclamation simultaneous with the joyful leap the foetus in her womb makes (Luke 1:44). Like Mary, Elisabeth seems also very familiar with prophecies; she declares that one reason Mary is blessed is that she 'believed that there would be a fulfilment of what was spoken to her from the Lord' (Luke 1:45). In Luke, after Elisabeth makes this declaration, Mary sings the Magnificat, amplifying and restating the prophecy of her miraculous pregnancy first suggested in Isaiah 7:14. Mary is similarly mirrored by her mother, Anna, who also becomes pregnant miraculously and gives birth to one who is 'alone of all her sex'.[64] As we note the way in which supposedly unique characteristics – characteristics definitive of some of the foundations of Christianity – are amplified by being repeated in several characters, we also get a glimpse of the diffuse web at the base of singular miracles. As the ideal is represented in the reproduction of faith, it is pluralized; thus, even as faith grows, the unity of trans-cendence is undermined.

Such diffusion is allied with the parodic, exaggerated extremes of *The Wife of Bath's Prologue*, for these texts all participate in faithful repetition. As a character Alisoun is constituted by repetition. By her own admission, the Wife embodies some of the anti-feminist stereo-types against which she rails. For instance, after calling the words of clerks 'lyes' (3. 302), she describes herself as the typical woman of appetite, greedy after money and sex, adding that she 'ne loved nevere by no discrecioun' (3. 622). Her repetition, then, is more than verbal; it is forcefully literal and physiological. In both the life that she describes living and the argument she makes against the conventions of anti-feminism, Alisoun repeats those conventions. Indeed, the Wife is herself a conventional, even a stock, character. A quick survey of the explanatory notes in any standard edition of the *Canterbury Tales* will teach that the main source for her character is that of La Vieille in Jean de Meun's portion of *Le Roman de la Rose*. La Vieille is an old 'trot', a woman too old to participate in the game of love any longer but who still associates herself with sexual pleasures, often by instructing young women in everything from proper table-manners to cosmetics, from how to catch a man to how to abort a child.[65] Alisoun also repeats the words of Jerome, the mysterious Theophrastus and Walter Map. The existence of the Wife, thus, is more than textual:[66] it is intertextual, a relation of infinitely complex stories.[67] Such intertextuality illustrates the potency of a single repetition of a discourse, because what we will see is that to repeat is not merely to reinscribe.[68]

In the Marian mode, the faithful have recourse to the truth created and upheld by the Christian narrative, but when Alisoun of Bath begins to hold forth, truth seems to disappear, broken into little bits and scattered. Such are the effects of making intertextuality apparent. Her story, like Mary's, uses and undermines notions of unity. The Wife's description of herself, her life and her motivations, with its emphasis not only on the Christian God, but also on the gods of romance and war, Venus and Mars, and human reasoning about gods – not to mention that this all is told in 'pleye' (3. 192) – illustrates how rhetorical authority of any singular discourse breaks apart in the texts of everyday life. Additionally, if to name something is to categorize it and, thus, control it, then surely the taxonomic appellation 'The Wife of Bath' implies a unity of character, or at least a unity of purpose in naming.[69] Yet Alisoun's very existence is pluralized even within her *Prologue* and *Tale* by the existence of characters who mirror her. Most apparent is the Wife's 'gossib' (3.529), who is also named Alisoun and who shares the Wife's 'privetee' (3. 531), as Elisabeth did Mary's. This gossib – meaning both 'confidante' and 'gossip' – doubles the Wife in name, in knowledge and in practice, aiding her charge in landing her fifth husband. In the tale she tells, the Wife is doubled by Midas' wife in the excursion the tale makes into Ovid, by the old woman who knows the secret of what 'wommen moost desiren' (l. 905) and even by the young woman into which the old one turns at the tale's end.[70]

As a wife, Alisoun mirrors Mary in several ways. The belief in Mary and Joseph's chaste marriage forced medieval legal theorists to reformulate marriage law so that even those who did not have sex could be considered to be legally married.[71] Earlier investigations in this chapter have illustrated ways in which Mary and Joseph's legal union took on some typical characteristics of marriage because even the pedagogical cycle dramas used anti-feminism to educate their viewers. One way in which Alisoun mirrors Mary is in her first three marriages to older men. The marriage type of the old husband married to a young wife, of which Joseph and Mary's marriage is the prime example, is one that Chaucer used in several of the *Canterbury Tales*; the Miller's 'legende and . . . lyf / Bothe of a carpenter and of his wyf' (1. 3141–2) of John and Alisoun[72] and the Merchant's tale of January and May are two of the most well known. The *Wife of Bath's Prologue* and *Tale* repeat and vary this type in some revealing ways. With her first three husbands, Alisoun is the young wife, married to the older mistrusting husband. Joseph's mistrust of his young wife is a mainstay of the plays that deal with 'Joseph's Troubles'. Under pressure from her husband who anxiously wishes to know who impregnated the youthful Mary, who had been left at home alone, Mary has recourse to ask her serving maids to speak for her, to provide evidence in support of her assertion that she had done nothing wrong. Similarly, Alisoun takes 'witnesse of [her] owne mayde' (3. 233) when accused of misdoing. Mary must go beyond her maids' testimony, as in the 'Trial of Joseph and Mary', and rely on the prophecies about the incarnate God, as well as her bodily knowledge of them, to instruct Joseph and the Jewish community, as Joseph plays his part as the typical, if not stereotypical, Old Cuckold.[73] Mary waits silently for the outcome of God's divine plan while, in contrast, Alisoun does everything but keep silent about her husbands' lack of perception. Instead she uses it to gain control of her life. All images of the Wife, in combination with all of the self-stylized pictures of her own life and opinions on commerce, society, religion and men and women, combine into a character named 'The Wife of Bath', at the same time that they disperse that title. In such a dispersive reinscription, the idea of what a wife is and who *this* wife is cannot remain unchanged, nor can the idea of binary gender that underlies the concept of marriage itself. And we can now see that in the cycle-drama version of Mary's story and in Alisoun's autobiography the stories have similar results: all the characters are shown to be reacting in conventional ways. This conventionality of characters and their reactions evidences the conventional existence of the rhetorical authority of many of the discourses propounded by the church as reality, as self-evident truths.

A similar process near the end of the Wife's *Prologue* allows us another glimpse of this conventionality. By the end of her *Prologue* and in the penultimate episode of her *Tale*, Alisoun has reversed the Mary/Joseph, young bride/elder husband type. She and the old 'wyf' of her tale (3. 998, 1066, 1082, 1086, 1088, 1090) marry young men, a scenario that allows for other narrative possibilities to be worked out rhetorically. Likewise, Mary's role is reversed as her life story and the narrative of salvation grow. Mary was understood to be not only Jesus' mother but also his daughter and wife.[74] As the story goes, since Jesus came to save humanity, he saved, or gave life to, all humans, including Mary; in this way he was a maternal figure.[75] Additionally, as an emblem of human perfection, Mary came to represent the future perfection of humanity, specifically the church, which Christ would wed upon his return to earth. Such rhetorical devices, standard practices in the church, make an intertextual maze of Mary's life. Joseph may be stereotyped as an Old Cuckold for the purposes of heightening drama, but Mary can be seen as a symbol and a body just waiting for significance, significance that the church adds rhetorically as needed. Again, we can understand the fictionalized character of her existence. More revealing, however, is the way that this fiction depends upon an underlying concept of binary gender. Joseph's jealousy and anxiety over his marriage to the young Mary are outgrowths of the anti-feminist tradition, while Mary's own virginally pregnant body con-stitutes the sublation of the fears of this tradition. Mary's continuous repetition of phrases as thoroughly standard as 'it is Goddis will'[76] in reference to her pregnancy leads Joseph into his final acceptance of his wife's innocence and of the absolute singularity of the child she will bear. But without the threat offered and created by anti-feminism, this miracle would have little force. For the mortality and capriciousness instigated by Eve in the garden makes necessary Mary's miraculous pregnancy and gives it its profound significance.

The Wife of Bath with all her Eve-like characteristics, then, must also be understood as part of the context in which Mary can signify so powerfully. Their alliance, though, is not just in their being yoked together as representative opposites; they also share similar narrative styles. Not only is Alisoun a character built upon repetition, as is Mary, but she also creates a character in her story who repeats standard, if not proverbial, bits of wisdom. The 'loathly' lady in the Wife's tale teaches her young felonious husband a lesson about 'gentillesse' (3. 1109) in a sermon so filled with examples and authority that any cleric would be proud to call it his own. Besides calling on the name of 'Jhesus' (1181), she invokes the names of 'Dant' (1126), 'Valerius' (1165), 'Senek', 'Boece' (1169) and 'Juvenal' (1192). With all these examples to support her point about character being more important than birthright, her wedding-night speech to her husband recalls the form and concerns of a sermon, like those of the *Parson's Tale*, which also touches upon gentilesse (10. 460–74). This sermon is matched by the concerns of the tale that surrounds it for this tale is a romance, a genre that often carries within its conventions the desire for wish fulfilment, a control through narratively derived miraculous magic that brings individual and cultural salvation.[77] What happens to transform this knight into a 'gentil man' (1116) is set 'In th'olde dayes' (857) when the land was full of 'fayerye' (859), mysteries and miracles; when women could transform men and themselves. The young knight, a proven rapist doomed to death for his crime, saves his life by listening to the secrets of an old 'wyf' (3. 998). To 'keep [his] nekke-boon from iren' (3. 906), the knight is charged with learning 'What thyng is it that wommen moost desiren' (3. 905). As he searches for an answer to this question in his attempt to save himself from certain death, in a clearing he sees 'ladyes foure and twenty and yet mo' dancing (3. 992). He draws towards them in order to learn their 'wysdom' (3. 994), but as he draws near, they all disappear leaving only the old 'wyf'. In the same way that 'the pillars of male authority, the discourse of Church, government and the written word' strive towards consolidation,[78] the twenty-four seem to be turned into one stereotype from the doctrine of anti-feminism – an ugly old woman who wishes to marry a young man. The knight plights his troth to her, not yet knowing she will ask for marriage from him, and she gives him the life-redeeming information: 'Tho rowned [whispered] she a pistel [message] in his ere / And bad hym to be glad and have no fere' (3. 1021–2). Recalling representations of the Incarnation with its emphasis on the ear, redemption and the messenger's assurance that there is nothing to fear, this scene exemplifies Alisoun's allusive and intertextual storytelling strategy. The old woman becomes a threat in this scene as she becomes an alternate source of authoritative information. She becomes, then, another of the Wife's attempts at miming and displacing the authoritative discourse of church and clerks. We can see in the end of the tale yet another example of this strategy. The young knight, repulsed by the idea that he is now married to such an old poor woman, refuses to acknowledge the wisdom of his wife's sermon on 'gentillesse' and so the 'loathly' lady offers her new young husband a choice. She says

> Chese now . . . oon of thise thynges tweye:
> To han me foul and old til that I deye,
> And be to yow a trewe, humble wyf,
> And nevere yow displese in al my lyf,
> Or elles ye wol han me yong and fair,
> And take youre aventure of the repair
> That shal be to youre hous by cause of me,
> Or in som oother place, may wel be. (3. 1219–26)

The 'either/or' character of this offer seems clear from her command to choose only one option and the decisiveness of 'elles'. Yet, like the 'both' of Alisoun's description of the functions of our 'thynges smale' (3. 121), 'elles', instead of being divisive, proves to be more a copula as the old wife makes the choice for her young husband and becomes 'both' (3. 1240).

In her essay 'The subversive discourse of the Wife of Bath', Ruth Barrie Straus suggests that the overriding motivation for making meaning in the Wife's text is that of masculine desire. She theorizes that the tale and the women in it double this desire. Thus the tale and its characters illustrate the fallacy of the question of what women most desire since that question posits a single, unified desire in women – a typical male fantasy. Certainly, having a beautiful, young, true wife could also be understood as fulfilling male desire. Yet to conclude with Straus that all the Wife's *Prologue* and *Tale* do is 'double the imagination and desire of masculine discourse',[79] even to subvert it, is to conclude that phallocentric discourse has the power it claims. Instead, what we have discovered is that the notion of doubling itself is problematized in the Wife's way of talking.

Doubling or repetition does not constitute replication. Each iteration of a discourse has power that comes not only from the conventional rhetorical power of the discourse itself but also from the context that produces the specific iteration. Surely, for example, the Wife's claim that all women lie (3. 228) has a different significance than a clerk claiming the same thing. The Wife illustrates what happens when the generalizations of 'auctoritee' are mimed within a context specific to one character's body, her desires and her experience. Overtly Alisoun's language contains

> an 'other meaning' always in the process of weaving itself, of embracing itself with words, but also of getting rid of words in order not to become fixed, congealed in them. For if 'she' says something, it is not, it is already no longer, identical with what she means. What she says is never identical with anything [original emphasis].[80]

When Alisoun says of her fifth husband, Jankyn, that 'in oure bed he was so fressh and gay, / And therwithal so wel koude he me glose, / Whan that he wolde han my *bele chose*' (3. 508–10), her previous use of the word 'glose' in relation to body parts and functions must inflect this usage; we are reminded that body parts and the gendered behaviours attached to them constitute merely one set of signs employed in Christian discourse, given meaning by and providing meaning for Christianity. The Wife's coupling of glossing with the euphemistic *bele chose*[81] to refer to her most intimate body parts calls attention to the quality of her body that is always textual, indeed, always intertextual and so never entirely apprehensible or categorized by any single way of making meaning.

When Alisoun narrates her life with Jankyn, she tells of the emotional pain he caused her by reading aloud to her out of his book of evil wives. But when Jankyn is hit in the face and thrown into the fire as he and Alisoun struggle over the book, astute readers understand that such a man has also already been inscribed by the dominant discourses of gender. Under 'Adam's mark' he could not help but be. The repeated narration of their lives illustrates, however, not only the power of discourses to mark, define and even deafen bodies but also the possibilities that arise from a singular intertextual repetition of any discourse. For in such repetition, what becomes inescapably apparent is the personal and cultural histories that come into play each time orthodox or heterodox texts and readings of them are brought to bear on bodies. The Wife of Bath's gender, as well as that of her husband and those variously described by the church, then, can be said to be neither true nor false, normal nor anomalous; instead, in being precisely what it is, the Wife's performance reveals the uncertain necessity of an oppositional understanding of gender differences in the midst of the church's self-definition.

3

Dispersing Faith:
Seinte Marherete, Maternal Bodies, and Telling Stories

In contrast to the gender- and genre-bending performance of the *Wife of Bath's Prologue* and *Tale*, the Middle English life of St Margaret is about keeping boundaries in place. This work is found collected with the lives of Sts Katherine and Juliana and with the treatises 'Ancrene Riwle' (Anchoress's Rule) and 'Hali Meiðhad' (A Letter on Virginity) in two manuscripts dating from the early thirteenth century. Such texts collaborated in the construction of an image of the medieval pious woman: virginal, selfless, devoted to God, like the ultimate example of female piety that was the Virgin Mary. Yet this representation of virtuous life was, in fact, riven by contradiction throughout its existence, for this view of virtue is one that is always split by the very thing by which it is manifested: the often-employed figure of the sealed(-in) female body.[1] Although Margaret's body was virginal, she was associated with birth, specifically the symbolically most violent of births, Caesarean section. In the most famous scene from the Middle English version of her life, she is eaten by a dragon that then bursts open because the saint has crossed herself. The scene is the reason for Margaret's association with Caesarean birth – even though *she* is the one who is symbolically (re)born – and it provides the best example of the conflation of bodies that takes place in this text. Margaret's body, Christ's crucified body, the dragon's body and the bodies of women in labour everywhere join to form a series, not just of bodies but also of signs connected through violence. Ultimately, this chapter argues that the violence and permeability of the virgin saint's body are factors that constitute the very notions of purity and sanctity, for without a body that can be razed and dispersed, the sealed-in body would not signify purity so powerfully.

Margaret's particular association with Caesarean birth and the way her story is pulled out of the theological register into the parturient one – in prayers to her during difficult childbirth – suggest a constant re-emergence of fleshiness in the process of making meaning. Her association with the Holy Virgin Mary via their similar intercessional functions during labour provides another layer of figuration in this investigation of the status of the flesh in the formation of Christian ideology. Margaret's story never forgets the torment and rending of bodies associated with producing ideology, nor does it overlook its own production. *Seinte Marherete, þe Meiden ant Martyr* is a work concerned with the business of storytelling. In the staging of its own composition, *Seinte Marherete* can be read as intimately concerned, both on the narrative and dramatic levels, with reproducing faithful bodies. As such, this story marks itself as part of the generic translation of a biography, specific to time, place and material existence, into an example of eternal verity. In so doing it claims for itself the status of metaphor of salvation. Yet, given the structure of metaphorical logic, which works by searching for likenesses only by recalling differences, *Seinte Marherete* fails to negate the difference between the body of the saint and itself as a body of intertextuality. In the prayers of every labouring mother to St Margaret, the in-between-ness, or the contingency, of the narrativized body as a figure is made apparent. We must see, then, how the living on of Margaret's story of torture and death in the dangerous occurrence of childbirth denies the negation of the body posited by the notion of the transcendence of the Word over the Flesh, even as the very staging of her story is an act that seeks to demonstrate the effects of this negation. Instead, Margaret's virginally sealed yet publicly exhibited body illustrates the divided quality of an ideal of transcendence dependent upon this slippery fleshy stuff as its medium.

Other than depictions of Mary's experience with pregnancy, the New Testament presents childbearing in only the most ambivalent of terms:

> In like manner also, that women adorn themselves in modest apparel, with shamefacedness and sobriety; not with braided hair, or gold, or pearls, or costly array. But (which becometh women professing godliness) with good works. Let the woman learn in silence with all subjection. But I suffer not

a woman to teach, nor to usurp authority over the man, but to be in silence. For Adam was first formed, then Eve. And Adam was not deceived, but the woman being deceived was in the transgression. Notwithstanding she shall be saved in childbearing, if they continue in faith and charity and holiness with sobriety. (1 Timothy 2:9–15)

The passage echoes and recuperates the curse placed on Eve in Genesis 3:16: 'I will greatly multiply thy sorrow and thy conception;/ in sorrow thou shalt bring forth children'. In its attempt to inscribe a firm position for women in the new church, the Pauline verse marks not only female sin and its connection to flesh but also the redemptive potential of fleshly (re)production. The connection between fleshy sin and mistaken language was one that held much currency in the Middle Ages. Paul has attempted to recuperate both aspects of Eve's sin and to bring woman's more greatly fallen nature back within the bounds of salvational possibility. In contrast to men who may voice their supplications to God (1 Timothy 2:8), women should let their attire and deeds speak for them. Their profession, or public declaration, of religion becomes publicly quieted, displaced to the signs their bodies carry. Clothes and deeds replace their silenced voices and their profession, or vocation, becomes the veiling of the bodily processes that may save them.

The danger of errant language, emphasized in the Pauline passage, remained a concern throughout the early history of Christianity and well into the Middle Ages. Eve is beguiled by the words of the serpent in the garden (Genesis 3:13) and Adam is cursed by God for having 'hearkened unto to the voice of [his] wife' and eating from the tree 'of which I [God] commanded thee, "Thou shalt not eat of it"' (Genesis 3:17). God's curses on the first humans make explicit the connections, in the biblical framework, between language and physical existence: the serpent's subtle words to Eve are translated into increased desire for her husband and the consequent pain of childbirth, while Eve's words – not narrated in the text of Genesis – are translated into the man's constant toil to make the ground produce food. Permeating biblical revisions of the story of the Fall is the underlying idea that listening to words from the wrong source creates dangerous situations. The passage from 1 Timothy attempts to put rules in place that would prohibit occasions in which the new church might hear from the wrong source, the mouth of pain and desire that is the fecund woman. Yet the passage posits this very fecundity as salvational. Only with the coming of God in human form via a virginally sealed body can salvation be found in reproduction.[2] With the Incarnation, the 'treasure' of life is put into the 'earthen vessels' of mortal bodies (2 Corinthians 4:7). Humans are

> always bearing about in the body the dying of the Lord Jesus, that the life also of Jesus might be made manifest in our body. For we which live are always delivered unto death for Jesus' sake, that the life also of Jesus might be made manifest in our mortal flesh. (2 Corinthians 4:10–11)

In response to the positive potential now available in the flesh, Pauline theology posits a maternal metaphor that recuperates Eve's original sin and its punishment of multiplied sexual desire and pain in childbirth. Thus, a woman can be saved by having children 'if she continues in faith and charity and holiness with sobriety' (1 Timothy 2:15). In some ways, the passage from the second letter to the Corinthians enlarges the concept of maternity to be descriptive of all Christians. This appropriative attempt, however, does not negate the difference that female physiology inherits from the story told in Genesis. To recall the passage from Timothy and the sentiments, prevalent in the Middle Ages, that it spawned, the Christian woman is both cursed and blessed with childbirth: it remains a mark of Eve's sin and curse, at the same time that it is personally and, via Mary, culturally salvational.

It should not surprise us then that patristic writing about maternity and reproduction often refers negatively to childbirth even as it bases the continuation of faith on the ever-present reinscription of labour pain. According to St Thomas Aquinas in *Summa theologica*, the command in Genesis to 'Be fruitful and multiply' (1:28) was an injunction to be not only spiritually prolific, but also physically so:

> The precept given as to generation looks to the whole multitude of men. This multitude must be not only multiplied bodily, but advanced spiritually. Therefore, sufficient provision for the human multitude is made, if *some undertake the task of carnal generation*. (*Summa theologica*, 2–2. 152. 2, reply to obj. 1)[3]

Aquinas describes a process in which carnal generation seems an a priori constituent in the process of spirituality, even as his statement devalues the physiological. And Aquinas was not alone in this mode of thinking in which salvation supplants but is dependent on the maternal body.

The same sort of necessary negation takes place in the story of Mary. During the Middle Ages Mary's spiritually necessary body was an object of constant study. Questions over whether and how Mary remained ever-virgin and whether she menstruated and lactated persisted as perplexing areas of disputation. Such strongly held beliefs as the Incarnation/Annunciation, Mary's own Immaculate Conception, her perpetual virginity and her bodily Assumption into heaven suggest that hers was not conceived of as an ordinary human body. Such theologies and their popular celebrations in feast days tended to erase many of the attributes that would define her as the human mother of God. According to medieval medicine, typical women participated in the final constitution of the child by providing the raw matter, the menses, out of which the child was formed by the guiding principle of the male's semen.[4] Thus, the woman participated, albeit to an inferior degree, in the final constitution of the child. Against this scientific background, the question of whether or not Mary menstruated became a central concern. If Mary is denied original sin, via the notion of her Immaculate Conception, she does not share the curse of Eve and being without the spot of sin[5] she must also be without the monthly 'spot' of menstruation. If given such a perfect body, she was nothing more than a vessel that received and nurtured the divine seed, adding nothing of herself and, therefore, putting the humanity of Christ into question and threatening to destabilize the salvational significance of the Incarnation. The disputation over the characteristics of Mary's body evidences a culture's attempts to define itself discursively, and in such conversations we can discern some of the boundaries the early Christian church set up for itself. In the contentions over the precise nature of Mary's physiology, the culture's repulsion of menstruation[6] and the narrative necessity of God's absolute purity constitute two opposite, hierarchically situated poles of difference. We come to understand that this thing called 'Mary's body' is as much a product of the desires and anxieties of the culture that employs it as it is a vehicle for the values of that culture.

An investigation of the medieval belief that Mary lactated and suckled her child will enable me to clarify this point further. From the earliest first-century images of her, Mary has been represented as a nursing mother. The *Protevangelium* describes a midwife witnessing the appearance of the child which then 'went and took the breast of its mother Mary'. Augustine also wrote about Mary breastfeeding Jesus: 'Suckle, mother, our food; suckle the bread coming from heaven and placed in a manger as the provisions of devout beasts of burden.'[7] A thirteenth-century lyric, 'I Sing of One that is Matchless', praises 'þe suete broste þat hire sone sec',[8] while another lyric of the same period, 'Our Lady Help us at our Ending', blesses 'þe pappis þat godis sone sauk' (68:3). This popular tradition continued and grew in the fourteenth century. In 'Marye, Mayde Mylde and Fre' the 'melke of [Mary's] breste'[9] has the power of taming the wild unicorn and a 'Song of Love to the Blessed Virgin' reminds readers that the Christ child was dependent on his mother's milk, which he 'sek . . . of hire brest' (111:13).[10] Since medieval medical practice connected the process of lactation with that of menstruation, these images prove to be very revealing. Incorporating ideas from Arabic medical writings, medieval doctors accepted and fostered the basic idea that milk is formed from menstrual blood.[11] In this scenario the reminder of the death curse is turned into nourishment, locally with each infant born and nursed and culturally in each picture or poem in which the Virgin offers her breast to Christ. The incorporation of the forbidden fruit and, thus, of sin and death in Genesis is, therefore, translated via the formless matter of the menses into salvation. This story makes clear how medieval Christianity has predicated its notion of human existence, salvation and eternal life on components it defines as deadly, evil and dangerously errant. My examination later in the chapter of a specific medieval medical text, the *English Trotula*, will illustrate this point further. The cursed body of Eve, although constantly reinscribed with the 'Ave' of Mary, never disappears in the equation; reminders and remainders of the matter of Mary's female body, so closely tied to its salvational purposes, recur in the disputations we have already examined, so central to the church's understanding of its very purpose and functioning, as well as in such displays as that of Mary's *mikveh* or tub where she washed away the defilement caused by her period, still a popular part of the tour at the Church of the Annunciation in Nazareth.[12] Analogously, part of St Margaret's torture at the hands of the pagan Olibrius is to be bound and thrown into a vessel of water, a translated purification of another woman whose narrative purity is never questioned yet always anxiously put to the test.

The connection of the curse to procreation and salvation brings us back to the passage from 2 Corinthians cited above. Whether it is Mary's, Jesus's or any Christian's, the body described by the Bible carries both life and death. This body is a permeable thing, a conglomeration of insides and outsides in which boundaries are transient and significations are contingent upon contexts. To be sure, the idea of a discrete human body, bounded firmly at all points, is a prevalent one, else the tales of martyred saints like Margaret would have little force. Through the violation of such boundaries identity formation takes place; through pain and separation, humans and the societies in which they function define themselves.[13] Yet, as the interdependent nature of the relationship between Mary, mother of God, and Eve, mother of mortality, makes evident, unbounded flesh is never far outside the frame. According to the medieval Christian frame, upon addition of the most pure of all bodily substances, sperm,[14] the unformed matter of maternal bodies is supposed to produce the paradigmatic: an able-bodied Christian man. But as a further look at some medieval medical concepts will exemplify, this notion of identity formation from matter does nothing so effectively as displace and multiply the effects of the unformed matter. Whether one considers the texts of the lives of Eve and Mary or those of a myriad of historical women struggling in childbirth daily, the excessive potential of the flesh remains. The stories about Eve and her connection to Mary at once try and fail to translate her body into punishment and desire – else why would there have been such a vehement misogynistic tradition in the Middle Ages, the vestiges of which are still discernible in today's media representations of women? At the same time the maternal body is potentially a medium of salvation with even pain serving a function. In their very urge to write away Mary's body – one way of doing this is by establishing her as anti-Eve – the stories that create Mary as *Theotokos* illustrate this displacement and the desire for unity that caused it to proliferate. What is the necessity that compels the patristic fathers to continue their discussion over Mary's physiology if they are so assured of the truths they desire her body to signify? In light of our investigation of Mary as Virgin/Mother, we can now understand that the origin of their anxious compulsion lies somewhere within the process that turned trope into truth, a compulsion shared by the narrator of *Seinte Marherete*.

It should not surprise us that medieval medicine was also a discipline of troping, of bodies signifying many things in addition to physiology, making them the matter of transcendence. Asserting most meticulously an opinion that grew to have great currency in the Middle Ages, Galen (130?–201?) postulated the interrelatedness of the sexes, suggesting a hierarchy of male over female but doing so via a logic of accident. As part of his reasoning about why women are less perfect than men,

Galen asserts that the female reproductive system was just like the male's, only turned outside in:

> in women the parts are within [the body], whereas in men they are outside. Consider first whichever ones you please, turn outward the woman's, turn inward, so to speak and fold double the man's and you will find them the same in both in every respect.[15]

Galen then develops in detail the exact matches between body parts, correlating scrotum with uterus, testicles with the ovaries, penis with vagina and prepuce with labia. According to Galenic logic, based largely on the four humours, the reason a female child is formed, that is, the reason why the organs remain inside the body, is that the female is colder than the male. Due to this *'defect* in the heat' (2. 630; my emphasis)[16] the organs could not emerge and perfect themselves. Galen asserts, though, that this lack proves beneficial to humanity:

> this, though making the animal itself that was being formed less perfect than one that is complete in all respects, provided no small advantage for the race; for there needs must be a female. Indeed, you ought not to think that our Creator would purposely make half the whole race imperfect and, as it were, mutilated, unless there was to be some great advantage in such a mutilation. (2. 630)

While making the masculine body the model of humanness, a concept of gender difference based not on the replication of perfection but on the reproduction – 'purposeful' though it may be – of mutilation destabilizes classical concepts of the superiority of the soul over the flesh and the man over the woman. Galenic texts and medical discourse more generally are concerned with marking boundaries in undifferentiated flesh, finding the divine reasons for the empirical differences and yet the subtextual accident of gender and the overlay of theological, scientific, philosophical and semiotic explanations must remind us of the errant and indeterminable basis of such concepts as 'human', 'natural' and 'without sin'.

Implied in this notion of accidental gender is an underlying notion of the human body as not discretely bounded. In this system of conceptualizing bodies, the prime physiological markers of gender, the genitalia, are perceived as essentially mobile, or more precisely, interchangeable. Given that this interchange is perceived as a movement between what is presumed to be inside and outside, we must recognize that the notions of a distinctly bounded body and the individual gendered identity that may go along with such a body come from somewhere besides physiology. The most basic dichotomy, that of inside/outside or I/not-I, must, then, be looked at not as foundational components but in the light of a web of interchangeableness and semiotic currency.

Specific medieval medical practices tended to bear out a concept of the body different from the modern post-Freudian body, in which specific processes of establishing bodily boundaries are associated with identifiable family figures and moments in time. The medieval medical body both had an internal coherence and extensive, overdetermined connections to the world outside it. Astrology is one pathway by which such connections were made. Chaucer's 'Doctour of Phisik' exemplifies the mixture of empiricism, planetary motion and daily practice that constituted a major discursive perimeter of medieval medicine:

> In al this world ne was ther noon hym lik,
> To speke of phisik and of surgerye,
> For he was grounded in astronomye.
> He kepte his pacient a ful greet deel
> In houres by his magyk natureel.
> Wel koude he fortunen the ascendent
> Of his ymages for his pacient . . .
> He was a verray, parfit praktisour.[17]

This is a mode of medicine in which the patient appears not as a individual but as an assortment of attributes, or 'ymages' discerned in the movements of the heavens. Perhaps the Doctor's patient needed some blood let; before proceeding, the doctor would have to recognize and interpret the astrological signs, as well as the climatological, spiritual and physiological ones.

Again, from the literary realm, Chaucer illustrates popular understanding of medical practice, and the need to interpret signs, in words the Man of Law speaks:

> For in the sterres, clerer than is glas,
> Is writen, God woot, whoso koude it rede,
> The deeth of every [one], withouten drede. (2. 194–6)

Medieval medical writings are full of attempts at learning to read this so-called writing, and so it is not surprising that the practice of etymological investigation marked much medical knowledge of the Middle Ages. As medieval etymology was largely a quest for the essential truth of any signifier, that signifier's purpose for being what it is, so medieval physiological research focused on the purpose of any organ, the way it received, held and passed on the spirits that animated it. From this teleological perspective, organs become the physical mani-festations of what are perceived of as essential *pneuma* that provide a human with intellect and connections to divinity.[18] Organs, which may be perfect or not, situate each expression of the essential in this way.

From Augustine, Bonaventure and Albertus Magnus to Thomas Aquinas and Vincent of Beauvais, medical thinkers proposed various and often contradictory theories concerning the active potential of the zodiac and the heavens to influence human lives and reproduction of them. One way this influence was figured was through the metaphor of the microcosm/macrocosm. This perspective, based on Pythagorean theories and elaborated with Arabic notions of planetary influences over specific parts and functions of the human body, situated the human as a representative in miniature of the universe, in tune with all its rhythms and influences. In *Figures of Life and Death in Medieval English Literature*, Philippa Tristram includes a typical representation of such influences, a picture of zodiac man from an early fourteenth-century English manuscript illustrating the various connections between signs of the zodiac and specific parts of the body. From Aries the Ram's government of the head to Scorpio's association with the groin and Pisces' charge of the feet, the system was a complete one.[19] Additionally, each of the four humours and its corresponding disposition was associated with a planet: phlegmatic with Venus, sanguine with Jupiter, choleric with Mars and melancholic with Saturn. Beyond this, however, as Constantinus Africanus writes in his treatise on coition, 'God can grant' what he will.[20]

Chaucer's Alisoun of Bath justifies her appetites and conduct by claiming such affinities with the planets, saying

> I hadde the prente of seinte Venus seel . . .
> For certes, I am al Venerien
> In feelynge and myn herte is Marcien.
> Venus me yaf my lust, my likerousnesse,
> And Mars yaf me my sturdy hardynesse; . . .
> . . . have I Martes mark upon my face (3. 604, 609–12, 619)

This passage exemplifies the way different discourses intersected to produce perceptions of a human body even in popular contexts. A physiological aspect of the body, the birthmark or 'Venus seel', is translated into the astrological register, which is itself a way of talking about the Wife's 'likerous' social behaviour. Yet the birthmark is not the cause for Alisoun's behaviour; it is a mark of previous planetary influence, the 'vertu of [her] constellacioun' (3. 616). In this complex of displacements and replacements, cause/effect logic is apparent in the verb 'yaf' and yet it is not clear what is the cause and what is the effect. For the birthmark seems to be equally the signifier of the ostensibly causal astrological influences and of the resulting behaviour in the Wife. In her astrological explanation, Alisoun of Bath uses the same deductive logic to explain her socially active body as that which a surgeon would use to comprehend the body laid out before him for surgery, a body any good surgeon would not dare incise when the moon was waxing for fear he might not be able to staunch the bleeding.

Alisoun of Bath's description and the general medical practices of the era, like the ones we have examined so far, indicate to us the way in which medieval science investigated and defined bodies within a complex web of various discourses. So for medieval practitioners of medicine, 'natural' causes of disease were not necessarily physiological causes. In fact, medieval aetiology was just as often concerned with astrology, divine influence, social behaviour and the way diseases were named and taxonomized as with examination of urine, pustules or body parts. The social and sexual, procreative body was one term in the series that gave the bodies significance and not the innocent origin of these significances. What we will see in *Seinte Marherete*, though, is that this body, created by discourses, will be employed as a vehicle to manifest the very truths that are purported to exist transcendent of time and space.

The history of dissection illustrates this point more precisely. In northern Italy evidence exists illustrating that dissections on human bodies were carried out as early as the end of the thirteenth century, while it was not until the late fourteenth century that dissections were officially sanctioned in France. Only in 1478 was the first human body dissected in Paris.[21] Many early medical descriptions of the human body were therefore based on descriptions of other types of bodies, those of animals. For instance, what was known about the female reproductive system was based not on the study of women but on the dissection of sows. Also involved was the teleological paradigm which emphasized the mechanism of any organ over its exact physical properties, that is, which emphasized the organ's situating of the essential life-giving quality over its material function or dysfunction in the particular body of its origin. In other words, even as it became a more regular part of medical training, dissection was carried out not to uncover new knowledge about human physiology but to demonstrate and pass on what was already known, what had been already proved by the ancients and the precepts of the church.[22]

What fascinates a modern reader about this scientific research is the overt recognition within the discourse of ways that medieval medicine took from and added to a series of different culturally situated discourses: philosophical, etymological, scientific and theological, to name but a few that we have already examined. In many ways this semiotic network reveals a prevalent desire to control and delimit the human body by explaining its functions in as many varied registers as possible. But the very complex and often contradictory nature of medical discourse, this 'magyk natureel', illustrates a continuing confusion over and mystification of human physiology. Aristotelian binary logic and the Galenic science founded on it may have described a dual existence, divided into spirit and body, male and female, the I and not-I, and yet we can now see the cultural forces that came into play as the conflation of many discourses makes these concepts seem natural and God-given. So even as practitioners of medieval science continued to advance new theories, to treat disease more effectively and to understand the mechanisms of organs more fully, physiology was yet being mystified. Indeed, the truth of the human body was known to medieval doctors and surgeons, and even midwives, but this was a truth synthesized from the anxieties, desires and cultural inheritances passed down and filtered through ages.

One way in which such knowledge was passed on was via daily medical practice. A typical example of a vernacular medical text is a work now generally known as the *English Trotula* or the fourteenth-century redaction of the *De passionibus mulierum curandarum*. It is impossible to authenticate the existence of one woman named Trotula after whom this work was named[23] because literary and historical evidence provide us with various explanations for the name. There may have been a historical Trotula who was an eleventh-century student at the medical school at Salerno. That women practised medicine and were associated with the great medical schools from at least the eleventh century to the fourteenth, both on the continent and in England, is supported by government and school records.[24] Yet the name also had a substantial literary significance. Like *La Vieille* in *Le Roman de la Rose* and Chaucer's Wife of Bath, old women in literature who were still sexually active and liked to talk about their lives, especially when doing so would instruct younger women in the 'art of the olde daunce', were called 'trots'. There is slipperiness, then, built into the title of this work, an interchangeableness between a scientific discourse and a prurient one. Indeed, Beryl Rowland, editor and translator of the *English Trotula*[25] for modern readers, suggests that the popularity of Trotula texts, including this one, may have been due to their 'pornographic' character, with science providing a justification for the salacious view of female physiology.[26]

So, despite the uncertainty of its authorial origins, the *English Trotula* serves as one avenue to investigate how the opinions of the learned doctors were translated into vernacular common practices and attitudes. Exemplary of medical manuals for women, the *English Trotula* reifies Aristotelian, Galenic notions of the female as an inferior being, by nature susceptible to more disease than the male. As such she has special medical needs appropriate only for other women to investigate and treat. The *English Trotula* suggests:

> For as moche as there ben manye women that hauen many diuers maladies and sekenesses nygh to þe deth and thei also ben shamefull to schewen and to tellen her greuaunces unto eny wyght, therefore I schal sumdele wright to herre maladies remedye, praying to God ful of grace to sende me grace truly to write to þe plesaunce of God & to all womannes helpyng . . . And thowgh women have diuers evelles & many greet greuaunces mo than all men knowen of, as I seyd, hem schamen . . . And yf women be in dissese, suche men haue hem in despyte & thenke nought how moche dysese women haue or þan they haue brought hem into þis world. And therefore, in helping of women I wyl wright of women prevy sekenes the helpyng and that oon woman may helpe another in her sykeness & nought diskuren her previtees to suche vncurteys men.[27]

The subtexts in this passage are now quite apparent to us: we can easily note the repercussions of the accidental quality of woman's existence, an inferior life by far, and the scientific and Christian emendations that tend to bring this 'naturally fallen' state back into the fold of humanity and God's timeless plan for it.[28] Even shame becomes a useful part of female existence, helping to keep boundaries of appropriate topics of discussion and examination firmly in place and reinscribing gendered spheres of influence.[29] And yet, even as this work in its entirety repeats this discourse of shame, it also describes the female body in overt terms. This text that ostensibly protects the modesty of women also describes procedures that put body parts on display and, like Galenic medical discourse, such procedures illustrate the transiently over-determined boundaries of the female body. Many treatments described for various maladies indicate the outward influence on inner health. One section describes how suppositories designed to be inserted into the 'prevy membres' must be 'bounde with a threde abouten oon of thyes' lest they be drawn completely inside. Another provides the midwife with instructions about how to insert her hands, anointed with certain oils, to correct the position of a foetus during childbirth. The *English Trotula* gives exact prescriptions for fumigations to be held near the nostrils and/or vaginal opening to ensure the correct position of the uterus and for various ways to cure prolapse, or 'travelling', of the uterus.[30] Like any medical text, this one attempts to make the secrets of the body known and connects these secrets with a myriad of outside forces.

Similarly, bodily revelation of secrets comprises an important part of Mary's story. Her behaviour after the Annunciation revolved around keeping secrets about her body. For instance, the *Protevangelium* describes Mary's behaviour after the archangel visits her with the news: 'Mary was afraid . . . and hid herself from the children of Israel . . . when these mysteries came to pass' (12:3). Then after the visit of the shepherds at the Nativity, she secretively 'kept all these things, pondering them in her heart' (Luke 2:19). In her initial reaction to her pregnancy, Mary's response arises from the same discourse of shame that constitutes the palimpsest for the *English Trotula*, and it is a way of comprehending women's bodies with which her older husband is quite familiar. For even though Mary attempts to hide herself from her community and keep her secrets, her obviously pregnant body reveals to Joseph at least one truth of her interior condition. In the network of the holy couple's community values, which I am about to describe, we will see re-statements of the medical and ethical discourses so common to the period. More specifically and revealingly, we can begin to understand how the bodies of typical women were made to signify in Judaeo-Christian culture and how Mary's pregnancy, as well as the maternal body in general, manifests the way in which a culture's anxieties become appended to that culture's notion of transcendence.

In the apocrypha, when Joseph returns home after travelling for some time and first sees the pregnant Mary, his shame is so great that he begins to mourn his reputation. He claims that his wife has acted as degenerately as Eve by declaring that in him the story of Adam has been repeated (*Protevangelium*, 13:1–2). Not only is the yoking of original sin and salvation apparent in this declaration but Joseph's focus on his own status in the community also illustrates the existence of Mary's body as one component in an ethical system that provides physiology with meaning(s). In the *N-Town* and *York* cycle-dramas, a similar displacement of the meaning of Mary's body on to the status of Joseph occurs. In the *N-Town*, he fears being known as an 'Olde cockwold' and threatens to return Mary 'To þe busshop . . . / Þat he þe lawe may here do / With stonys' what is appropriate.[31] The *York* cycle's 'Joseph's Trouble about Mary' begins with the elderly Joseph's complaints about having to take a young wife. The motivation for his complaints is the fear of being shamed by what a young woman living in his house might do, and his fears come true upon his view of his pregnant wife whose 'sidis shewes she is with childe'.[32] He begins to fear that he will 'dare loke no man in þe face' (l. 147) and that he will have to 'bere þe blame' (l. 181) of her pregnancy. He tells her

> But Marie, all þat sese þe
> may witte þi werkis ere wan,
> Thy wombe all way it wreyes þe,
> þat þou has mette with man. (163–66)

We can recognize here that Mary's obviously pregnant body signifies what is at stake for Joseph, an upstanding member of the Galilean Jewish community. His view of her pregnant body makes her physiology part of a culturally constructed semiotic system of values – of shame and sin. Indeed, Joseph's refusal to consider other possible interpretations of what he sees when he looks at the pregnant girl who stands before him – such as a miraculous pregnancy, the outcome of divine prophecy – illustrates the way in which cultural and religious constructs produce bodies. The verb *wreyes* is important here. It means both 'publish' and 'betray', as if the mere fact of not keeping her pregnancy secret is in itself some type of betrayal. Therefore, Joseph says that Mary's body *publishes* her sin and so *betrays* her secrets to the town. And within the values of this community, certainly a girl who becomes pregnant while her husband is away is in store for countless trials and much abuse. Yet this scene and 'Joseph's Doubt' also make something else public. The *York* cycle spends 236 lines on Joseph's confusion over Mary's pregnancy while the *N-Town* spends the whole of the play 'The Trial of Joseph and Mary' and 125 lines of 'Joseph's Doubt'[33] on failed attempts to bring Mary's pregnancy within discursive areas that will make it sensible or, in other words, that will make the physical experience of it comprehensible intellectually. More specifically, Joseph's and the priests' constant reiteration of the question, 'Whose is the child?', illustrates the limits of this community's ability to make Mary's words of innocence and virginity match what seems to be her body's obviously breached state. Surely the Jewish judges and Joseph knew of the prophecies, foundational to their religion, that a young girl would give birth to the Messiah and yet when faced, in the flesh, with the culmination of their history, they end up seeing only a pregnant 'ȝonge damesel' before them.[34] It takes a lot for them to shift their perspective: they have to remember other semiotic systems, specifically the eschatological prophecies of the Messiah, before they believe what Mary says of her own body, before her body becomes intelligible to them. As these plays were performed for an audience already familiar with the end of the story, as any reader of *Seinte Marherete* would be with her story, given the formulaic nature of the saint's-life genre, the Jews and Joseph become stock characters, as we all know, laughable in their ignorance and refusal to believe. For such an audience, Mary's sexuality and procreative capability, then, signify not only the timeless narrative of salvation, past, present and future, but also the very time-bound cultural attitudes of hatred and ridicule towards the Jews, prevalent in both liturgical drama and secular works like miracles of the Virgin and Chaucer's *Prioress's Tale*.[35] This anti-Semitism cannot be extracted from the doctrine these plays intend to put forth, nor can the underlying danger of sexuality, Mary's inheritance from Eve. Even as a text like the *N-Town* tends to appropriate maternity and annul its physicality, it also makes something else clear in the figure of Mary: access to transcendence and eschatological certitude is solely figural. The significances the character of Mary is made to bear as a figure in a play about Christian teleology and in the salvational narrative as a whole cannot exist without the physiological figure of her pregnant body. However, pregnancy is in no way, according to this same narrative frame, dependent on moral goodness or transcendent purpose. Instead, what is built into this system is the accident of reproduction, a quality that proves to be an effective foundation upon which to build an

idea of perfection and purity with no mistakes. And yet this uncontrollable and ultimately unknowable foundation, this fleshy otherness which is still part of each Christian, also must remind us that
something always lies outside our (pur)view. It is not so much, then,
that the cultural anxieties we have been examining have been appended
to, or are some by-product of, the idea of Christian transcendence, but
rather define and, indeed, constitute the very idea of transcendence.

Still, as anyone who has read Freud, Foucault, Lacan or Kristeva
will argue, albeit from different theoretical perspectives, cultures
produce bodies by establishing the paradigms by which members of
any culture can comprehend human physiology. Surely, that is what
our earlier view of medieval astrology and Galenic medicine exemplified for us. A further look at the *English Trotula* will help me to clarify
the relationship between culture and physiology because, with its
objective discourse of science, the *English Trotula*, unthinkingly – that
is, without needing to consider the motivations behind statements –
mixes in culturally based presuppositions about appropriate treatment
and behaviour. In addition to the statements throughout that leave
medical matters to the grace of God, the *English Trotula* situates its
expertise within a specific moral and legal framework. For instance, in
suggesting what to do for a woman whose uterus has travelled so far as
to press against her heart and lungs and suffocate her, the text claims
that one remedy is

> to haue company with man. But þus vnderstonde: in lawefull
> companyying, as with her housebandes and with none other; for in
> certayn it were better for a man other for a woman to haue þe grettest
> sekenesse of þe body the whiles þei leven than to ben helyd thorough a
> dede of lechery other ony other dede ayenst goddis hestys.[36]

This statement of propriety simply marks in the text another form of
cure. It is preceded by detailed descriptions of the aetiology of the
disease and of the extent of the pain in which it puts a woman; it
precedes several rigorously described recipes for prescriptions and
other techniques for replacing the uterus in its appropriate location.
We can infer from this statement and others like it that those
practitioners who used this manual would have accepted what is
'lawefull' simply as another part of medicine that unquestionably falls
within and helps define the scientific purview. The text began with a
buried reminder of the curse of Eve, so it should not surprise us that it

comprehends, as part of its reason for being, the morals and laws that make Christianity intelligible. We must remember, though, that a society would not be in need of moral codes – reminders of goodness – if morality were truly transcendent, for if it were, all would know it innately. Instead, morally behaving bodies remind the faithful of what is understood to be good. So in this focus on morals we can see one avenue by which medieval culture produced itself and, in so doing, produced this concept of errant female physiology. The stereotypical, anti-feminist concept of women as heirs to all Eve's faults becomes, in this moral system, an outside force against which a culture defined itself as proper, lawful and unified. The discourse of shame constitutes a constant reminder of the risky, secret or 'prevy' aspects of the flesh.[37] And yet this exterior 'other' is also *part of* the culture; like her ability to give birth, one's mother, sister, lover or wife always had this digressive potential *inside* her. We can see now how this narrative translates the dangers of the unpredictable into the perilous secrets of femininity and how these secrets then become shame, the basis of a moral code and a system of accompanying laws.

In this narrative process of substitution we can discern the several discourses that created the empiricism of medieval medicine and the teleological, etymological, mechanistic medical body. Within this spectrum, a body could signify many things – among others, Galen's teachings, planetary movements, a blessing from God, an etymological chain. So what we can now recognize is that such knowledge – accepted as natural, a transcendent part of God's first book, Creation – was, instead, knowledge created, not discovered, by the bodily metaphors employed by medicine and theology. And what we must now recognize is that these domains of knowledge, like the bodies that symbolize them, exist and thrive, at least in part, because of the holes that permeate them.

Saints'-lives tales worked in a similarly appropriative manner: they put the narrated body in pain and make the pain signify Christian faith and salvational history.[38] In *The Body in Pain: The Making and Unmaking of the World*, Elaine Scarry defines a relationship between pain, appropriation and power. She argues that since pain, of itself, resists language because it seems to refer to nothing but itself, it is most often figured by objects that inflict it. Thus, pain is represented by that with which it is inflicted or those who inflict it. In her investigation of various modern transcripts of sessions of torture for political reasons, Scarry discovers that such objectifying representations have allowed pain to be appropriated by those wishing to consolidate their power. In such an appropriation, bodily pain is figured as the ability to inflict said pain. Therefore the body in pain becomes a medium for those, like Olibrius, who gain power by creating the spectacle of pain.

We can see that medieval empiricism was also appropriative, a realization that should not surprise us since we have already discovered that this empiricism was also a morality, a cosmology, a legal system and a theology, all systems that made bodies to signify for their own narrative ends. What we can also discern in this webwork of discourses is a constant recursive urge to establish cultural identity. The discourses that we have examined illustrate particularly the way in which medieval Christianity had as one of its foundational components physiology and, more specifically, the workings of the female body. The desire for identity operates by excluding, delimiting and negating difference, and the long-lived authority of the church through the ages indicates the potent effects of these narrative practices. Yet within texts as various as the prescriptions of Galen and the early church fathers, the narrated lives of Alisoun of Bath and the Trotula woman, vestiges of difference remain and appear as both the sublated potential of predication and the risk of dissemination.

Turning to the story of St Margaret, a crystalline example of virtue, will enable us to understand some of the specific ramifications of these differential vestiges, remainders which remind us of the very material existence of narrative and the rhetorical authority based upon it. The Middle English *Seinte Marherete* is a typical text in that it attempts to appropriate the pain of the saint as a way to (re)produce Christianity and its transcendent values. In its narrative urge to control and translate differences – like women's bodies, Asian princes and their followers, and even heresies of black demons from hell[39] – it represents the unified and unifying ideas of culture. Yet it also narratively and historically illustrates how the pain of mothering resurfaces in unpredictable and uncontrollable ways.[40] So, being a typical example of the hagiographic genre, it repeats Christian dogma and doctrine, illustrating the efficacy of repetition in reinscribing culture and yet, with its own particular history of reception and the intertextuality out of which the story is woven, it reminds us of the veiled threat that iterability poses to the dominant tropes of culture. A close reading of *Seinte Marherete* provides us with another opportunity to see some specific repercussions of medieval Christianity's reliance on the reproductive, female body as one of its dominant textualized tropes; such tropes are at once reflections of a culture's belief in transcendent values and excessive reminders of how such precepts were created as transcendent.

Seinte Marherete begins by highlighting Christianity against that which it is not, thus, outlining part of the complex process that produces Christian faith and those who hold it. Christians do not worship 'heðene mawmez, of stockes ant of stanes werkes iwrahte' (heathen idols, wretched things made of sticks and stones).[41] Instead, Christians worship Jesus who deigned to live for a time 'bimong eordliche men' (among earthly men) and who 'botnede blinde, þe dumbe, te deaue, ant to deade arerde to lif ant to leomen' (cured the blind, the dumb, the deaf and raised the dead to life and light). The faithful are those who 'beoð of Crist icleopet, swa ʒef ha nutteð hare nome' (are named by Christ, such that they deserve [or profit by] their name). This they do by 'deð dreheð for [Christ], oðer eni nowcin' (suffering death for Christ or any hardship) (p. 2). In this brief setting of tone for the piece, we see the constitutive position of bodily existence in the realm of salvation and how the propriety and prosperity of the name of God is made manifest through the mutability of bodies. In this generically standard passage, the intersection between the ongoing discourse of 'godes lay' or 'God's law' (2) and its individual iterations – the story of Margaret and also of her story's singular narrator, Teochimus, who names himself even before naming Margaret – makes clear the doubled structure of Christian faith. The overt quality of such faith is represented in the story's focus on torture and the introduction's censure of 'licomes lustes' or 'lusts of the body' (2); these characteristics reflect the Neoplatonic disdain for the flesh and translate fleshy suffering and sensuality into proof of God's existence and grace. In other words, the introduction exemplifies standard Christian doctrine about the inferior place of the body in salvation. Yet the overzealous, nearly anxious, focus on the interweaving of body and law, which is the defining hermeneutic upon which the genre of hagiography operates, highlights the *articulations* of this salvific system, that is, its joints. 'Articulate' is from the Latin verb *articulare* meaning 'to divide into parts' or 'to be jointed'. Modern physiological discourse still speaks of one bone articulating with another, so this is a usage not lost to modern readers. So as *Seinte Marherete* articulates – that is, speaks – God's law, it also structures all the truths of salvation, jointing them together into what then appears to be a seamless narrative. Like Mary, who doubly thus articulated the Word of God, *Seinte Marherete* illustrates that the only manifestations of salvation are its bodily ones.

   Seinte Marherete does this by focusing intensely on the saint's bodily
existence. Four specific, interrelated aspects of the way the text describes
her body prove to be particularly revealing in terms of our central
question concerning the relation between matter and transcendence: the
physical torture she undergoes, her body's virginally sealed state, her
body's relation to Christ's and the Caesarean birth she experiences in a
displaced manner. These aspects prove to be revealing because of how
closely they are aligned with narrative practice and anxieties over
authorship of Margaret's story, a story of her faith. *Seinte Marherete* is
the story of a young, beautiful Christian woman of Antioch, taken
captive by a visiting pagan prefect, Olibrius. Olibrius first wants her for
her beauty and wants to marry her, but when, out of a desire to protect
her virginity, she refuses this request, he requires her to worship his idols
and renounce the Christian God. The story offers few surprises for
anyone familiar with the saint's-life genre; Margaret refuses Olibrius's
requests, which increase in frequency and in coercive force as he begins
to torture her. He has her stripped naked and whipped. When this does
not achieve the desired effects, he has her suspended in the air and rent
with swords and iron hooks. Then she is hung up again and burned with
candles, subsequently bound hand and foot and thrown into a deep
vessel of water to drown. Finally, Olibrius is forced to have her killed by
cutting off her head. In between torture sessions, she also suffers and
survives being visited by demons from hell. Even though she dies in the
end, her death brings the conversion of thousands of Olibrius's followers
and her status as a saint becomes firmly established.
   Since Margaret experiences the act of torture and spiritually over-
comes it, *Seinte Marherete* repeats the discourse of disdain for the flesh
even as it is through the saint's body that divine grace is made
perceptible and that Margaret proves her faith in God. Margaret can,
with no hint of contradiction, at once easily ask for protection from
'fleschliche fulðen' or 'fleshly defilement' *and* emphasize the physicality
of her spirituality. She says of her relationship with Jesus that she has
given to him her 'meiðhad iʒettet, & luuie as leouemon & leue as on
lauerd' (virginity intact and love[s] [him] as a lover and believe[s] as on a
lord) (9).[42] The impact of physiology is made apparent in this example
which is one of many in the text.[43] Margaret makes clear the significance
of sensuality as part of the Godhead when she instructs her tormentor,
Olibrius, about the Christian God. She tells this Asian prefect that what
makes Jesus effectual is precisely his physiology, which stands in
marked contrast to the pagan deities' existence; she describes them as

'witlese wihtes . . . blodles ant banles, dumbe & deaue' (senseless beings
. . . bloodless and boneless, dumb and deaf) and, therefore, quite
ineffectual (43). As doctrinally sound as it is, Margaret's description
nevertheless calls attention to the ambiguity built into the Christic body:
the ability to be efficacious in salvation seems to arise out of the
coincidence of flesh and grace, not solely from the latter.

That Christian eschatology is dependent on such risky, mutable
matter as flesh is one reason that virginity became such an integral part
of the salvational narrative. Because of Eve, the female and, more
specifically, the maternal body is a cursed one,[44] in need of constant
recuperation, like that which Paul and the early fathers provide.
Virginity becomes a way of recuperating female physiology, a positive
inversion of the risk of dissemination Eve's sin originated. Female
virginity, then, provides one avenue of control over that risk. It is no
wonder, then, that most female saints are virgins, even when, like Mary
and Margaret, they are also mother figures. Virginity is the path to
God, not only for the virgin herself but also for those who believe in
the truths for which her sealed body stands. Margaret describes her
own virginity as follows: 'Mi lauerd haueð mine limen sunderlich
iseilet, & haueð, to me ʒimstan þat ich ʒettede him, iʒarket ant iʒeve me
kempne crune' (My lord has especially sealed my limbs and, for the
gem-stone that I granted him, has prepared and given me a champion's
crown) (43). This is one of several times that Margaret makes claims to
have a sealed, crystallized body. At the beginning of the tale as she sees
the threat Olibrius brings to her, she prays to the lord to protect her
'deor ʒimstan . . . mi meiðhad ich meane' (precious jewel . . . my
virginity, I mean) (7). Again, as Olibrius presses her to worship his
idols, she claims that Jesus 'haueð iseilet to him [her] seolf & [her]
meiðhad' (has sealed [her]self and [her] virginity to him) (11). After
Olibrius threatens her with physical torture, Margaret defines her
special relation with Christ: 'He haueð his merke on me iseilet wið his
in-seil, ne mei unc nowðer lif ne deað tweamin atwa' (He has his mark
on me, sealed me with his seal, nor may death or life divide us again)
(13). This apparently closed crystalline body, however, becomes the
doorway for others to enter heaven. For example, after being bound
and thrown into a cauldron of water to drown and being saved by her
own prayer, the suffering Margaret converts 'fif þusent men' (five
thousand men) (45). All these converts are immediately put to death by
the prefect and they ascend to heaven praising God out loud, sensually.

When Olibrius forces Margaret into the water, many readers would have recognized this mode of torture as a perverted translation of the ritualized bath, the *mikveh*. A community as concerned with and repelled by the menstrual process as was the early and medieval Church would have been cognizant of rites of purification from and protection against the perceived uncleanness of menstruating women. Specifically, the *mikveh* was prescribed in Leviticus for cleansing away bodily impurities associated with, among other things, childbirth and menstruation. Historically, even Mary participated in this ritual.[45] During the Middle Ages, Christian women and men participated in their own rites of purification, practices which kept the taint of original sin cyclically present in the minds of anyone who might have regular casual contact with fertile women. The irony of the situation into which Margaret is thrown is that she obviously is in no need of purification; her body is Christ's perfect crystal. The seal on her is so potent that she will not heed the words of the devil or of the 'feondes an foster' (the devil's own child) (7), Olibrius. She is, therefore, safe from the errancy of spirit and body to which Eve damned all women, and so flesh is once again brought back within the fold of God's mantle. Even Olibrius's vicious modes of torture, which rupture the boundaries of her body, do not change the parameters of her faith. She has been sealed and is unchangeable, and so she is very different from other women. One demon who visits her in her cell remarks that she is 'ne nawhit . . . wommon ilich' (in no way like [other] women) (31). Exactly like Mary, she also is alone of all her sex.

And, like Mary, she is the animator of faith. As such she supplements the Christic body and its salvational functions, which the text invokes at its beginning and which Margaret invokes each time she crosses herself. Allied with Christ, Margaret would seem to be the crystal-clear reflection of mature faith in God needed by this narrative to represent complete understanding of God's divine plan.[46] So, even though she is not like any other woman, Margaret's lifestyle is to be emulated. This argument is further supported by the fact that the manuscript of *Seinte Marherete* is bundled with two other texts about virginal service to God: *Ancrene Riwle* and *Hali Meiðhad* ('Anchoress's Rule' and 'Letter on Virginity'). For Teochimus, our narrator, for the genre of the female saint's life and within the many stories of the Holy Virgin, the figure or monument of the virginally, Christ-ally/crystally sealed female body constitutes a prime symbolization for major tenets of medieval Christianity.

As such a mode of representation and through its dissemination,

female physiology becomes a site where one type of knowledge is
narratively translated and transubstantiated into another type, authorized and yet jeopardized by this very transformation. In St Margaret's
story, the saint's pain becomes proof of God's grace, Olibrius's
foolishness becomes proof of God's justice and Teochimus's compulsion to tell the story becomes proof of God's eternal narrative of
salvation. In fact, everything becomes proof of the Christian ethic of
transcendence. In such a complex of authentication, reanimation and
materialization, the effects of world-building and of the ascription and
maintenance of authority are potent. The church's existence as the
most influential of institutions in the Middle Ages evidences this. Yet
once we realize that this compulsion towards proof is a narrative urge,
we can see the many other narrative forces at work in this story, social,
historical, physiological forces, that have created the figure of the
virgin as such. We must also recognize, then, the role such culturally
bound forces play in filtering perception of transcendent truths and,
indeed, in creating the very notions of 'transcendence' and 'truth'
themselves. Each time Mary is called upon to right femininity by
righting the name of Eve, each time Margaret's actions prove she is not
like other women who spread the curse around and each time female
physiology is recuperated from prurience, the subtextual vagrancy of
this fleshy existence is recalled. But more importantly, we can note the
various semiotic displacements and substitutions that intersected to
form such a vagrantly, narratively, transcendently useful institution.

In such a culturally bound process, that a virgin is figured as the
mother of God is not surprising.[47] Nor should it surprise us that the
ecstatic suffering of the virgin martyr, Margaret, becomes emblematic
of Caesarean birth and that Margaret herself becomes a patroness of
childbirth. To be sure, what first connects Margaret's story with childbirth and labour is not apparent. In his collection of saints' lives, the
Legenda Aurea, Jacobus de Voragine simply states that while the saint
prayed before her beheading, she added 'a prayer that any woman who
invoked her aid when faced with a difficult labour would give birth to a
healthy child'.[48] De Voragine does not explain why Margaret is
associated with childbirth. Nor does the Middle English life provide
any exact explanation for the association between the virgin martyr
and mothering. It does, however, expand on Margaret's prayer and
puts the words of that prayer into a direct quotation from the saint
herself, in a conversation with her God:

I þe hus þere wummon þineð o childe, sone so heo munnið mi nome, hihentliche help hire ant iher hire bene; þat i þe hus ne beo iboren nan misbilimet bern, nowðer halt ne houeret, noðer dumbe ne deaf ne ideruet of deoulen. (47 and 49)

(In the house where a woman pains with child, as soon as she remembers my name, quickly help her and obey her prayer; that in that house is born no deformed child, neither lame nor hunch-backed, neither dumb nor deaf nor plagued by the devil.)

Why does this unquestionably virginal woman consider herself to be – and why was she accepted as – especially capable of intervening in childbirth, particularly in times of trouble? The answer to this question lies in the complex of displacements surrounding one of Margaret's tests while in prison – her defeat of a demon in the form of a dragon.

The dragon scene begins with Margaret in her cell praying for, among other things, the chance to see and challenge the devil face-to-face. Soon enough her prayer is granted, even though she is so frightened that she 'forʒet hier bone þat heo ibeden hefde swa þat ha moste iseon þen unsehen unwiht' (forgot her request that she had prayed that she might see the unseen devil) (23). A hairy dragon with a long beard and flames flickering from his mouth appears. He wraps his long tongue around his shoulders as he advances on Margaret. He arches over her and widens his mouth, preparing to swallow her whole. As any protagonist in a saint's life would, Margaret prays to God in this time of danger; then she 'droh þa endelong hire, ant þwertouer þrefter, þe derewurðe taken of þe deore rode þat he on reste' (drew on herself along downward and across thereafter, the beloved token of that precious cross on which He rested) (25). The dragon nevertheless uses his tongue to flick her into his mouth and then he 'for-swalh into his wide wombe' (completely swallows [her] into his wide belly) (25). But

þe rode taken arudde hir readliche, þat heo wes mid iwepnet, ant warð his bone sone, swa þat his bodi to-barst omidheppes; & te edie meiden allunge unmerret, wið-uten euereuch weom, wende ut of his wombe, heriende on heh hire hehe healent in heouene. (25)

(the sign of the cross with which she was armed delivered her quickly and straightway became (the dragon's) slayer, in such a way that his body

burst asunder through the middle; and the blessed maiden completely
unharmed, without any spot, walked out of his belly, praising her exalted
saviour on high in heaven.)

This scene functions in two different but complexly related ways. One
thing the presence and actions of the dragon do is to distinguish
Margaret's story in a specifically negative sexual way. Several factors
participate in creating this aspect of the story. The Antichrist was often
represented as a dragon and imagined as a lascivious seducer. Also
dragons were associated with violent procreation. A prominent belief
in the period held that dragons or vipers give birth through deadly
force: the young bite their way through the mother's belly to emerge. In
addition, the procreation of viper young causes the death of the father,
as Rabanus Maurus explains. While the female dies during birth, the
male is killed by the female during intercourse; she is so frenzied during
coition that she bites off the male's head.[49] Such extremely negative
allusions to sexuality in a saint's life, of course, are not unexpected, but
the image of Margaret's birth from the serpent provides a unique
mapping of theological bodily appropriations and repudiations as well
as providing a picture of how that theology endlessly generates itself.

Margaret's violent, rupturing rebirth from the dragon's 'wombe'
suggests the violence and double nature of Caesarean birth in the
Middle Ages. Vaginal birth could also be a violent and dangerous time,
as evidenced by the pages and pages of the *English Trotula* focused
solely on this one topic. Indeed, the idealization of female virginity in the
fourteenth century may have been one realization of the typical dangers
of pregnancy and childbirth.[50] Caesarean birth marked a particularly
acute occurrence of this dangerous time. Only in desperation were
Caesarean births performed. The surgery usually cost the mother her life
and often was not sufficient to save the life of the child, who might
survive only long enough to be baptized. In fact, midwives were
constrained by the church to perform the procedure if they thought a
foetus might be alive after its mother's death so that the
child might be baptized and saved. The responsibilities of the midwife,
then, were not solely medical. She was charged in such life-and-death
situations with making decisions that could influence the eternal state of
the child's soul. She who surgically delivered a child that died before it
could be baptized, condemned that child to burial in unconsecrated
ground. She who decided not to deliver a child surgically might be
charged with murder of the child and held ethically responsible for its

unbaptized state. As with other medical practices, several different and often contradictory discourses converged around the Caesarean procedure, defining, inscribing and delimiting it. In this web of practices and meanings, the Caesarean procedure, more so than vaginal delivery, marked the translational character of the maternal body. Defining the body on one side were the urges, pains and drives of physiology, while on the other side were the constraints of theology, medical practice and law.[51]

The Caesarean procedure could foist upon its viewers and patients some unlikely and thought-provoking images. It might provide the picture of life, complete, being pulled from the husk of death. When the mother survived the surgery, as sometimes she did, the procedure of breaching her body to remove another discrete life complicated the notion of distinct identities.[52] The necessity of having to perform the procedure itself could be a reminder of the uncontrollable principle of female flesh, even as proscriptions against sacrificing the mother for the sake of the child reified the idea of discrete personalities and subject-ivities.[53] In such figures as those initiated by the Caesarean procedure, we can now recognize that the boundaries between life and death, the self and the other, indeed the very boundaries that establish personal and cultural identity are contingencies and contiguities. The highly prescribed, increasingly complex offices surrounding the physiology of the Caesarean procedure[54] – efforts at control – point to the anxiety at the foundation of this medical, legal discourse, an anxiety over the unpredictable quality of each birth specifically and of the maternal body in general. A woman undergoing a Caesarean procedure was as much created and delimited by the various semiotic practices of that procedure as she was a reminder – in her pain and suffering as well as in her life-giving potential – of the ways such discourses can never get at the ultimate truth of the maternal body. They only keep producing endlessly disseminated concepts of this thing called 'the truth'. We may also discern the role that medical, legal and ethical intentions play in creating the certainly overdetermined concept of personal identity. At birth, vaginal or Caesarean, all of history, past, present and future, can be understood to bear down upon who that child will be.

Once again, then, Caesarean birth constitutes a specifically intense reminder of the culturally constructed figure of the liminal, maternal body. Within the Christian narrative, Margaret serves locally as a site through which the 5,000 can enter heaven while Mary as intercessor for humanity serves universally as the gate of heaven for all who seek her services. In such narratives of conversion, Christianity writes itself through such figured bodies. Striking visual representations of Mary exist that call attention to this figuration and ally it with Caesarean birth. In a surgical birth, of course, the mother's body is cut open so that the child may be pulled directly from the womb. Mary's body is similarly opened in statues called *vierges ouvrantes*. When closed, such statues simply depict the virgin humbly seated, but these statues are designed to open, to be split down the middle of the Virgin's body from collarbone to feet. Inside, Mary might be holding depictions of Jesus enthroned, the Trinity, or the whole of salvational history, often from its very beginnings at the Fall in the garden to its ultimate effect in the New Jerusalem.[55] In such a form of devotion, the centrality of the maternal body becomes apparent: it is the matter upon which life, mortal and eternal, is predicated. Yet this origin is often obfuscated for reasons that are now apparent to us – the culturally bound definition of women as inherently inferior. The motherly connection is mutable and excessive, the female body with its monthly bloody discharge a reminder of Eve's original mothering of mortality. So femininity becomes a move away from the unity posited in Genesis or in any history of origins. This dangerous aspect of femininity is recalled in *Seinte Marherete* as Olibrius becomes progressively more insane with each view he has of the saint's beautiful body and the ravages it undergoes. He exteriorizes his anxiety over someone not believing in his world-view on to the body of a woman. In so doing, he hopes to rewrite the world the way he knows it ought to be. In narrating such a story, Teochimus attempts the same thing, using the figure of the virginal body to reify the ideal of a univocal God.

But the *vierges ouvrantes* and the complex of discourses and practices that constituted medieval Caesarean birth have shown us another aspect of this ideal. While it produces ideals of behaviour, emotional and physical, there are also things that extrude from within the discursively constructed boundaries that have created this ideal, things like the belief systems of Asian princes and the potential that a child might be born 'misbilimet' or deformed.[56] In each prayer to the Virgin Mary or St Margaret for help during difficult labour, extrusion takes place as pain, accident and dissemination; all these things surface as defining aspects of experience and put into question boundaries of experience that have been taken for granted. The figures of Mary and Margaret as mothers, particularly with their stories' striking similarities to Caesarean birth, are figures that illustrate a breaching of the boundaries of female bodies, but even in such a breaching the boundaries are recalled and reinscribed. At the same time, though, such imaginative, theological, medical and legal conceptions belie the 'naturalness' or truth of the bodies to which they claim to refer transparently. What is at work here, in the Pauline and Mariological recuperations of the original biblical curse on Eve, in the complex of discourses and secrets that surround medical practice on women's bodies, and specifically in the web of differences that create Caesarean birth as a surgical practice, is a discursive construction of what is natural. This process works by instigating certain attributes of physiology. In other words, the discourses of Christianity instigated the notion of the inferiority of women. This idea became so accepted that it influenced the ways in which bodies were conceptualized; certain physiological characteristics that reinforced the inferior status of women came to be expected as naturally belonging to women. Any woman who seems in some way not to fulfil these expectations, then, like Mary or Margaret, is not really a woman. We can see how such a process institutionalizes authoritative and normative notions of natural and proper characteristics. The idea of 'maternity' that such processes have created is a particularly potent figure because it highlights both the 'natural', controlling consequences and the semiotic processes that produced the idea of 'natural'. In each representation of a mother, we can see the ways medieval society wrote and thought about mothers, birth, women, sexual intercourse, etc. Now we can also see how such representations create for those things rhetorical authority and so create and reinscribe cultural identity. And yet we must also now recognize how each term simultaneously and endlessly escapes this controlling desire.

In Margaret's story, however, we see no doubts over cultural or spiritual identity, even though she is embroiled in a test for her life and of the validity of her faith. She emerges from the belly of the dragon unharmed. Her Caesarean birth is a completely successful one in that she not only survives it but easily sloughs off the demon that would take her identity from her, just as she successfully rebuffs all of Olibrius's seductions. Her identity has been so firmly founded in this narrative and metanarrative rebirth that she is not even threatened by the next demon that appears. She defeats him with ease and gets him to reveal all his secrets to her while holding her heel on his throat. By stepping on this demon and controlling him, Margaret recuperates the curse of enmity God put on the serpent and Eve in Genesis 3:14–15, an enmity repeated in Revelation between the pregnant woman 'clothed with the sun, with the moon beneath her feet and a crown of twelve stars on her head' (12:1) and the 'great red Dragon, with seven heads and ten horns' (12:3). This woman was a type of Mary – as queen of heaven[57] – and served as another figuration of her righting the name of Eve. Like Mary, Margaret is a virgin who experiences childbirth. Like Mary, Margaret is blessed among women.[58] Like Mary, Margaret's faith and actions are unique but meant to produce endless if different repetitions, the purpose of hagiography being to teach ideal behaviour. Like Mary, who is the *specula sine macula* and who in some important ways seems to have sloughed off the curse of childbirth levied against Eve, Margaret, 'wið-uten euereuch weom' (without any spot) emerges reborn from the discarded maternal body of the dragon, signifying her having left behind the (stereo)typical painful, desiring, transient female body. Margaret's body becomes the sealed, crystalline and transparently intelligible body deployed by Christianity to reify its system of values and enable its ethic of transcendence.

Yet as the series of displacements, replacements and substitutions within this sacrificial and appropriative system indicates, the very foundational place of such ultimately uncontrollable and endlessly disseminated components, like the procreative body, unmasks the ideological agenda of categorization, particularly strategies of forming identity by separation and bounding. Even in its efforts to crystallize the Christian identity it sets forth, Margaret's story highlights how theological thinking, medical practice and writing and hagiography bound bodies variously, identifying them via often contradictory semiotic practices. *Seinte Marherete* is particularly forceful because it illustrates how such contradiction is concomitant with and, indeed, constitutive of dominant discourses. From this perspective we will return to the scene of Margaret's issuance from the dragon and the second way in which this scene functions.

As the scene's covert sexual implications suggest, even Margaret's most standard employment of the sign of the cross exposes the narrative frame that makes this sign signify as it does. The narrative strategies used by both Margaret and Teochimus in the scene heighten this expositive effect. To start, the scene is a series of displacements and substitutions, intermingling bodies and signs and making one of the other. The scene focuses attention on Margaret's body, which she inscribes with the cross and recalls for readers that this was 'þe deore rode þat he on reste' (the dear cross on which He rested) (p. 25). The dragon swallows her, but the cross on her body saves her and makes the dragon's body burst open so that she can emerge, bodily unharmed. Margaret's spotless body, then, emerges as the sign of Christ's grace and, in some important senses, replaces Christ's body as a signifier. The scene recalls the incarnate existence of God only to reanimate that existence with Margaret's body. In thanks for her delivery from the dragon, Margaret praises her saviour in heaven aloud – that is, sensually – emphasizing the materiality of the scene's significance. This significance arises from the narrative strategies employed in the tale. Bodies in this tale clearly become signifiers that work in a series instigated at the tale's beginning and reinscribed and reinvested with meaning throughout by Teochimus's original claim to authority, itself reinvested via the process of his storytelling. Margaret also participates in this anxious desire for maintaining authority by telling and retelling stories. After she defeats the dragon and begins her mostly verbal battle with the black demon who next appears to test her, she retells the story of her triumph over the dragon as part of a prayer praising Jesus' power in her salvation.[59] This is an authority that works by negating difference and desiring unity, an authority that has worked in *Seinte Marherete* by reifying the soul/body dichotomy and producing the unified figure of Margaret's 'sealed' body. It would seem Teochimus's gaze transcends the vulnerability of the female body and even the body of the text, the physical book that he narrates, but this dominance cannot be sustained because the scene of Margaret's issuance from the dragon, and those scenes that follow, evidence nothing so clearly as the way in which the very act of authoring in this story is an act of making the truth material. The truth of Teochimus's faith and of 'godes lay', God's law (p. 3), lies ultimately in not only the suffering, sealed body of Margaret, but also in the sloughed-off reproductive flesh of the dragon, that dangerous, supplemental formless matter, which the narrator's text(s) can conceive of but not hold on to completely. For this dragon scene calls to mind many of the other stories that give significance to Margaret's particular circumstances. In some important ways, then, the dragon scene reminds us of the intertextuality of the general hagiographic undertaking. The body of this specific virgin/mother has been weighted by medical practice and writing, Mariology and its connections to Eve, theologies of salvation and damnation and acts of propriety, diffusion and dissemination. While Margaret does become the symbol Teochimus wishes her to be, the reliance on her physicality – by its nature an intertextual existence – undermines the transcendence of the narrator's beliefs and even of Margaret's own faith.

Seinte Marherete is filled with concerns expressed over the business of storytelling, particularly the business of the narrator's authorship and authority, and in this way evidences its intertextuality. Teochimus establishes his authority from the outset by claiming both knowledge of God's law and personal knowledge of Margaret; he constantly reminds readers that he is telling a story from his own lifetime. All these claims to have seen what he writes about demonstrate an underlying anxiety over the believability of his story. So like a good lawman, he further attempts to establish his authority in this scene by making clear how it is that he knows what Margaret suffered while in prison. He provides eye-witness testimony: the saint's 'uoster-moder' (foster-mother) has been caring for her during her imprisonment and 'Heo . . . ant monie ma biheolden þurh an eilþurl' (she . . . and many more watched through a window) (p. 21) as the dragon came upon the maiden. Jacobus de Voragine calls Margaret's being swallowed by the dragon 'apocryphal and not to be taken seriously',[60] so perhaps the English author felt a particular need to establish the validity of his version. Jacobus' more canonical story is that the dragon threatened Margaret but disappeared when she made the sign of the cross. The Latin tradition of the story relates that Margaret was vomited by the dragon, which was irritated by the sign of the cross she had made before being swallowed.[61] Teochimus's anxiety over establishing the facts of how he knows the truth of Margaret's story, so that even the most unbelieving of sceptics can find no hole in the proof he offers sealed in his book, reveals the worldly quality of the theological discourse he takes so for granted. This anxiety also reveals a dispersal of his authority.

Yet he continues to claim sole responsibility for Margaret's story. He declares that he alone is answerable for the spread of Margaret's story. He declares himself in no uncertain terms as Margaret's author:

> Ich ah wel to witen þis, for, i pine of prisun þer ha wes iput in, ich hire fluttunge fond, & fleschliche fode; & ich iseh hwer ha faht wið þe feorliche feont, & hire bone wes þat ich hit write on boc-felle, & hire liflade lette don o leaue, & sende hit soðliche iwriten wide ȝont te worlde. (p. 53)

> (I surely ought to know this, because I supplied her with provisions and food for her body where she was kept in pain in prison; and I saw where she fought with the fearful demon, and her wish was that I write it on parchment and have her life story set down on pages, and send it truthfully written widely throughout the world.)

Such statements make clear the way in which Margaret and her story are made into points of transition between physiological dimensions and theological as well as cultural ones. In its staging of the translation from bodily pain to leaves of vellum, to continue the tale's authority the passage reifies the hierarchical dichotomy between text and body. The statement follows the typical Christian, Neoplatonic teleologic course of humanity: from a body weighted with pain and in need of sustenance, Margaret becomes immortal through her story and her faith as the angels carry her soul to heaven at the tale's end,[62] while Teochimus carries the story through the world. But at the same time, the passage's translational, narrative functions point us towards the articulations that have created the naturalized, hierarchical distinction between soul and body. Additionally, Teochimus's tale of male lust and female virginity highlights this distinction as also being one of sexual difference; even as the tale inverts the classical notion of the male as representative of intellect and the female of emotion and appetite, it recalls this notion. But we can see that Margaret undermines the closure of such neat binary logic even as she serves as its vehicle: she is a body that is all soul, is alive in her death and is a woman who is not like any other woman. Margaret is the matrix upon which such binaries are predicated, while the intertextuality of her story reminds us how this matrix was produced culturally. To make his point and illustrate the truths he believes to be self-evident, Teochimus must foreground Margaret's liminality. In other words, *Seinte Marherete* is exemplary of the hagiographic genre; her story is standard theology. And yet the figure of Margaret's sealed-up, liminal body is the very thing that exposes the limits of the narrative, the theological frame that strains towards the rhetorical authority to define the world.

By following narrative practices standard to the genre and providing ample proof for his story, Teochimus attempts to establish *Seinte Marherete's* rightful position in the genealogy of English Christianity. Yet, if his story is dealing in eternal truths as he claims, why would he think that there might be a mistake about this genealogy and what he is trying to communicate? His anxieties reveal why. The tale's attempts to negate difference and circumscribe unity – which mirror larger theological, philosophical and political attempts – reveal the already divided nature of the story that the tale so much wants Margaret's sealed body to signify. *Seinte Marherete* stamps and restamps its seal on Margaret's body in its attempts to make her signify in one crystalline way. Yet in these repetitions – copies upon often imperfect copies which are nevertheless intrinsic to the (re)production and continuation of Christian faith – lie all the intertextual references that divide and disperse the sign 'Margaret's body' and indicate that it exists also somewhere outside (intersections of) discourse. From this perspective, faith and salvation seem to lie in this dispersal itself. Even though the prevalent desire revealed in *Seinte Marherete* is the desire to prescribe faith and ways to attain salvation, the figure that St Margaret becomes must remind us of the very worldly quality of the story's claim to truth. The seal on Margaret's body, which is meant to be its transcendent signifier, is necessarily dispersed by its very claim to truth, for such a claim, specific to time, place and materialities of bodies, languages and texts, does nothing so much as suggest the absence of access to any such transcendence. Faith, then, must be located in the very specific moments of intersection between 'bodi . . . ban . . . [and a] boc of . . . pine' (body . . . bone . . . [and a] book of . . . pain).[63] That is, faith and the salvation it predicates seem to exist in a vast web of disseminative semiotic practices and various physiologies, texts and moments in time. Specific intersections produce doctrine and dogma or the events from which these things are instigated. But the uncontrollable and ultimately unknowable extent of this web – knowable, indeed, if at all, only at its intersections – necessitates the constant repetition and variation of articles of faith. Margaret's sealed-up body is a crystalline monument to a system ever trying to petrify itself – by its own signs, by its own guardians, by the way it surveys and keeps knowledge. But the invocation of Margaret's name when something is going wrong during the delivery of a child or when labour pain is so great that it is unspeakable implies the 'always also somewhere else' quality of flesh. And it is this possibility for 'elsewhereness' that splits the seal on Margaret's body and on any claim to rhetorical authority which it may be called on to represent.

4

Mary, the Maiden and Metonymy
in *Pearl*

God should not be said to be ineffable, for when this is said, something is said. And a contradiction in terms is created, since if that is ineffable which cannot be spoken, that is not ineffable which can be called ineffable. This contradiction is to be passed over in silence rather than resolved verbally.[1]

O n the most basic level, symbols surrounding the Holy Virgin attempt to name the unnameable. Mary becomes paradoxical in such attempts: metaphorically she is, for example, at once bride of her son, mother of her father, and sister and mother to all of humanity.[2] Similarly, the inexpressibility topos in *Pearl* paradoxically expresses and foregrounds the gap between time- and space-bound human language and the total otherness of divinity. The poem's recapitulative formal qualities, embodying the central spherical metaphor of the poem, the eponymous jewel, heighten this feeling of difference between mundane things and the perfection of divine things, even as the poem speaks of bridging this gap. The poem uses the pearl image and many other metaphorical figures, comparing the ineffable to worldly things, in order to represent this otherness.

It is no wonder, then, that many interpretations of this poem have focused on the logic of metaphor.[3] However, it is sometimes forgotten that metaphors work only by preserving a sense of difference both within and beyond the establishment of metaphorical likenesses.[4] Pseudo-Dionysius, who with Augustine had a profound influence on medieval allegorical thought, understood that no metaphor can totally annihilate either of its terms because it can function only to the extent that it states, not negates, its own reality of difference.[5] So we are reminded that metaphors actually preserve the status quo, crossing categorical boundaries only by recalling those very boundaries, and yet we can also recognize that there is another logic at work in *Pearl*, a metonymic logic, which tends to pluralize the heaven of the poem, connecting it fluidly to human desires and bodies.

Metonymy exploits the contiguity between categories, that is, between something and its attributes, its surroundings and its components. From the perspective of medieval Christianity, which understood that 'For [God's] invisible things, from the creation of the world are seen, being understood by those things that are made: his eternal power also and Divinity' (Romans 1:20), God inheres in the things of the world; that is, the transcendental signified is metonymically immanent and manifest, contiguous with its creation. Thus, an investigation of metonymy in *Pearl* can lead not only to an understanding of the poem different from one focused on metaphor as a defining trope but also to a different understanding of the way the poem treats the categorical differences between humanity and divinity.

Before we turn to an analysis of the *Pearl* maiden's ostensibly salvific words and the poem's symbolism and form,[6] considering representations of Mary will help shed some light on the logic at work in the poem and more generally in Christianity and its narratives, since Mary can be seen to highlight divinity's metonymic relationship to mundane things. The Annunciation, the Incarnation and the Assumption can be taken as metonymic representations when we understand them as figurations within the narrative of salvation that foreground the contiguous[7] nature of flesh and the divine, of things and faith. An investigation of certain depictions of Mary as both artefact and queen of heaven will evidence an underlying fluidness of signification, in which each term in the semiotic network is dependent on others. From the perspective of metonymy we can understand the idealism of *Pearl* other than in the ostensibly appropriate metaphoric form of humanity versus divinity. For in so doing, we can understand the import of *Pearl*, which lies not so much in its tour de force of form but in its textual refusal to idolize or monumentalize its accomplishments.[8] In the same way that Mary physiologically manifests the interdependence between flesh and salvation, the pearl, shifting in meaning from context to context, is a figure that metonymically marks the contiguity between divine and human, and, more remarkably, between purity and poetic representation.

Called the 'wyndow' and 'yate of hewen' (Brown 41:24 and 27),[9] Mary is a trope on the boundaries between heaven and earth, translating things of one sphere into another. For instance, the *vierges ouvrantes* constitute one example of the theme of Mary as the *sedes sapientiae*, the throne of Wisdom: via the Incarnation, she translates the Word and Wisdom of God into the mundane realm. She who held the Word within her becomes iconographically his seat or support.[10] This theme is part of a larger one that reminds the faithful of the connection of Mary's flesh to Christ's and therefore ultimately to salvation. A late thirteenth- or early fourteenth-century *vierge ouvrante* from the Middle Rhine represents a crowned and enthroned nursing Madonna when closed. The statue opens to reveal the adult Christ enthroned, holding a crucifix and surrounded by scenes of salvational history.[11] Such representations, along with others, like monstrances in which the host is held in the body of Mary,[12] remind the faithful of the necessary, liminal quality of the Holy Virgin and more generally of the female body within this salvational narrative.

Mary, then, is the contiguous figure between the failure of the old law and the inauguration of the new incarnational one. Her explication of Word into flesh initiated the redemption of human language; as Anne H. Schotter explains: 'for if language had fallen with Adam, it had been redeemed by Christ's condescending to take on human flesh – and therefore human speech'.[13] She is, according to a fourteenth-century lyric, a 'tokne þat pays [peace] scholde be / By-tuexte [between] god and manne' (32:15–16), the medium through which the light of God must pass and be refracted to be apprehensible to humanity.[14] An investigation of such passive roles in relation to her didactic and regal functions will reveal a narrative necessity that Mary remain a trope that never attains any one all-subsuming significance. In this liquescence, the medieval faithful, like Dante's pilgrim who reaches Paradise at last, wrote 'nostra effige' on to the face of God (33:131). Via the pathway of Marian imagery we will see how, even if he does not see himself reflected in the New Jerusalem his sight enters, the *Pearl* narrator is productive of that landscape.[15]

Five aspects of the history of Marian figuration are especially relevant to *Pearl*: stories about her life after Jesus's death; tales surrounding her own death and Assumption; and her roles as queen of heaven, throne of Jesus and vanquisher of evil. The *N-Town* 'Assumption of Mary' begins with a collection of Jews discussing the threat Mary still poses to their society after Jesus's death:

> . . . of on thing I warne yow at the gynnyng:
> His [Jesus's] dame is levyng, Mary that men call;
> Myche pepil halt hire wythall.
> Wherfore in peyne of reprefe,
> Yif we suffre hyre thus to relefe,
> Oure lawys sche schal make to myschefe and meche schame
> don vs sche schall.[16]

One threat she poses is her 'hie lore', or 'high learning' (l. 137). As representations of the Annunciation make clear, Mary was believed to be a woman of serious and complete education in Jewish law.[17] The *N-Town* 'Assumption' play indicates that Mary was also a teacher, that her 'fayre speche' has 'bredyn' belief in the resurrected Christ (71 and 70). Bynum notes several late-medieval visual representations of Mary as a priest.[18] Such images undoubtably emanate from early writings of the church. Apocryphal sources show the Virgin in a position of authority, albeit not a strictly ministerial one, as she continues to have the ear of several of the Apostles. We see her in the position of teacher to John, Peter and James in the 'Twentieth Discourse of Cyril of Jerusalem'. The text reveals that, as Mary is about to die, she calls these Apostles before her 'reminding them of the life of Jesus' and instructing them, according to the wishes of Jesus, to build a 'great church' over her grave.[19] Similarly, the 'Discourse of Theodosius' has Mary preaching to the Apostles, this time about the horrors of death and how they will be extinguished.[20] In the 'Discourse of Saint John the Divine' Mary takes on the clerical function of burning incense and directing John in prayers about her death.[21] Additionally, in a role that was to become traditional, Mary becomes an intercessor for humanity, even at her own death, praying:

> I beseech thy name which is greatly extolled, O Christ, God, King of the ages, only-begotten of the Father, receive thine handmaid, thou that didst vouchsafe to be born of me the lowly one to save mankind by thine unutterable dispensation. Every man that calleth upon or entreateth or nameth the name of thine handmaid, grant him thine help.[22]

This intercession is strikingly similar to that provided by the priest via the mass and confession. Again, we see Mary as a translational term within the process of salvation. As intercessor Mary is also active, suggesting a potent, if overwritten, aspect of the medium in which the Word was made manifest.

After recognizing the threat Mary's power poses to their society, the collection of Jews in the *N-Town* 'Assumption' plot her death. The priests and leaders of the Jewish community consider the power of her corpse as they plan to 'brenne here body and the aschis hide, / and don here all the dispith' (ll. 84–5) they can devise. In this Christian pedagogical piece, even the Jews recognize the power of Mary's flesh in reproducing faith. They believe further that, once Mary is dead and her body done away with, they can safely 'sle tho disciplis' without having the 'comownys', or the common people, rise up against them (86 and 81). The disappearance of Mary's body would have political efficacy, offering no more 'myschefe' to their 'lawys'.

The Jews want Mary dead and their plans coincide, not surprisingly in this piece of dramatic Christian didacticism, with God's plans: Mary is already dying and her death will once again prove God's power and mercy. Mary prays to be reunited with Jesus in heaven, beginning her request by reminding her son that he is 'god and man of [her] bodye' (l. 105), a request granted by Jesus, here named Sapientia. As in apocryphal accounts, Mary has some time – here three days – to prepare herself before her death.[23] She asks to see the Apostles and they appear magically at her door. Throughout this recounting, as in the *York Plays* and the apocrypha, the bodily nature of Mary's death is stressed. The verb used is the common one, 'to d(e)ye', as in ll. 139 and 257 in the *N-Town* and 44, 104 and 132 in *York*. 'The Death of Mary' in the *York* cycle additionally emphasizes the 'peynes' and 'sikenes' Mary suffers.[24] Also following apocryphal sources, each play recounts the double nature of Mary's death. First her 'flech . . . feble be nature' (*N-Town*, l. 302) dies and then it 'expirand' (l. 129) – or expires transitively – her soul: '*hic exiet anima marie de corpore in sinu[m] dei*' (stage direction between ll. 329 and 330). As her soul thus rises into the *sinu[m]* or 'fold' of God, Mary is left on earth as a corpse, about which Jesus gives the Apostles explicit directions for burial and protection from the scheming Jews. But, then, even Mary's corpse is prolific: her soulless body, that is matter without form, converts those outside the fold and increases the faith of those already within it. In the *N-Town*, even as the Apostles pray to the 'swete soule of mary' (l. 313) for Jesus's grace, the Jews scheme to take the body and make of its immolation a public spectacle. As the Apostles carry it towards the grave site, one of the Jewish leaders attempts to snatch the body off its bier, resulting in painful consequences:[25] 'Allas, my body is ful of peyne! / I am fastened sore to this bere! / myn handys are ser [withered] bothe tweyne' (ll. 395–7). The 'Latin Narrative of Pseudo-Melito' goes into further detail describing how 'his hands dried up from his elbows and clave to the bier. And when the apostles lifted the bier, part of him was hanging and part clave to the bier.'[26] The way in which Mary's body has power over others in contiguity with it creates a network of bodies. In the case of *Pearl*, the jewel will have a similar function.

The incident of the Jew's withered hands is strikingly similar to a midwife's attempt to make trial of Mary's virginity, a story recounted in the *Protevangelium*. After her test of the new mother's virginity, the midwife's hand fell off her 'in fire' (20:1) and she called out in pain. Like the Jewish leader of the *N-Town* who asks Peter for 'sum medycyn' (l. 403) to cure his problem, Salome, the midwife, calls out for aid. Both receive it when they profess their belief in the miracle of Jesus's birth and life as a human. Peter tells the Jew that he must 'beleue in Jhesu criste oure saveyour / and that this was his moder' (ll. 406–7) and 'honure' the body on the bier before him (l. 409). Such moments, which reproduce faith, recall the threatening quality of the maternal and translational body. This threat is reinstated in the *York Plays* in the references there to the efficacy of a prayer to Mary during the pains of childbirth, the intercessional functions of which recall her sacerdotal functions.[27]

Even recuperated here within the Christian narratives of salvation and conversion, Mary's body has physiological and psychological potency, a potency more striking in Assumption texts since her soul is already in heaven. We can see how Assumption texts incorporate and attempt to sublate Mary's flesh and yet make of it this dangerous, slippery matrix upon which so much of the narrative is founded. This system's own definition of such matter as prototypically outside the bounds can teach us to listen and read in ways other than in good form(s)[28] by understanding the semiotic networks that produce and enact the idea of heaven, as in the cases of the Christian salvational narrative and of *Pearl* and, more generally, the authority of images upon which these narratives rely.

Mary's soulless body is one site where this semiotic process can become visible because it is a body comprehending a contradiction: it must be completely human, if God is indeed to be truly incarnate, and yet the corpse, conceived without spot, that had once been the home of God should not, believers held, be subject to decay and consumption by worms.[29] Mary's body was believed to have been created and purified immediately upon the addition of her soul, sent pure from heaven.[30] Therefore, Mary was pure in body and soul from conception onwards, for only from so pure a human source could God/man have arisen. A similar logic founds the stories of Mary's Assumption. The 'Latin Narrative of Pseudo-Melito', popular in the West by the tenth century despite its enigmatic origins,[31] reveals a typical application of this narrative teleology. As the Apostles lay Mary in her tomb, Jesus arrives and accosts them. Peter tells him that, since Mary was his 'immaculate chamber', he should 'raise up the body of [his] mother and take her . . . into heaven' (16:2). In the same way that the *Praeredemptio* seemed a logical necessity in the Incarnation, since Mary's was such a unique incorporation, her bodily assumption also became a necessity.

The period played out this logic in shared representational features. During the Annunciation Gabriel visited the young Virgin, while at the elder Mary's death an angel comes to announce that her prayers to be with her son have been answered.[32] Even the greetings are similar. Gabriel, of course, greets the young Virgin with 'Hail, O favoured one, the Lord is with you!' (Luke 1:28). Following apocryphal sources, the *N-Town* has an angel sent straight from Jesus to greet the dying Mary with the following:

> Heyl, excellent prynces, Mary most pure!
>   Heyl, radyant sterre, the sunne not so bryth [is]!
> Heyl, Moder of Mercy and mayde most mure!
>   The blessyng that God yaf Jacob vpon you now lyth [is].
> (ll. 117–20)

The *York Plays* add to this similarity by having the greeting spoken by Gabriel himself ('The Death of Mary', ll. 1–4).

Even more striking, however, is the way in which both moments have to do with specifically human concerns being suddenly thrust into a divine or at least superhuman context – a technique of which *Pearl* will make full use. In the Annunciation, of course, Mary is confused about how she, who knows 'no man þat shulde haue fyled / [her] maydenhode' (*York Plays*, 'The Annunciation and Visit of Elisabeth to Mary', ll. 173–4), could be with child. This short-lived anxiety is dilated in Joseph's fear of shame and in the Jewish judges' misbelief and trial of the couple.[33] In the Assumption texts, Mary prays 'Wyth all [her] herte and sowle be natures excitacyon' for her death in order to be with her son; all creatures, she knows, want to be with him but, 'myche more owe I, youre moder be alye [kindred], / Syn ye wern born God and man of my bodye, / To desyre yowre presens, that were our ferste formacyon' (*N-Town*, 'The Assumption of the Virgin', ll. 101 and 104–6). Following apocryphal and literary sources,[34] this passage indicates the very human, physiological affiliation she feels for Jesus, whom she also calls a 'gloryous lord' (l. 72). This passage is striking because it begins with a catalogue of the Godhead's power and attributes, yet it returns to the physical connection to and reliance upon maternal flesh of 'saluacyon' (l. 69). Again here, Mary's death is doubly potent: even as Assumption texts tend towards a sense of timeless history connected to salvation, Mary's body continues to return as a specific, material site upon which this narrative of transcendence is figured, contiguous with the transcendent.

Narratives of Mary's death continue this focus on situational specificity. Early Syriac versions of the Virgin's passing to heaven actually do not describe her death; instead, she is translated into heaven attended by the three others who have been thus glorified – Enoch, Elijah and Jesus.[35] However, later texts, including all those apocryphal and dramatic texts so far cited in this chapter, specifically emphasize a bodily death of Mary. The 'Discourse of Theodosius' makes clear the contextual reasons why Mary's passing turned from a *Transitus* into an Assumption.[36] As James synopsizes: 'Jesus spoke [to the Apostles] of the necessity of death. If [Mary] were translated, "wicked men will think concerning thee that thou art a power which came down from heaven and that the dispensation [the Incarnation] took place in appearance."'[37] As Jesus and Mary talk before her death in the *York Plays*, the terms of her death are made clearer still. She asks her son that she be spared the horrifying experience of seeing the devil when she dies (l. 134). Jesus cannot grant this request, however. He refuses her, saying:

> But modir, þe fende must be nedis at þyne endyng,
> In figoure full foule for to fere þe;
> Myne aungelis schall þan be a-boute þe.
> And þerfore, dere dame, þou thar noȝt doute þe,
> For douteles þe dede schall noȝt dere þe. (154–8)

In other words, the fiend must be there so that her death will be completely human and the salvational narrative will continue.

The myth of Mary's death correlates meticulously with the period's reading of the Song of Songs and creates of her a metonymic link between the whole of humanity, specifically the faithful of the church, and the redemptive power of heaven. In an allegorical reading of the Song, the bride is understood to represent the church and the canticle itself becomes an expression of God's love for the faithful. Ambrose (?340–97) was the first father of the western church to connect the bride of the Song, the church, Mary and each individual Christian.[38] While the Song was used for a variety of purposes, one of the foremost among which was the veneration of virginity, its significances were certainly not mutually exclusive and Mary as church and bride of Christ was a popular image. An 'Autumn Song' of the early fourteenth century calls upon this prevalent imagery in describing Mary's place in heaven as that of 'bo maiden ant wyue' (50:10).[39] This paradoxical figuration, connected in such an intimate way with Mary's death, betokens that her death is also *not* typical. That her body would not be subject to decay after death is one indication of the narrative's failure to sublate even as the Assumption is a narrative necessity.

Such comprehensively contradictory figuration continues as Mary becomes queen of heaven. In section 8 of *Pearl*, the maiden attempts to explain to the narrator her relation as *a* queen of heaven to Mary, whom the narrator understands to be *the* Queen[40] from whom all 'grace . . . grewe' (l. 425). The *Pearl* maiden also calls Mary the 'quene of cortaysye' (l. 456) but adds to this a feudal connotation:

> Þat emperise al heuenz hatz –
> And vrþe and helle–in her bayly;
> Of erytage ȝet non wyl ho chace,
> For ho is quen of cortaysye. (441–4)

(That empress has all heaven, earth and hell within her castle walls [dominion]; she will chase none from their heritage because she is the queen of courtesy.)

Mary's queenship was a traditional aspect of poetic figuration. In his praises of the Virgin, Richard of St Lawrence describes her as queen of three provinces, 'coelestium, terrestrium, et infernorum', just as our poet does.[41] Brown's lyric collections contain thirteen references to the title 'quen[e]' in thirteenth-century[42] and five in fourteenth-century lyrics.[43]

That Mary reigned bodily in heaven was a commonplace and, as with the other forms Mary takes, as queen of heaven she is meant to continue reproducing faith. In an 'Orison of the Five Joys' dating from the first half of the fourteenth century, for example, a petitioner prays to 'marie, quene of heuene' (26:1) to take his 'saule to heuene, þer-in a place to fille' (26:56). Whereas this sinner believes in his soul's potential to gain heaven, the poem's tenth stanza makes clear the embodied state of Mary's residency:

> Marie, for þat swe[te] ioye wan þou from erþe was tan,
> In-to þe blisse of heuene with aungeles mani an,
> & i-set bi swete ihesu in fel [skin] & flecsch & ban,
> Þou bringe me to ioyes þat neuere schal be gon. (26:37–40)

In her role as heavenly intercessor between humanity and the God-head, she is the term of contiguity between human and divine realms according to many literary and theological texts. But the contradiction of Mary's materially spiritual procreation must remind us of her originally sinful predecessor, Eve, for Mary was not the first woman to come face to face with the devil. Even in her moment of triumph over Satan and the triumph it suggests for all humanity, Mary's role as vanquisher of evil is intricately associated with Eve and the Fall in the garden. This role arises from allegorical readings of several seemingly disparate Old Testament verses and from these readings being associated with the first five verses of Revelation 12, verses upon which the 'Madonna of Humility' type was based. The relationship between Mary and the serpent of evil begins with a remarkable mistranslation of the curse on humanity in Genesis 3:15: 'I will put enmity between thee and the woman and thy seed and the seed of her: she shall bruise thy head in pieces, and thou shalt lie in wait of her heel.' Hirn describes the mistranslation as follows: 'The great prophecy in Genesis . . . has been rendered in the Vulgate by "Ipsa conteret caput tuum, et tu insidiaberis calcaneo ejus" – "*She* shall bruise thy head, etc."'[44] Instead, the original states that the seed shall bruise the head of the serpent, not the woman. The confusion over the gender of nouns in the translation served to add to the Holy Virgin's reputation in the salvational narrative. Another image added to this reputation still further. Psalms 91:13 is part of a meditation on God as protector of the faithful which states that believers 'will tread on the lion and the adder' and 'will trample under foot' 'the young lion and the serpent'. Allegorical readings of this verse represented Mary as riding atop a lion and/or serpent. Schiller describes an Adoration compositional type prevalent from the mid-twelfth century in which the Virgin, enthroned, rests her feet atop a bull, a lion and/or a serpent, signifying her conquering the dragon of Psalms 91:13.[45] Such readings, founded on mistranslations and built up narrative element by narrative element, call attention to the role context plays in signification. Each element, 'mistaken' or based on standard theology, plays a part in determining the significance of all other elements and the structure of the whole narrative of salvation, as well as Mary's place within it. Again, our attention is turned to the contiguity between the elements of this system, a contiguity which *Pearl* will foreground in a similar manner.

Additionally, the snake had other more widely disseminated significances that survived in some form the Christian appropriation. A complete description of snake cults is outside the bounds of the present project, but, briefly, the snake was believed to be born anew each time it shed its skin and thus was connected to the moon, reborn every month. Thus, the snake and the moon are associated with immortal life and the menstrual cycle. We see these connections deeply buried in the myth of the Fall in Eden: humanity lost eternal life at the subtle bequest of the serpent, who claimed to know the secret of eternal life, and part of the curse was menstruation.[46] In her righting of humanity from original sin, Mary serves as a vehicle for the recuperation of the serpent into the Christian narrative. However, as even this brief history of the appropriation of the serpent metaphor and the resurfacing of its more ancient implications makes clear, the palimpsest upon which the salvational narrative is written can never be completely denuded of its traces of other narratives, myths and the cultures that produced them.

Images – like the 'Madonna of Humility' and the Adoration type – in which Mary is simultaneously mother and queen, crowned and barefoot, Old Testament prophecy and New Testament fulfilment, indicate the medieval exegetical urge towards final signification in which ultimate salvation and the Second Coming subsume all other narratives. Yet as the metonymical and intertextual relationship between the units of the story of salvation makes clear, this desire for final signification seems always to be unrealized. The series of substitutions and mistranslations that produce Mary as the vanquisher of evil and queen of heaven evidences nothing so much as the allegorical reading process itself; as it does so, it evidences also the desires of its individual practitioners, enraptured by the ideology of Christianity and the possibility that they might, like the Virgin, be comprehended and be made comprehensible by it.

Consequently, 'The Death of Mary' in the *York Plays* ends with a chorus of angels, including Gabriel and *'uno diablo. . . . cantant antiphona scilicet Aue regina celorum'*, 'a devil . . . singing, naturally, the antiphon "Ave! Queen of Heaven"' (following l. 194). The devil, a reminder of the serpent, is brought under the canopy of heaven's powers. In the *N-Town*, demons arrive to carry off the scheming Jews to hell, clearing the way for the Holy Mother's Assumption. Then the Assumption scene itself follows. It includes Apostles, angels and God, bodies and souls, heaven and earth. Jesus commands his angels to descend with him to earth 'To reyse the body of [his] moder terestyall' (l. 492) and bring it to him so that she can know 'the vnyte' of heaven (l. 494).[47] Christ arrives at the sepulchre in his 'manhede clere' (l. 498) and greets the Apostles gathered there. John and the archangel Michael take on the task of convincing *Dominus* to raise Mary by reuniting her with her soul, which he has been keeping in heaven. John makes the parallel between mother and son explicit by saying 'Lord, as thou rese from deth . . . / So reyse thou this body' (ll. 501–2). Michael urges that God 'fest' or 'fasten' her soul back to her 'blissid body' (l. 506) since 'sche bare . . . God in [his] mythtis' (l. 508). *Dominus* does so, saying,

> Go thanne, blyssid soule, to that body ageyn.
>   Arys now, my dowe, my nehebour and my swete frende,
> Tabernacle of joye, vessel of lyf, hefnely temple, to reyn.
>   Ye schal haue the blysse wyth me, moder, that hath non ende.
> For as ye were clene in erthe of alle synnys greyn,
>   So schul ye reyne in hefne clennest in mend. (ll. 509–14)

(Go then, blessed soul, to your body again. Arise now, my dove, my neighbour, my sweet friend, tabernacle of joy, vessel of life, heavenly temple, to reign. You will have bliss with me, mother, that has no end. For as you were clean on earth of all the marks of sin, so shall you reign in heaven, cleanest in mind.)

With this scene, the *N-Town* ends with a tour de force of discursive sublation, yet in this ending's attempts to be all-comprehensive we can read the contingencies of this world-building – the accidents, desires and untraceable myriad of circumstances that have been solidified into Christianity.

John makes clear the human logic at work in what is supposed to be one of the most profound mysteries of faith; after his request of God, he reasons about the propriety of raising Mary, concluding that to 'Vs semyth this ryth is' (l. 504). Michael similarly calls on something in addition to the transcendent truths of heaven to sway God, saying 'Hefne and erthe wold thynke this the best now' (l. 507). The earth may be, according to Augustinian sign theory, the book of creation in which the *signa* of God are manifest;[48] yet it is also the place of mis-interpretation and the babble of many languages, languages created by God in response to a threat from the humans for whom 'nothing . . . will be impossible' with a common language (Genesis 11:6). Such languages suggest different systems of logic and understanding, yet John's and Gabriel's pronouncements reflect the desire to have unity, as does the ultimate idea of Mary's soul being forever reunited with her body, as Revelation promises each Christian's will be. Similarly, this is the type of unity for which the *Pearl* narrator struggles but which he never grasps, although the poem, in both form and content, tends towards it.

The eponymous pearl, a 'perle wythouten spot' (pearl without spot) (ll. 12, 24, 36, 48), begins the tale allied with the *specula sine macula* image of Mary. At first the poem presents a jewel lost; the pearl that was once 'clanly clos in golde so clere' (cleanly set in gold so clear) (2) and is now 'clad in clot' (dressed in dirt) (22). And so the 'Joylez Juelere' (Joyless Jeweller) bewails his loss near harvest time, 'In Auguste in a hyȝ seysoun, / Quen corne is coruen wyth crokeȝ kene' (In August in a high season, when corn is cut with keen sickles) (39–40). Scholars have linked this seasonal timing, as well as the herbs growing in the 'erbere' or garden (9), with the Holy Virgin, the fifteenth of August being the feast day of the Assumption.[49] The *Pearl* maiden is multiply framed by these opening lines.[50] Connected to the Holy Virgin more than with just these and other textual references, the image of the pearl is similarly a transitional image.

When the narrator falls asleep and begins his dream vision, he enters a magical landscape where we begin to see metonymic logic at work more precisely. The pearl image next appears as a part of this land-scape. As the narrator walks, gazing at the 'crystal klyffez so cler of kynde' (crystal cliffs so naturally clear) (74) and the trees with trunks 'as blwe as ble of Ynde' (as blue as blue of India) (76) and leaves like 'bornyst syluer' (burnished silver) (77), he hears the crunching of gravel under his feet. He looks down to find that it consists of 'precious perlez of oryente' (precious pearls of Orient) (82). These pearls – recalling the whole of the poem and figuratively allied with every other pearl in this vision – metonymically represent the character of this landscape, a place where the narrator recognizes the fixtures and yet realizes they are in a context completely new to him. Where the pearl was before singular, a lost object of grief, the image has now been multiplied and translated from the grave-like 'huyle' or hill where the pearl had fallen (41) to the expansive landscape of the dream. This landscape, in between the human world of death and harvest and the timeless, heavenly New Jerusalem, is indebted to both the religious and the erotic visionary traditions.

Precedents like John's apocalyptic vision and Dante's *Commedia* abound on the religious side. In addition, Eden and the *hortus conclusus* are models for the magically artful landscape of *Pearl*, as Patricia Kean has written.[51] From the erotic tradition, the love garden or the garden of *Deduit* from *Le Roman de la Rose*, the fallen Eden, offers a precedent.[52] This alliance of spiritual and secular analogues provides us our first glimpse of the intertextual and often contradictory nature of the setting of this dream vision. The image of the pearl focuses and manipulates such intertextuality. Given the semiotic weight of pearls in the period, the poem's translation of the pearl image offers a metonymic glimpse of the indeterminacy of this highly intertextual setting, as allegorical and lapidary texts would indicate.

In the Middle Ages, pearls were called Margarita stones, connecting them to the purity and virtues of St Margaret. In his *Testament of Love*, Thomas Usk translates the physical value of pearls – their capacity to provide bodily comfort, to protect against passions of evil men and to staunch blood – into the virtues of purity, humility and the healing effect of beloved on lover.[53] Lapidary lore describes similar virtues. Pearls are made 'of þe dewe of heuen' and have powers 'aȝens rennyng [running] of blod, & aȝens þe flyx [flux] of þe wombe' and powers to comfort 'lymes & membris' because they can cleanse away 'superfluite of humors & fasten the lymes'.[54] Such virtues coincided with medieval exegetical practices, but from the biblical perspective pearls had both a positive and negative weight. Matthew 13:45–6, for example, relates the parable of the pearl of great price: 'the kingdom of heaven is like to a merchant man, seeking good pearls. And having found one precious pearl, he went his way and sold all that he had and bought it.' Similarly, Matthew 7:6 associates pearls with attaining and protecting God's kingdom: 'Give not that which is holy to dogs; neither cast ye your pearls before swine, lest perhaps they tread them with their feet and turning, to tear you.' Additionally, pearls appear as part of the kingdom itself, as the gates of the New Jerusalem (Revelation 21:21).

On the negative side, Revelation 17:4 describes the whore of Babylon as 'gilded with gold and precious stone and pearls', while after the destruction of Babylon, the town's merchants are themselves 'Joylez Juelere[s]' (*Pearl*, 1. 252), mourning their lost 'merchandise of gold and silver and precious stone and pearl' (Revelation 18:12). Additionally, as Dolores Frese argues in her work on Chaucer's *Pardoner's Tale* and its relation to *Le Roman de la Rose*, the gravel that covers the river bed in the garden of *Deduit*, like the pearly gravel in the *Pearl*'s magical landscape, is suggestive of semen. As a sign, semen can have negative or positive connotations because, as Augustine says, in the 'torrent of the human race, both elements are carried along together – both evil which is derived from him who begets and the good which is bestowed by Him who creates us'.[55] Within these few examples are evident the various natures of the pearl as image; it is a symbol of perfection and transcendence and, at the same time, of mutability and moral corruption.[56] All that distinguishes a good pearl from a bad one, it seems, is the setting of the pearl, the semiotic context that provides it with signification. Like the translated 'dewe of heuen' that forms a pearl, the image of the pearl is itself fluid; and this fluidity, infusing and infused by each context in which it signifies, operates in *Pearl* as a collateral logic to that of the poem's dualism. Indeed, what we will see is that such a primary indeterminacy, like that of Mary's position within the figurations of the church, founds the artistic urge to monumentalize the ideality of Christian logic and turn 'Gilofre, gyngure . . . gromy-lyoun' (gillyflower, ginger . . . gromwell) (43) and their wafting 'fayrre reflayr' (fair odour) (46) into the 'bornyst syluer' (77) icons of dogma.

The conflicted history of the interpretation of this poem and its central figure illustrates the difficulty such fluidity poses to coming to some final understanding of the poem. Those who would read the poem via Augustine's four-tiered strategy of allegory understand the pearl to have spiritual significance right from the poem's beginning.[57] There are those who understand the pearl to be a symbol, believing that the poem provides its own exegesis, no outside systems being necessary.[58] Those who do what might be called a psychological reading understand the pearl to be secular and personal at the poem's beginning but increasingly endowed with changing significance throughout the work.[59] The importance of these various and contradictory readings to my project is not in using one or the other of them to uphold yet another interpretation of the pearl image; instead, these readings help us to focus on *how* the poem works, how it calls attention to the process of signification by repeatedly relocating and reinterpreting the pearl image.

We next see the pearl in the clothing of a 'faunt' or 'child' (161) the narrator notices in the magical landscape. Gradually it becomes clear that this child is the pearl that the narrator lost in the garden. The narrator sees the maiden on the other side of a stream, which he realizes is 'a deuyse / Bytwene myrþez' (a device between joys) (140) planned to divide him from 'paradyse' on the other side (137). Even this naive narrator realizes the fabricated, divisive quality of his surroundings. The narrator is amazed to see 'A mayden of menske, ful debonere' (A maiden of honor, completely debonair) in a 'Blysnande whyt' (shining white) gown (162, 163). Like the jewel that he once possessed 'clanly close in golde so clere' (completely imbedded in gold so clear) (2), she looks like 'glysnande golde' (glistening gold) (165) sitting on the opposite bank with a face as 'whyt as playn yuore' (white as plain ivory) (178). He fears (losing) her 'gostly' (ghostly) presence (185) even as he solidifies her through description:

> Þat gracios gay withouten galle,
> So smoþe, so smal, so seme slyȝt,
> Rysez vp in hir araye ryalle,
> A precios pyece in perlez pyȝt. (189–92)

(That gracious, gay [one] without gall, so smooth, so small so seemly slight, rose up in her royal array, a precious piece in pearls fixed [or arrayed].)

These lines echo the original description of the first stanza in which the narrator describes his lost pearl as 'rounde', 'smal', and 'smoþe' (5 and 6). Stanza 17 intensifies the pearl imagery in its description of the maiden's white gown which is 'with precios perlez al vmbepyȝte' (with precious pearls completely surrounded) (204). Stanza 18 describes her crown 'Of marjorys and non oþer ston' (Of Margerys [pearls] and no other stone) (206). However, stanza 19 makes most clear the metonymic logic at work in this landscape and in the relationship between the dreamer/narrator and the maiden as well as between the poem and its readers; in this complex the poem teaches another lesson in how signification occurs. It describes the most remarkable pearl that arrays the maiden's gown:

> Bot a wonder perle withouten wemme
> Inmyddez hyr breste watz sette so sure;
> A mannez dom moȝt dryȝly demme
> Er mynde moȝt malte in hit mesure.
> I hope no tong moȝt endure
> No sauerly saghe say of þat syȝt,
> So watz hit clene and cler and pure,
> Þat precios perle þer hit watz pyȝt.
> Pyȝt in perle, þat precios pryse. (221–9)

(But a wondrous pearl without spot, in the middle of her breast was set securely; a man's judgment could rapidly fade, before a mind could speak it in moderation; I think no tongue could endure nor sweetly say a word of that sight, so clean, clear and pure it was, that precious pearl where it was fixed, that precious prize fixed in pearl.)

The narrator then addresses her as 'perle . . . in perlez pyȝt' (pearl . . . in pearls surrounded) (241). Even, it would seem, in this magical land-scape where the narrator's gaze turns everything into art,[60] there are some things that are inexpressible, things that make judgement fail. Yet as the maiden becomes what the narrator sees her wearing – that is, she becomes the *Pearl* maiden as he recognizes and describes all the pearls she wears – conventionality of representation becomes apparent, even in the basic convention of the inexpressibility topos. Additionally, her being 'withouten wemme' reminds us of her inter-textual, contiguous relationship with Mary and the cultural matrix she disseminates.

The pearl on the maiden's breast seems to represent her met-onymically just as she represents that paradise across the stream meto-nymically, as the text later reveals. The above passage is remarkable, however, for the way in which it foregrounds the reciprocal process that produces meaning; as it foregrounds the failures of language, it uses language and invokes the fluid processes of signification. Such processes are indicated most powerfully in the circular 'Þat precios perle þer hit watz pyȝt. / Pyȝt in perle þat precios pryse.' Repeating the verb 'pyȝt', 'to fix' – forms of which are also used in descriptions of the maiden's dress – reveals the urge in this signifying system to make this pearl mean something, to fix it in time and space. But the way in which this passage and the several stanzas that precede it actually make the pearl into the pearl illustrates that this longed-for fixity is only a rest-stop in the web that gives the passage meaning. As the various intertextual affiliations align the description of setting and maiden with various scriptural, theological and romance texts, meaning is made and yet dispersed by the very vehicles of poetic representation used.[61]

By noting how the metonymic characteristics of the first stanza's pearl become the maiden of the landscape, we can understand the way in which the poem foregrounds its own artifice and conventionality, teaching us to read in ways other than simply passing over in silence with our judgement faded. What the metonymic construction of the maiden illustrates is not so much what the ideal is like, but rather how the notion of 'the ideal' itself is reached. Since metonymy and contiguity can also be understood as placing things into serial relationship, looking at a series of substitutions in the text will help me to clarify this perspective further.

In this poem, pearls are substituted for pearls and each variation becomes the focal point for a new context. When an image, and not an ostensibly external, transcendent idea, becomes such an anchor for a context, the narrative urge towards plenitude becomes more apparent. In other words, as characteristics aggregate into this character, the ideal is being *articulated*, not transparently *represented*. In the same way that Mary articulated the Word – that is, gave it intelligibility by giving it the jointed form of the human body[62] – this poem attempts to make the transcendent intelligible through the physicality of form and sound; the primary paradox of the poem becomes, then, the realization that 'the ideal world, which is meant to transcend time and space, is represented here by its very contradiction, an image, an artifact of time and space'.[63] However, in the same way that Mary fills the role of the translational site or the term of contiguity between heaven and earth, the metonymic logic of the poem undoes the logic of paradox, the logic of duality, the logic of metaphor, on a fundamental level.

The *Pearl* maiden calls on metaphoric logic and exegetical practice when she cites Matthew 13:45–6, the parable of the pearl of great value. In ll. 730–4, she retells the parable adding that this

> makellez perle þat boȝt is dere . . .
> Is lyke þe reme of heuenesse clere –
> So sayde þe Fader of folde and flode –
> For hit is wemlez, clene and clere,
> And endelez rounde and blyþe of mode,
> And commune to all þat ryȝtwys were.

> Lo! euen inmyddez my breste hit stode:
> My Lorde þe Lombe þat schede Hys blode,
> He pyȝt hit þere in token of pes. (733–42)

(this matchless pearl that is bought dear . . . is like the realm of bright heaven, so said the father of earth and flood, for it is spotless, clean and clear and endlessly round and joyous in mood and common to all who are righteous; Lo! even in the middle of my breast it remains; my lord the lamb that shed his blood, he fixed it there as a token of peace.)

Just as the figure of Mary is inserted in a narrative to represent humanity or divinity depending on context and narrative necessities, the above passage sets up a series of substitutions. As Sarah Stanbury has so forcefully pointed out in her investigation of the poem's scopophilic tendencies, this passage metonymically allies the maiden's body with the lamb who reigns in the poem's New Jerusalem.[64] But the series is not just a dual one between maiden and her 'make' or mate, the lamb (759); it also includes the 'fader', the earth and seas, the pearl itself and the biggest of all celestial bodies, heaven. In such metonymic relationships figurative bodies continue to reappear, recuperated but ever-present.

As Kevin Marti has pointed out in *Body, Heart and Text in the Pearl-Poet*, Christ's body is the spatial centre of medieval culture.[65] In the ritual re-enactment of the Incarnation that is the Eucharist, each Christian's body participates in the Christic redemption of the flesh. Scholars point to ll. 457–68 of *Pearl*, which relate the biblical similitude of Christians to the limbs of Christ, and the poem's allusion to the sacrament in ll. 1208–10 as the loci of understanding the poem as itself incarnational.[66] Formally, the poem attempts to incarnate its central symbol, the pearl, in its recapitulative aspects. The poem is tightly constructed throughout, connecting five stanzas at a time by the use of *concatenatio*, or the repetition of key words in the beginning and ending lines of each stanza. These five-stanza groups are linked by the repetition in the first line of the next stanza of the concatenating words of the previous stanza group.[67] The poem concretizes this circularity by ending upon virtually the same phrase with which it began: 'Perle plesaunte, to prynces paye' (Pleasant pearl for prince's payment) (1) and 'Ande precious perlez vnto His pay' (And precious pearls for His payment) (1212).

Formally, therefore, the pearl and *Pearl* maiden are connected with the matter of the text, its physical properties, and the poem itself becomes another term in the metonymic series. White and round, inscribed with the Word of God, pearl and poem both have a tendency to be sublated in service to the transcendent presence even as they manifest that transcendence, calling our attention to its absence. As with figures like the 'Madonna of Humility' and representations of the queen of heaven, embodiment remains an issue. Metonymically, the poem connects and interchanges bodies, texts and textual represent-ations with transcendent truths and timeless ideals. Before we can understand the poem's reflexive attitude towards this contiguous relationship, we should first look at how the text speaks about bodies, primarily the maiden's and the lamb's, but with Mary's curiously allied to both.

The apocryphal texts and cycle dramas have illustrated the potency of Mary's body, with and without its soul and its imperial powers even in its mothering roles. *Pearl* couples the heavenly functions of the *Pearl* maiden, the 'bryd'[68] of Christ and 'quene in blysse' (415), with those of Mary. But the text allies the two in more ways than just their titles as queens and brides. The *Pearl* maiden is, in body and name, a twin of her who was 'neuere in two to be twynnand' ('The Death of Mary', *York Plays* 182).[69] In his signature study of the poem's allegory, Jefferson B. Fletcher describes the most obvious exegetical ways the poem associates the two characters. He cites *Pearl*, ll. 763–4, 'Cum hyder to Me, My lemman swete, / For mote ne spot is non in þe' (Come hither to Me, my sweet love, for there is neither speck nor spot in thee) as a Middle English translation of Song of Songs 4:7–8 about the spotless bride from Lebanon, commonly thought of as a precursor to Mary.[70] Additionally, the image of the white pearl set in gold recalls Richard of St Lawrence's descriptions of the lily-white Virgin's virtues adorning her '*quasi aurum*',[71] virtues the *Pearl* maiden, 'coronde clene in vergynté' (crowned purely in virginity) (767), shares. In a close study of Richard's *De Laudibus Beata Mariae Virginis*, Fletcher finds many instances in which Mary is described as bedecked with pearls and shining with pearl-like luminescence.[72] Such portrayals create of the *Pearl* maiden a twin of her who was not to be made into two. In this multiplication, another logic becomes apparent: the logic that must use repetition to conceive of its idea of singularity. In the same way that the Eucharist replicates the body of Christ, *Pearl* replicates the body of Mary in the *Pearl* maiden, who herself is replicated exponentially in the poem's final vision when she is in a procession

Of such vergynez in þe same gyse
Þat watz blysful anvunder croun.
And coronde wern alle of þe same fasoun,
Depaynt in perlez and wedez qwyte;
In vchonez breste watz bounden boun
Þe blysful perle with gret delyt. (1099–1104)

(Of such virgins in the same guise as was the narrator's blissful crowned
one; and all were crowned in the same fashion, adorned in pearls and
white clothes; on the breast of each one was fixed ready the blissful pearl
with great delight.)

All fall at the feet of the lamb in praise. Even the narrator feels 'delyt'
in gazing on the scene from across the stream (1116 and 1117). The
passage operates on the assumption that the lamb is the eschaton of the
action, the focus of this story and of the history of salvation towards
which the poem has been progressing all along. And yet, the lamb's
serial relationship with the body of the *Pearl* maiden and, now, with all
these identical maidens illustrates that the lamb is one term in a
metonymic series, allied with figuration and physiology.

The *Pearl* maiden's alliance with Mary is more, then, than just
titular and exegetical. Their stories share the bodily foundation of
figuration at the same time that their bodies are inscribed by the discourses of salvation and virtue that they legitimize. Like Mary, whose
story necessitated she not rot in the earth, the *Pearl* maiden seems not
to be rotting either since she is in the physical presence of the narrator.
Yet the narrator had his doubts about the bodily fate of his lost pearl
at the poem's beginning. He believes his pearl has left him, his 'priuy
perle withouten spotte' (very own pearl without spot) (24) having gone
from him, or 'fro [him] sprange' (13), in a particular 'spote' (spot) (13).
Now he mourns 'To þenke hir color so clad in clot' (To think of her
colour so clad in dirt) (22), her 'rychez to rot . . . runnen' (riches run to
rot) (26). Later, however, he meets the maiden, manifest in all of her
expanded, redoubled presence in the magical landscape. Through the
blazon of the maiden and her shining white clothes (stanza group 4, ll.
181–240) the pearl reappears as the *Pearl* maiden, embodied for
readers as a human character, not a figuration of grief, for the first
time. Her 'wemlez', or spotless, body in all its glory seems anything but
dirty and rotted. And as the metonymic qualities of this scene
illustrate, her body is multiplied exponentially by the pearls on it – that

become it – and this first vision of the *Pearl* maiden foreshadows the multiplicity her body will take on in the New Jerusalem at the feet of the lamb.

However, even this immaculate pearl knows the vicissitudes of death. She tells the narrator that his 'corse in clot mot calder keue' (corpse must rot more coldly in the dirt) (320) before he can enter the paradise he sees across the stream. Her own body 'in clottez clynge[s]' (in clots remains) (857), as does the body of each who 'beren þys perle vpon [her] bereste' (bears this pearl upon her breast) (854). But of course, this pearl of heaven knows the teleology of her death; it mirrors and depends upon that of the lamb, who was 'to þe slaȝt þer lad' (led to the slaughter there) (801) and who overcame sin and death, to exist bodily in the New Jerusalem. This point in the story when the salvational narrative seems so clear and clearly efficacious, however, is one of the most intertextually revealing. The *Pearl* maiden calls on John's vision of the Apocalypse as the authority for what she describes. Within the five stanzas of stanza group 14, she invokes this vision, this other text or 'trw recorde' (true record) (831), four times. John, she says, had his visual apotheosis on the 'hyl of Syon þat semly clot' (hill of Sion, that seemly soil) (789). This 'clot' reminds us of the one where the narrator mourns his loss at the poem's beginning and portends the ones that the maiden describes surrounding the bodies of all the *Pearl* maidens. Most interesting, however, is the connection between this passage, with its teleology and sublation of bodily death, and the earlier passage in which she explains to the narrator that he must be surrounded by clots before he can enter paradise. She continues to explain the reason for this condition:

> For hit watz forgarte, at paradys greue;
> Oure ȝorefader hit con mysseȝeme.
> Þurȝ drwry deth boz vch man dreue,
> Er ouer þys dam hym Dryȝtyn deme. (321–4)

(For it (the body) was destroyed, in the grove of paradise; our fore-father did misuse it; each man is driven through dreary death before the Lord deems him over this stream.)

The maiden later retells the same story, adding the details of how the biting of the apple by 'Oure forme fader' (Our former father) 'forfete[d]' (forfeited) (639–40) the 'delyt' (delight) of paradise (642). She also extends this story forward to include the Crucifixion (646), the Harrowing of Hell (651), baptism (653) and the Eucharist (647). She retells the salvational narrative three times, each time correlating the terms of salvation with those of original sin. By thus inscribing salvation as contiguous with the originary moment of loss, a moment repeated in the narrator's loss of his pearl, the poem calls attention to the slippery potential of generation and reproduction, even of faith. Curiously, Eve is absent from these scenes of original sin, but in their focus on inheritance of this already stained body, the stage for the scenes has been set by another passage occurring much earlier in the poem. If we return to our first view of Mary in the poem, we again see this emphasis on 'erytage' (443), that is, on genealogical serial contiguity. As illustrated by the 'Madonna of Humility' and the *vierges ouvrantes*, even when Mary is crowned and enthroned as 'emperise' (441) of heaven, the fecundity of her body is never far behind. This picture of her with heaven, earth and hell in her dominion strains towards the idea of unified and self-identical existence, yet the focus on heritage and its connection to bodily reproduction and transgressions calls the spectre of Eve forth. Her body seems to be one missing term upon which this vision of perfection is based.

The conflicted histories of Mary's conception, birth, motherhood and death and her relation to Eve must, then, impact on the following lines about the Holy Virgin spoken by the narrator: 'We calle hyr Fenyx of Arraby, / ψat fereles fleȝe of hyr Fasor' (We call her the phoenix of Arabia, that blameless of her form, flew *or* unique from her creator, flew) (430–1). In the Middle Ages the tradition of the phoenix was familiar from both popular and learned writings. For instance, the narrator of Chaucer's *Book of the Duchess* calls the White Queen the 'soleyn fenix of Arabye' (l. 982) (see also lines 15,948–64 in *Le Roman de la Rose*). Such citations often emphasize the solitary existence of the bird, just as Mary was, of course, alone of all her sex. Yet the myth of the phoenix from *Metamorphoses*, which would have been the most well-known form of the story in the period, also emphasizes another aspect of the bird's existence – its singular reproductive capacities. It gives birth only to itself over and over, with only one phoenix existing at any time. Once again, we are drawn to see how Mary is made to signify differently – often in ways contradictory to each other – in various contexts for various purposes. This image of such singular birth seems antithetical to Mary's metonymic role as gate of heaven, that point of translation between human and divine, productive of the

salvation of innumerable faithful; as such, Mary was figured as the
mother of all humanity. And as the poem itself has revealed, Mary is
neither so limitedly reproductive nor so singular. The *Pearl* maiden, a
metonymic reflection of the Holy Virgin, reminds the narrator that it
was from Mary that 'Jesu con spryng' (Jesus did spring) (453).
Similarly, the poem's subtle emphasis on heritage calls to mind the
contiguous nature of sin and salvation, death and life, bodies and
immaculate pearls.

   In this way, this image of the phoenix focuses the poem's self-
reflexive qualities as it suggests the extent to which any formal tropo-
logical classification of images is bound to lead to crossed or confused
categories at certain points. Representations of Mary as the architecture
and furniture of heaven, her relationship to Eve and her inheritance of
cultural anxieties about maternity intimate the supplementary nature of
flesh and figuration to faith in transcendence. Even in *Pearl*, Mary's
body is seemingly comprehended into the *telos* of the heavenly vision.
The *Pearl* maiden falls on her knees to worship the Holy Mother,
calling her the empress of heaven, but nowhere does the Holy Virgin
appear as a character in the plot. In the same speech in which the *Pearl*
maiden prays to her, Mary is replaced by the *corpus mysticum* of ll.
457–68, which relate the Pauline doctrine of Christians being the limbs
of Jesus (Romans 12:4–5). During the vision of the New Jerusalem, only
attributes of her appear: the virginal *Pearl* maidens and the 'hyȝe trone'
(high throne) on which the lamb sits (1051) suggest her metonymically.
It would seem that sublation is complete, that the dangerous supplementarity of flesh and figuration has been put in its proper place in
service to the truth of the lamb and his grace.

   Yet the poem has taught its readers early on how certain types of
figuration do not work, even though it uses this figure of the phoenix.
It is this phoenix and her metonymic representative, the *Pearl* maiden –
repeated and diffused as I have shown her to be – that articulate the
poem's concomitant logic of transcendence. This metonymy, even
mirrored by the poem's own formal characteristics, creates what could
be a mystifying web of signification. To prevent readers from becoming
lost like the 'dased quayle' (dazed quail) (1085) the narrator becomes
within this web, the poem calls readers' attention to its underlying
logic. Returning to an earlier passage will enable me to clarify this
point further. In the *Pearl* maiden's retelling of the parable of the pearl
of great price, she names God as 'þe Fader of folde and flode' (father of
earth and flood) (736), bringing this web to the surface on the levels of

letter and word. The metathesis involved in changing 'folde' to 'flode' is remarkable for it calls attention to the part context plays in signification. In the same way that the passage substitutes one body for another in what seems to be a seamless and logical progression, the letters make sense in context. However, the similarity between these words illustrates the fundamental indeterminacy that underlies language. The same five letters in different serial relation to each other can mean two different things. Their self-identical but reproducible quality and their ability to be cited and translated into other contexts, like the bodies of Mary and the *Pearl* maiden, evidence the divisive consequences of figuration. The *Pearl* maiden is self-identical, being easily recognizable to the narrator as his pearl when he first sees her.[73] Yet, she is the epitome of multiplicity: her clothes repeat her metonymically; she repeats and is repeated by the 'Hundreth þowsandez' (Hundred thousands) in the procession of maidens (1107); and she stands in for the body of that singular phoenix, Mary and her offspring, the lamb that is Christ. It is the repetition of her sameness, stemming from the idea of the unity and plenitude of heaven, that undoes the figure of the maiden, authorizing yet jeopardizing that very sameness.

The metonymy of the poem thus allows us to see the fold in the immaculate pearl, or the ways in which its multiple representations of perfection undermine its purity. The narrator feels some vexation upon looking at the *telos* of this purity, the New Jerusalem, where his sight can penetrate the walls but his dreamer's body cannot. Driven by 'luflongyng in gret delyt' (love-longing in great delight) (1152)[74] upon spotting his 'lyttel quene' (little queen) (1147) among the multitudes in the heavenly city, he attempts to cross the stream that separates the magical landscape from paradise. Instead of fulfilling his desire to be with his queen, however, he awakens from his dream to find himself in the garden in which he began. Having been specially chosen to experience a vision of ostensible completion and perfection, his desire is nevertheless 'to maddyng malte' (to folly dissolved) (1154) and is still singularly focused on the one facet of that plenitude. And he forfeits it all. His experience marks the dissolute but dangerously necessary effects of figuration as he chooses his one *Pearl* maiden – that is, one piece of the story – and not the whole of the salvational narrative.

My investigation in this chapter of metonymy, Mary and the *Pearl* maiden and the investigations I have undertaken in previous chapters of this project have illustrated that myriad discourses created the certainty of salvation, of Christianity itself. Tenets about gender and physiology, upon which a remarkable portion of the Christian narrative is based, prove to be both the very media through which this narrative is told and the places where it is most contentious. If Mary, Constance, Alisoun of Bath, Margaret, the *Trotula* woman and the *Pearl* maiden can teach us anything about how the medieval church conceived of the relationship between gender and talk of the divine, the lesson is that concerns about gender have always been part of Christianity because they are part of the lives of believers. All of these characters – whether those in the popular imagination, those of the religious didactic tradition, or those, like the *Trotula* woman in medical discourse – illustrate the intimate connections between the divine and the human. Despite Augustine's interdiction to pass over in silence what cannot be said, we have seen that believers tried over and over again to draw the ineffable into something tangible or legible, indeed, into the mundane world of birth, death, law, love, marriage, travel, grief and any number of other human realms. Augustine's words that began this chapter themselves reveal the period's mistrust of words to do all that writers would have them do, yet no one has stopped writing. The conclusion of *Pearl* reminds us of the constant refiguration of the ineffable and the narrative of salvation 'in þe forme of bred and wyn / . . . vch a daye' (in the form of bread and wine . . . each day) (1209–10) and in each act of taking communion. Metonymy, then, proves to be an important trope, perhaps the signal trope, for understanding those aspects of medieval Christianity thus tied up with gender, bodies and the materiality of signification.

NOTES

Introduction

1 This translation of lines 21,543–552 is from Charles Dahlberg's edition (London: University Press of New England, 1983), p. 351; the Old French reads: 'Ainsinc va des contreres choses, / les unes sunt des autres gloses; / et qui l'une an veust defenir, / de l'autre li doit souvenir, / ou ja, par nule antancion, / n'i metra diffinicion; / car qui des .II. n'a connoissance, / ja n'i connoistra differance, / san quoi ne peut venir en place / diffinicion que l'an face.'

2 Ruth Morse, *Truth and Convention in the Middle Ages: Rhetoric, Representation, and Reality* (New York: Cambridge University Press, 1991), p. 2.

3 Ibid., p. 180.

4 Ibid., p. 4.

5 Ibid., pp. 231–2.

6 Ann W. Astell, 'Chaucer's "St. Anne Trinity": devotion, dynasty, dogma, and debate', *Studies in Philology*, 94 (1997), 395–416 (45 and 46).

7 Gail McMurry Gibson, *The Theater of Devotion: East Anglian Drama and Society in the Late Middle Ages* (Chicago: University of Chicago Press, 1989), p. 138.

8 Julia Kristeva, *Stabat Mater*, *The Kristeva Reader*, ed. Toril Moi and trans. León S. Roudiez (New York: Columbia University Press, 1986), pp. 160–86 (pp. 161–2).

9 For example, see his 'Signature, event, context', in *Limited Inc*, trans. Samuel Weber and Jeffrey Mehlman (Evanston, IL: Northwestern University Press, 1988), pp. 1–23.

10 *The N-Town Play: Cotton MS Vespasian D.8*, ed. Stephen Spector (Oxford: Oxford University Press, 1991), ll. 94–7. All references are to this edition.

11 Cf. V. A. Kolve, *The Play Called Corpus Christi* (Stanford: Stanford University Press, 1966), particularly his chapters on 'Religious laughter' and 'The invention of comic action'; on p. 134 Kolve argues, 'The Corpus Christi drama is an institution of central importance to the English Middle Ages precisely because it triumphantly united man's need for festival and mirth with instruction in the story that most seriously concerned his immortal soul.'

12 Gertrud Schiller, *Iconography of Christian Art*, trans. Janet Seligman (London: Lund Humphries, 1971), vol. 1, pp. 47–8.

13 Donald Attwater, *A Dictionary of Mary* (New York: P. J. Kennedy & Sons, 1959), p. 189. Marina Warner, *Alone of All her Sex: The Myth and the Cult of the Virgin Mary* (New York: Knopf, 1976), pp. 92–3, calls this passage a key to understanding the text of the Assumption mass, which celebrates 'the conquest of lust and putrefaction'.

14 For example, Schiller, *Iconography*, vol. 1, p. 41.

15 Gibson, *Theater of Devotion*, p. 8, argues that such images arise from the Franciscan devotional emphasis, 'a deliberate and conscious effort to objectify the spiritual even as the Incarnation itself had given spirit a concrete form'.

16 See 1 Timothy 2:9–15.

17 A method of writing in which the lines are inscribed alternately from right to left and from left to right; derived from the pattern of the turning of the oxen at the end of a ploughed row.

18 Julia Kristeva, excerpt from *Revolution in Poetic Language*, in *The Kristeva Reader*, ed. Toril Moi and trans. León S. Roudiez (New York: Columbia University Press, 1986), p. 98; Kristeva develops her theory of the thetic break on pp. 98–110.

19 For example, reading various apocryphal stories of the Virgin's Assumption into heaven or her Dormition will show that the later the text, the shorter the amount of time it took for her soul and/or her son to return from heaven to claim her body.

20 See Genesis 5:24 and Hebrews 11:5 for Enoch's story, Deuteronomy 34:5–6 for the mysterious circumstances of Moses' death and 2 Kings 2:11 for Elijah's story.

21 See Derrida, 'Signature, event, context', pp. 9–10.

22 All references are to the 3rd edn, *Riverside Chaucer*, ed. Larry D. Benson (Boston: Houghton Mifflin, 1987); fragment 2, l. 192.

23 Judith Butler, *Gender Trouble: Feminism and the Subversion of Identity* (New York: Routledge, 1990), pp. 128–41.

24 *Seinte Marherete, þe Meiden ant Martyr*, ed. Frances M. Mack (London: Oxford University Press, 1934), p. 34. All further references are to this edition.

25 Elaine Scarry, *The Body in Pain* (New York: Oxford University Press, 1985). Cf. also Gayle Margherita, *The Romance of Origins: Language and Sexual Difference in Middle English Literature* (Philadelphia: University of Pennsylvania Press, 1994), pp. 43–61.

26 Margherita, *Romance of Origins*, p. 43.

27 *The Poems of the Pearl Manuscript: Pearl, Cleanness, Patience, Sir Gawain and the Green Knight*, ed. Malcolm Andrew and Ronald Waldron (Berkeley: University of California Press, 1978), ll. 468. All further references to *Pearl* are to this edition.

28 Teresa de Lauretis, *Technologies of Gender* (Bloomington: Indiana University Press, 1987), p. 10.

Chapter 1

¹ In 'Oure tonges *différance*: textuality and deconstruction in Chaucer', in *Medieval Texts and Contemporary Readers*, ed. Laurie A. Finke and Martin B. Shichtman (Ithaca, NY: Cornell University Press, 1987), pp. 15–26 (p. 17), H. Marshall Leicester describes a similar process in *Troilus and Criseyde*, declaring that the text '*mimes* a certain sort of discourse in such a way as to bring out the assumptions that make it possible and to question them'.

² In *Narrative, Authority and Power: The Medieval Exemplum and the Chaucerian Tradition* (New York: Cambridge University Press, 1994), Larry Scanlon has dealt in detail with exemplarity in the Middle Ages and in Chaucer's writing in particular, yet my study of the Man of Law's use of exemplarity provides a different perspective on, a closer view of, the Man of Law's own use of exemplarity to reveal ways in which the tale he tells reveals more of himself than is at first apparent.

³ See the *Protevangelium*, 8:1; all subsequent references to New Testament apocrypha are from *The Apocryphal New Testament Being the Apocryphal Gospels, Acts, Epistles, and Apocalypses*, ed. and trans. Montague Rhodes James (Oxford: Clarendon, 1924).

⁴ See Gertrud Schiller, *Iconography of Christian Art*, trans. Janet Seligman (London: Lund Humphries, 1971), vol. 1, p. 42.

⁵ This common appellation for Mary originates in the Old Testament apocryphal work, Wisdom of Solomon, 7:26: 'For she is a reflection of eternal light, a spotless mirror of the working of God and an image of his goodness.' Similarly, Constance is said to be 'unwemmed', or immaculate (fragment 2, l. 924).

⁶ Marina Warner, *Alone of All her Sex: The Myth and the Cult of the Virgin Mary* (New York: Knopf, 1976), p. 236; Jaroslav Pelikan, *Mary through the Centuries: Her Place in the History of Culture* (New Haven: Yale University Press, 1996), p. 199.

⁷ In 'Chaucer's "St. Anne Trinity": devotion, dynasty, dogma, and debate,' *Studies in Philology*, 94 (1997), 395–416, Ann W. Astell has written of Chaucer's use of references to Anna, or more precisely to the 'St Anne Trinity' – the grouping of Anna, with her daughter and her grandson (Jesus) in medieval and renaissance iconography. Chaucer refers to the three together in *The Man of Law's Tale* and *The Second Nun's Tale*. On p. 395, Astell argues: 'Chaucer's juxtaposition of Anne's name with Christ's and his representation of Mary in the central, double role of daughter and mother form a neat chiasmus that mirrors the iconography of the St. Anne Trinity.'

⁸ André Grabar, *Christian Iconography: A Study of its Origins* (Princeton: Princeton University Press, 1968), pp. 129–31.

⁹ Donald Attwater, *A Dictionary of Mary* (New York: P. J. Kennedy & Sons, 1959), p. 122.

¹⁰ Yrjö Hirn, *The Sacred Shrine: A Study of the Poetry and Art of the Catholic Church* (London: Macmillan & Co., 1912), p. 221.

[11] Hirn, *Sacred Shrine*, p. 218; Pelikan, *Mary through the Centuries*, pp. 192–7. See Bernard's *In assumptione sermo et Epistola ad canonicos*, especially epistle 174.

[12] Hirn, *Sacred Shrine*, pp. 224–5.

[13] Warner, *Alone of All her Sex*, p. 242; on the same page, Warner makes the following conclusion on how such an act enhanced Christ's reputation as a healer. See also Pelikan, *Mary through the Centuries*, pp. 196–7.

[14] Grabar, *Christian Iconography*, pp. 128–9.

[15] See Hirn, *Sacred Shrine*, p. 238, for a fuller description and other examples of images of the embrace at the gate.

[16] See, for example, Isaiah 30:22, Lamentations 1:17 and Ezekiel 18:6.

[17] Charles T. Wood, 'The doctors' dilemma: sin, salvation, and the menstrual cycle in medieval thought', *Speculum*, 56 (1981), 710–27 (713–16).

[18] See Gail McMurry Gibson, *The Theater of Devotion: East Anglian Drama and Society in the Late Middle Ages* (Chicago: University of Chicago Press, 1989), p. 137.

[19] 'The Marriage of Mary and Joseph', *The N-Town Play: Cotton MS Vespasian D.8*, ed. Stephen Spector (Oxford: Oxford University Press, 1991), ll. 36–9. Further references are to this edition and will be given in the text.

[20] The original reads, 'In lateritiis vero tabulis arundinei styli ministerio, virgo varias rerum picturales sociabat imagines; pictura tamen subjacenti materiae familiariter non cohaerens, velociter evanescendo moriens, nulla imaginum post se relinquebat vestigia.'

[21] This line is from a fourteenth-century 'Ave Maris Stella', no. 45, l. 8, in Carleton Brown's *Religious Lyrics of the Fourteenth Century*, 2nd edn (Oxford: Clarendon, 1965). Unless otherwise noted, all lyric citations are from Brown's editions, with the number of the lyric in Brown followed by a colon and the line number(s).

[22] See Genesis 1:26 and 'God Creates Adam and Eve' in *The Plays Performed by the Crafts or Mysteries of York on the Day of Corpus Christi in the Fourteenth, Fifteenth and Sixteenth Centuries*, ed. Lucy Toulmin Smith (New York: Russell & Russell, 1963); all references to the *York* cycle are from Smith's edition.

[23] Cf. Meike Bal, 'Sexuality, sin, and sorrow: the emergence of the female character (a reading of Genesis 1–3)', *Poetics Today*, 6 (1987), 21–42.

[24] Carolyn Dinshaw, *Chaucer's Sexual Poetics* (Madison: University of Wisconsin Press, 1989), p. 6.

[25] Philo, *On the Creation*, ed. and trans. F. H. Colson and G. H. Whitaker (Cambridge: Harvard University Press, 1958–62), vol. 1, p. 119.

[26] *Malleus Maleficarum*, ed. and trans. Montague Summers (1928; repr. New York: Benjamin Blom, 1970), p. 44.

[27] Quoted in R. Howard, *Representations*, 20 (1987); R. Howard Bloch, 'Medieval misogyny', *Representations*, 20 (1987), 22.

[28] See Genesis 2:18–23.

[29] Bloch, 'Medieval misogyny', p. 11.

[30] Book 7, chapter 20; in the original, Augustine says that he had been 'admonitus quaerere incorpoream veritatem'.

[31] Gibson, *Theater of Devotion*, p. 139.

[32] Bal, 'Sexuality', p. 29.

[33] In *The Works of Philo*, trans. C. D. Yonge (Peabody, MA: Hendrickson, 1993), Philo understands the serpent, which he reads as a fallen representation of all bodily pleasures tied to mental capacity, to be the first entity to trope language; for example, see pp. 45–9.

[34] Grabar, *Christian Iconography*, pp. 128–9, collects several pictorial images in which the child is already present even as the angel speaks to Mary. Additionally, many of the religious lyrics of the fourteenth century collected by Brown, *Religious Lyrics*, reflect a similar idea. See, for examples, nos. 26, 41 and 45.

[35] One might add *pharmakon* to this list. See Jacques Derrida, 'Plato's pharmacy', in *Dissemination*, ed. and trans. Barbara Johnson (Chicago: University of Chicago Press, 1981), pp. 61–171, on the status of such permeable signifiers.

[36] See particularly 2. ll. 162–8 which invoke many of the tropes often used to describe Mary. For a collection of specific likenesses, see Juliette Dor, 'From a crusading virago to the polysemous virgin: Chaucer's Constance', in *A Wyf Ther Was: Essays in Honour of Paule Mertens-Fonck*, ed. Juliette Dor (Liège: University of Liège Press, 1982), pp. 129–40 (pp. 133–4). Similarly, Astell in 'Chaucer's "St. Anne Trinity"' asserts 'Custance becomes the altera Maria' (398).

[37] Dinshaw, Chaucer's *Sexual Poetics*, p. 95.

[38] Hirn, *Sacred Shrine*, pp. 250–70, and Attwater, *A Dictionary of Mary*, pp. 173–9, collect all these descriptions and more when they write of the childhood of Mary.

[39] See, for examples, Dyan Elliott, *Spiritual Marriage: Sexual Abstinence in Medieval Wedlock* (Princeton: Princeton University Press, 1993), pp. 178–9; Elizabeth Robertson, *Early English Devotional Prose and the Female Audience* (Knoxville: University of Tennessee Press, 1990), pp. 39–40; Anne Clark Bartlett, *Male Authors, Female Readers: Representation and Subjectivity in Middle English Devotional Literature* (Ithaca, NY: Cornell University Press, 1995), pp. 64–5.

[40] Dinshaw, *Chaucer's Sexual Poetics*, pp. 88–112.

[41] Dor, 'Crusading virago', pp. 131 and 138.

[42] Brown, *Religious Lyrics*, 16:19 and 31.

[43] On this word, see R. Allen Shoaf, '"Unwemmed Custance": circulation, property, and incest in the *Man of Law's Tale*', *Exemplaria*, 2 (1990), 287–302 (289) and *A Chaucer Glossary*, ed. Norman Davis et al., (Oxford: Clarendon, 1979).

[44] The *MED* suggests that the Middle English usage was a mixture of the Latin verb *indictāre* and the Old French verb *enditier* both meaning 'to declare, dictate, compose'.

45 Dinshaw, *Chaucer's Sexual Poetics*, p. 91, also suggests that the words 'endite' and 'thyng' from the portrait of the Man of Law in the *General Prologue* connect literary output with law since these words are commonly used in Chaucer to refer to literary creations.

46 See *Confessions* 2. 8, 7. 3 and 4. Boethius' *Consolation of Philosophy*, based on a Platonic notion of always striving for the true good in the world, operates on the idea of 'good as cause and sum' of all worldly striving (Prose 10); anything moving away from the good is evil. See Prose 12 for an explicit definition. And, of course, the whole of Dante's *Inferno* creates images of evil as deficiency, images which culminate in a vision of Satan frozen in the ice of Cocytus creating the very ice which imprisons him in silence.

47 Constance's prayer reflects portions of the Good Friday mass as well as the votive mass that invokes the help of the cross for travellers.

48 Dinshaw, *Chaucer's Sexual Poetics*, pp. 88–112; Dor; 'Crusading virago'; and Melissa M. Furrow, 'The Man of Law's St Custance: sex and the saeculum', *Chaucer Review*, 24 (1990), 223–35, discuss the contentions over Constance's sexuality.

49 This idea persists even in the modern Catholic church; according to Warner, *Alone of All her Sex*, p. 68, the prayer book authorized by the Second Vatican Council of 1964, for example, contains a prayer emphasizing Mary's virginity.

50 Elliott, *Spiritual Marriage*, p. 47.

51 Ibid.

52 Ibid., pp. 46–7. See also Christopher N. L. Brooke, *The Medieval Idea of Marriage* (Oxford: Oxford University Press, 1989), pp. 53–4 on Mary and Joseph's marriage and pp. 54–6 on Augustine's assertions.

53 Penny S. Gold, 'The marriage of Mary and Joseph in the twelfth-century ideology of marriage', in *Sexual Practice and the Medieval Church*, ed. Vern L. Bullough and James Brundage (Buffalo, NY: Prometheus, 1982), pp. 102–17 (p. 108). See also Elliott, *Spiritual Marriage*, pp. 137–8.

54 Gold, 'Marriage', p. 116.

55 Elliott, *Spiritual Marriage*, pp. 136–7.

56 Brown, *Religious Lyrics*, 11:11–12.

57 Ibid., 16:1–12.

58 Derrida, 'Plato's pharmacy', p. 104.

59 Cf. Elisabeth Bronfen, *Over her Dead Body* (New York: Routledge, 1992), whose main thesis is about the relation between death and aesthetics, and Jacques Derrida, 'Living on: border lines', in *Deconstruction and Criticism*, trans. James Hulbert (New York: Seabury, 1979), pp. 75–176, who writes of the way in which the belief in the fixity of the boundary between life and death founds the fixity of all boundaries.

60 Hirn, *Sacred Shrine*, pp. 380–1.

61 Cf. Herbert Marcuse, 'The ideology of death', in *The Meaning of Death*, ed. Herman Feifel (New York: McGraw-Hill, 1959), pp. 64–76, who writes of the social implications and uses of death.

[62] Cf. Hirn's chapter in *Sacred Shrine*, 'Mary's death and Assumption', Warner's chapter in *Alone of All her Sex*, 'The Assumption', and Pelikan's chapter in *Mary through the Centuries*, 'The Queen of Heaven, her Dormition and her Assumption'. Chapter 4 will look more closely at the rhetorical intricacies of Mary's death.

[63] Compare Louise O. Fradenburg, '"Voice memorial": loss and reparation in Chaucer's poetry', *Exemplaria*, 2 (1990), 169–202, and '"Our owen wo to drynke": loss, gender and chivalry', in *Chaucer's* Troilus and Criseyde: *Subgit to alle Poesye*, ed. R. A. Shoaf (Binghamton: Medieval and Renaissance Texts and Studies, 1992), pp. 88–106, who theorizes about the relationships between women and death in Chaucer's works.

[64] See the end of the tale, which in its 'Joye after wo' and wish for grace for the pilgrims 'that been in *this* place' (2. 1161 and 1162, my emphasis) suggests the interdependent nature of its telling and signification.

[65] See Derrida, 'Signature, event, context', in *Limited Inc*, trans. Samuel Weber and Jeffrey Mehlman (Evanston, IL: Northwestern University Press, 1988), pp. 1–23 (pp. 9–10), for his discussion on errancy of contexts.

[66] Again, Shoaf, '"Unwemmed Custance"', makes a similar point throughout his essay. My suggestion here is that this is a reading and writing practice used not only by the Man of Law but also as a world-building strategy by many readers.

[67] Robert T. Farrell, 'Chaucer's use of the theme of help of God in the *Man of Law's Tale*', *Neuphilologische Mitteilungen*, 71 (1970), 239–43, points out that examples in the first group were often used in the liturgy as part of the rites for those who were near death.

[68] As evidence of this tendency, see ll. 190–203 and 295–308 and the introduction of the tale itself, which is a conglomeration of astrological, philosophical, scientific and theological readings of the time of day.

[69] See for instance the *Second Nun's Tale* of St Cecilia or the *Prioress's Tale* of the little clergeon.

[70] In '"Unwemmed Constance"', Shoaf writes of such errancy using the vocabulary of circulation and corruption.

[71] The Man of Law ends his tale with a standard blessing for the pilgrims, suggesting an ever-ongoing discourse.

[72] Cf. Bronfen's chapter in *Over her Dead Body*, 'Preparation for an autopsy'.

[73] This incident may be compared to miracles of the Holy Virgin in which, typically, the Virgin appears in a vision to reinitiate proper Christian devotion and faith. See *The Middle English Miracles of the Virgin*, ed. Beverly Boyd (San Marino, CA: Huntington Library, 1964) and Jacobus de Voragine, *The Golden Legend: Readings on the Saints*, trans. William Granger Ryan, 2 vols (Princeton: Princeton University Press, 1993).

Chapter 2

1   Lee Patterson, for instance, in *Chaucer and the Subject of History* (Madison: University of Wisconsin Press, 1991), pp. 317–21, has argued that in fragments 2 and 3, as in fragment 1, the authority of text/the text of authority is put into question by various tales and their tellers. In investigating medieval rhetoric more generally, Rita Copeland in *Rhetoric, Hermeneutics, and Translation in the Middle Ages: Academic Tradition and Vernacular Texts* (New York: Cambridge, 1991), p. 4, argues that routine rhetorical practices 'actually constitute mechanisms for displacing the authoritative text'.

2   Alcuin Blamires's, *The Case for Women in Medieval Culture* (Oxford: Clarendon, 1997) is based upon the thesis that in the Middle Ages we can discover the 'roots' of the tradition of a long-standing defence of women. He argues, p. 47, that in *The Wife of Bath's Prologue*, 'Chaucer comes closest to combining an interest in the relativities of "authority" . . . with an interest in the subjectivity of misogyny'. And in reference to the Wife herself, he asks (p. 36), 'how is the defence to avoid perpetuating the belligerence which it is opposing?' This chapter provides one possible avenue to answering that question.

3   Cf. Anne Clark Bartlett, *Male Authors, Female Readers: Representation and Subjectivity in Middle English Devotional Literature* (Ithaca, NY: Cornell University Press, 1995) and Elizabeth Robertson, *Early English Devotional Prose and the Female Audience* (Knoxville: University of Tennessee Press, 1990); each of these projects as a whole deals with women as readers in the Middle Ages. Both argue that Mary became a prime model for women readers.

4   See the *Protevangelium*, 10:1; all subsequent references to New Testament apocrypha are from *The Apocryphal New Testament Being the Apocryphal Gospels, Acts, Epistles, and Apocalypses*, ed. and trans. Montague Rhodes James (Oxford: Clarendon, 1924).

5   Theresa Coletti, 'Purity and danger: the paradox of Mary's body and the en-gendering of the infancy narrative in the English mystery cycles', in *Feminist Approaches to the Body in Medieval Literature*, ed. Linda Lomperis and Sarah Stanbury (Philadelphia: University of Pennsylvania Press, 1993), pp. 65–95 (pp. 75–6).

6   See Charles T. Wood's famous essay on the physiological femaleness of Mary's body: 'The doctors' dilemma: sin, salvation, and the menstrual cycle in medieval thought', *Speculum*, 56 (1981), 710–27; Wood shows (p. 722) how through consideration of the need for Jesus to be fully human, Mary had to be fully human and so 'the Virgin would remain fully a woman, ever subject to the curse of Eve'.

7   See ll. 5–6; this and all subsequent references to York plays are from *The Plays Performed by the Crafts or Mysteries of York on the Day of Corpus Christi in the Fourteenth, Fifteenth and Sixteenth Centuries*, ed. Lucy Toulmin Smith (New York: Russell & Russell, 1963).

[8]   See ll. 82 and 83; this and all subsequent reference to *N-Town plays* are from
      The N-Town Play: Cotton MS Vespasian D.8, ed. Stephen Spector (Oxford:
      Oxford University Press, 1991); all further references will be given in the
      text.

[9]   Susan Groag Bell, 'Medieval women book owners: arbiters of lay piety and
      ambassadors of culture', in *Sisters and Workers in the Middle Ages*, ed.
      Judith M. Bennett, Elizabeth A. Clark and Sarah Westphal-Wihl (Chicago:
      University of Chicago Press, 1989), pp. 135–61 (p. 154); Gertrud Schiller,
      Iconography of Christian Art, trans. Janet Seligman, 2 vols (London: Lund
      Humphries, 1971), vol. 1, p. 42.

[10] The irony is, of course, that this is a Jewish temple and these events
      chronologically predate the birth of Trinitarian belief. Thus the scene is an
      example of the way in which teaching and texts defined who Mary was and
      was to become.

[11] Schiller, *Iconography*, vol. 1, pp. 41–2.

[12] See, for example, Gail McMurry Gibson, *The Theater of Devotion: East
      Anglian Drama and Society in the Late Middle Ages* (Chicago: University of
      Chicago Press, 1989), pp. 143–4.

[13] André Grabar, *Christian Iconography: A Study of its Origins* (Princeton:
      Princeton University Press, 1968), p. 128. See also Gibson, *Theater of
      Devotion*, fig. 1.1, representing a German sculpture of the Visitation (dating
      from 1410) in which both John the Baptist and Jesus are present and visible in
      their mothers' wombs – seen through 'wound-like slits' in their mothers (p. 8).

[14] Schiller, *Iconography*, vol. 1, p. 44; the following description of the icon is
      also from this page.

[15] This line is from a fourteenth-century religious lyric, no. 26, l. 6, in Carleton
      Brown's *Religious Lyrics of the Fourteenth Century*, 2nd edn (Oxford:
      Clarendon, 1965). Unless otherwise noted, all lyric citations are from
      Brown's editions, with the number of the lyric in Brown followed by a colon
      and the line number(s).

[16] Gibson, *Theater of Devotion*, p. 137.

[17] Schiller, *Iconography*, vol. 1, p. 41; fig. 86.

[18] For typical examples of this usage, see *Malleus Maleficarum*, ed. and trans.
      Montague Summers (1928; repr. New York: Benjamin Blom, 1970), p. 44,
      and line 219 of the *N-Town*'s 'The Parliament of Heaven'.

[19] Book 11, ch. 8; the original reads: 'hoc insonuit foris auribus hominum, ut
      crederetur et intus quaereretur, et inveniretur in aeterna veritate.'

[20] Marina Warner, *Alone of All her Sex: The Myth and the Cult of the Virgin
      Mary* (New York: Knopf, 1976), p. 210, traces the western development of this
      practice to Cistercian and Franciscan insistence on the humanity of Christ.

[21] See St Bernard's (1090–1153) *Sermo II in festo Pentecostes*, quoted in Yrjö
      Hirn, *The Sacred Shrine: A Study of the Poetry and Art of the Catholic
      Church* (London: Macmillan & Co., 1912), p. 298.

[22] *Opera Omnia*, ed. Bernhardo Geyer (Aschendorff: Westfalorum Monastery,
      1958), p. 171; the original reads: 'omnes homines erant sub peccato; ergo,

licet homo debuerit, tamen homo non potuit redimere; ergo oportuit, quod aliquis plus esset quam homo, qui deberet redimere. Sed INFRA probabitur, quod angelus non erat unibilis; ergo oportuit, quod esset deus et homo; ergo necesse fuit deum incarnari.'

23   Book 13, ch. 15; the original reads 'in aenigmate nubium'.

24   Augustine, *Confessions*, book 10, ch. 30; the original reads 'carnis fluxum'.

25   Ibid., book 7, ch. 20; Augustine calls the truth 'incorpoream veritatem'.

26   See particularly 'The body of Christ in the later Middle Ages', in Caroline Walker Bynum, *Fragmentation and Redemption: Essays on Gender and the Human Body in Medieval Religion* (New York: Zone, 1992), pp. 79–117; '"And woman his humanity": female imagery in the religious writing of the later Middle Ages', in *Fragmentation and Redemption*, pp. 151–79; and 'The female body and religious practice in the later Middle Ages', in *Fragmentation and Redemption*, pp. 181–238.

27   'Female body', *Fragmentation and Redemption*, p. 183.

28   From *con* and *capio* meaning 'taking or holding together'.

29   For example, *Cassell's Latin-English Dictionary* provides 'to express in a certain form', 'to repeat words after another', 'to publish, conclude', 'to take in', 'to fancy, imagine', and 'to comprehend, grasp'.

30   Julia Kristeva, *Stabat Mater*, *The Kristeva Reader*, ed. Toril Moi and trans. León S. Roudiez (New York: Columbia University Press, 1986), pp. 160–86 (p. 173).

31   On Mary as weaver of cloth and body, see also Gibson, *Theater of Devotion*, 156–169.

32   The *N-Town* goes a step further than the other plays, however, in staging both Mary's reflection on Gabriel's words – a stage direction demands the actors be silent as the young woman ponders her fate – and her acceptance of them and the Incarnation – another stage direction provides information for what Gibson, *Theater of Devotion*, p. 144, calls 'a dazzling visual spectacle' of the Trinity arriving at the point of Mary's accepting her role as mother of God.

33   See Schiller, *Iconography*, pp. 35–8 and figs 52, 71–3, 156 (with a basket of wool instead of a spindle). Even though these are works from the early church, Schiller contends that they influenced medieval representation, as the passages from lyrics I cite below illustrate.

34   Augustine, *Confessions*, book 13, ch. 15; the original reads 'attendit per retia carnis'.

35   Coletti, 'Purity and danger', p. 86.

36   Carolyn Dinshaw, *Chaucer's Sexual Poetics* (Madison: University of Wisconsin Press, 1989), p. 21.

37   In contrast, my research has shown that Mary is represented as actively engaging in several of these 'masculine' pursuits. She is the mediatrix between humans and her son, involved in interpreting his love and justice to them and their penitence to him. She is also often associated with the translational process of conversion.

[38] Dinshaw, *Chaucer's Sexual Poetics*, p. 9.

[39] Cf. H. Marshall Leicester, *The Disenchanted Self: Representing the Subject in the* Canterbury Tales (Berkeley: University of California Press, 1990), p. 118.

[40] Cf. Dinshaw, *Chaucer's Sexual Poetics*, pp. 113–31; in this chapter on the Wife, Dinshaw's main purpose is to illustrate the way that Alisoun is at once textual and breaks down the idea of textuality.

[41] Cf. Alcuin Blamires on excess, exemplarity and gender in 'Refiguring the "scandalous excess" of medieval woman: the Wife of Bath and liberality', in *Gender in Debate from the Early Middle Ages to the Renaissance*, ed. Thelma S. Fenster and Clare A. Lees (New York: Palgrave, 2002), pp. 57–78 (*passim*).

[42] Melvin Storm, 'Alisoun's ear', *Modern Language Quarterly*, 42 (1981), 219–26 (220).

[43] Ibid., 224.

[44] Melvin Storm, 'The miller, the virgin, and the Wife of Bath', *Neophilologus*, 75 (1991), 291–303 (297).

[45] Ibid., 291–92.

[46] Ibid., 292.

[47] Ibid., 293.

[48] Ibid., 297.

[49] Ibid.

[50] Cf. also Chauncey Wood, 'Three Chaucerian widows: tales of innocence and experience', in *A Wyf Ther Was: Essays in Honour of Paule Mertens-Fonck*, ed. Juliette Dor (Liège: University of Liège Press, 1992), pp. 282–91 (p. 290).

[51] Cf. Judith Ferster, *Chaucer on Interpretation* (New York: Cambridge University Press, 1985), pp. 3, 12–13, 122–38; Lisa Kiser, *Truth and Textuality in Chaucer's Poetry* (Hanover: University Press of New England, 1991), pp. 1–3, 136–41; Leicester, *Disenchanted*, pp. 26, 65–158; and Lee Patterson, '"Experience woot well it is noght so": marriage and the pursuit of happiness in the "Wife of Bath's Prologue and Tale"' in *Geoffrey Chaucer: The Wife of Bath: Complete, Authoritative Text with Biographical and Historical Contexts, Critical History, and Essays from Five Contemporary Critical Perspectives*, ed. Peter G. Beidler (New York: Bedford, 1996), pp. 133–54 (*passim*).

[52] Cf. Elaine Tuttle Hansen, *Chaucer and the Fictions of Gender* (Berkeley: University of California Press, 1992), p. 14, and Ruth Barrie Straus, 'The subversive discourse of the Wife of Bath: phallocentric discourse and the imprisonment of criticism', *ELH*, 55 (1988), 527–54 (*passim*).

[53] Danielle Jacquart and Claude Thomasset, *Sexuality and Medicine in the Middle Ages*, trans. Matthew Adamson (Princeton: Princeton University Press, 1988), pp. 7–47.

[54] See James Finn Cotter, 'The Wife of Bath and the conjugal debt', *English Language Notes*, 6 (1969), 169–72 (*passim*); Stewart Justman, 'Trade as pudendum: Chaucer's Wife of Bath', *Chaucer Review*, 28 (1994), 344–52 (*passim*); Kenneth J. Oberembt, 'Chaucer's anti-misogynist Wife of Bath',

Chaucer Review, 10 (1976), 287–302 (*passim*); and Lee Patterson, 'Feminine rhetoric and the politics of subjectivity: La Vieille and the Wife of Bath', in *Rethinking the* Romance of the Rose, ed. Kevin Brownlee and Sylvia Huot (Philadelphia: University of Pennsylvania Press, 1992), pp. 316–58 (p. 333), for examples of this type of reading.

55 Cf. Judith Butler, *Gender Trouble: Feminism and the Subversion of Identity* (New York: Routledge, 1990), pp. 16–25, on the fictive quality of what is perceived as an abiding substance of gender.

56 Mary Carruthers, 'The Wife of Bath and the painting of lions', in *Feminist Readings in Middle English Literature: The Wife of Bath and All her Sect*, ed. Ruth Evans and Lesley Johnson (New York: Routledge, 1994), pp. 22–53 (pp. 26 and 22).

57 See vol. 2, p. 628, of Galen, *On the Usefulness of the Parts of the Body*, trans. Margaret Tallmadge May, 2 vols (Ithaca, NY: Cornell University Press, 1968); this and all subsequent quotations from Galen are from May's edition.

58 Quoted in Bynum, 'Female body', p. 220.

59 Galen, *On Usefulness*, vol. 2, p. 630.

60 In contrast, see Hansen, *Chaucer and the Fictions of Gender*, pp. 30–1, who argues that the Wife is mystified by the language she uses and in very little control of it.

61 Leicester, *Disenchanted*, p. 10.

62 In 'Commodities among themselves', in *This Sex which is Not One*, trans. Catherine Porter (Ithaca, NY: Cornell University Press, 1985), pp. 192–7, Irigaray argues on p. 192, 'Heterosexuality is nothing but the assignment of economic roles: there are producer subjects and agents of exchange (male) on the one hand, productive earth and commodities (female) on the other' and wonders further what would happen if these commodities began to speak.

63 Cf. Kiser, *Truth and Textuality*, pp. 136–8.

64 The *Protevangelium*, 4:1, tells the story of Anna's blessing from God. After Anna prays to become pregnant, an angel appears to her, saying, 'Anna, Anna, the Lord hath hearkened unto thy prayer and thou shalt conceive and bear and thy seed shall be spoken of in the whole world.'

65 See *Medieval Woman's Guide to Health: The First English Gynecological Handbook*, ed. Beryl Rowland (Kent, OH: Kent State University Press, 1981), p. 4, for a more complete discussion on the etymology of this name; see also Patterson, 'Feminine', p. 321–2.

66 For an example of this critical position, see Kiser, *Truth and Textuality*, (pp. 58–9).

67 Cf. Ferster, *Chaucer on Interpretation*, pp. 2–3; Leicester, *Disenchanted*, p. 99; Patterson, 'Feminine', p. 333.

68 Cf. Jacques Derrida, 'Limited inc a b c . . .', in *Limited Inc*, trans. Samuel Weber and Jeffrey Mehlman (Evanston, IL: Northwestern University Press, 1988), pp. 29–110; Irigaray, 'This sex which is not one', in *This Sex which is Not One*, pp. 23–33; and Ferster, *Chaucer on Interpretation*, p. 13.

[69] Cf. Patterson, '"Experience"', *passim*.

[70] Cf. Ferster, *Chaucer on Interpretation*, p. 133; Hansen, *Chaucer and the Fictions of Gender*, p. 33; Leicester, *Disenchanted*, pp. 144–5.

[71] See Penny S. Gold, 'The marriage of Mary and Joseph in the twelfth-century ideology of marriage', in *Sexual Practice and the Medieval Church*, ed. Vern L. Bullough and James Brundage (Buffalo, NY: Prometheus, 1982), pp. 102–17, for a full description of some of these reformulations and their effects on married couples in the period.

[72] See Storm's 'The miller, the virgin and the Wife of Bath', 291–303, for a detailed analysis of further connections between Mary and Joseph and the Miller's Alisoun and John.

[73] Jonathan Nauman, 'The role of the blessed virgin in the York Cycle', *Philological Quarterly*, 70 (1991), 423–31, discusses fully this tradition and others that are used to represent Joseph's role in the York cycle.

[74] In her chapter 'The Song of Songs', Warner, *Alone of All her Sex*, gives specific examples of Mary both as child and bride of Christ, while Ann W. Astell, *The Song of Songs in the Middle Ages* (Ithaca, NY: Cornell University Press, 1990), pp. 42–62, and E. Ann Matter, *The Voice of my Beloved: The Song of Songs in Western Medieval Christianity* (Philadelphia: University of Pennsylvania Press, 1990), pp. 152–69, trace the historical development of Mary as bride of Christ.

[75] Cf. Caroline Walker Bynum, *Jesus as Mother: Studies in the Spirituality of the High Middle Ages* (Berkeley: University of California Press, 1982), *passim*.

[76] See, for example, 'The journey to Bethlehem; the birth of Jesus' in the *York* cycle, l. 38.

[77] Cf. Louis O. Fradenburg, '"Fulfild of fairye": the social meaning of fantasy in the "Wife of Bath's Prologue" and "Tale"', in *Geoffrey Chaucer: The Wife of Bath,* ed. Beidler, pp. 205–20, and Gayle Margherita, *The Romance of Origins: Language and Sexual Difference in Middle English Literature* (Philadelphia: University of Pennsylvania Press, 1994), pp. 1–14.

[78] Straus, 'The subversive', p. 530.

[79] Ibid., 549.

[80] Irigaray, 'This sex', p. 29.

[81] The same point can also be made about her use of the euphemism *quoniam* in l. 608.

Chapter 3

[1] The four texts bundled with *Seinte Marherete* all focus on women who have chosen to remain virgins or to confine themselves, as anchoresses often did, in order to be closer to and more worthy of God's love.

[2] Cf. Julia Kristeva, *Powers of Horror: An Essay on Abjection*, trans. León S. Roudiez (New York: Columbia University Press, 1982), pp. 113–32, who

posits the notion that the interiorization of Christic flesh into the Trinity parallels and exemplifies a movement from a concept of the threat of evil from without – indicated by Levitical prohibitions – towards a different speaking subject with the potential for defilement and evil always residing within.

3   Emphasis added. Aquinas makes this statement as part of his valorization of virginity and in so doing defines bodily procreation as spiritually inferior to the work of saving souls. Yet for Aquinas, bodily multiplication remains the stage upon which spiritual multiplication takes place. The original reads: 'Sed praeceptum datum de generatione respicit totam multitudinem hominum, cui necessarium est non solum quod multiplicetur corporaliter, sed etiam quod spiritualiter proficiat. Et ideo sufficienter providetur humanæ multitudini, si quidam carnali generationi operam.'

4   For a sampling of source materials see Vern L. Bullough, 'Medieval medical and scientific views of women', *Viator*, 4 (1973), 485–501; Danielle Jacquart and Claude Thomasset, *Sexuality and Medicine in the Middle Ages*, trans. Matthew Adamson (Princeton: Princeton University Press, 1988), pp. 48–86; and Charles T. Wood, 'The doctors' dilemma: sin, salvation, and the menstrual cycle in medieval thought', *Speculum*, 56 (1981), 710–12.

5   The Middle Ages read Song of Songs 4:7 as a prefiguration of Mary: 'You are all fair, my love; there is no flaw [spot] in you.' See Ann W. Astell's *The Song of Songs in the Middle Ages* (Ithaca, NY: Cornell University Press, 1990), *passim*, and E. Ann Matter, *The Voice of my Beloved: The Song of Songs in Western Medieval Christianity* (Philadelphia: University of Pennsylvania Press, 1990), *passim*.

6   This was an outgrowth of Levitical prohibitions (12:19–30) against un-cleanliness. Jacquart and Thomasset, *Sexuality and Medicine*, pp. 73–4, collect a series of popular beliefs about the power of the menses or a men-struating woman to taint and curse food, for instance.

7   'Lacta, mater, cibum nostrum; lacta panem de coelo uenientem et in praesepi positum uelut piorum cibaria iumentorum'; *PL 39*, 1655; quoted in Mary Clayton, *The Cult of the Virgin Mary in Anglo-Saxon England* (New York: Cambridge University Press, 1990), p. 12.

8   This line is from a thirteenth-century religious lyric, no. 31, l. 22, Carleton Brown's *English Lyrics of the Thirteenth Century* (Oxford: Clarendon, 1932). Unless otherwise noted, all lyric citations are from Brown's editions, with the number of the lyric followed by a colon and the line number(s).

9   This line is from a fourteenth-century religious lyric in Carleton Brown's *Religious Lyrics of the Fourteenth Century*, 2nd edn (Oxford: Clarendon, 1965), 32:66.

10 See also Margaret Ruth Miles, 'The virgin's one bare breast', in *The Expanding Discourse*, ed. Norma Broude and Mary D. Garrard (New York: Harper Collins, 1992), pp. 26–37.

11 See Jacquart and Thomasset, *Sexuality and Medicine* (citing Constantine the African's eleventh-century translation of a tenth-century text by Alβ ibn Abbβs and an eleventh-century text by Avicenna translated into Latin

in the twelfth century), pp. 43, 52, and 72; and Wood, 'The doctors' dilemma', 721. Although the physiological details of this transformation were debated during the era, the fundamental idea of the transformation itself was standard. In 'The body of Christ in the later Middle Ages', in *Fragmentation and Redemption: Essays on Gender and the Human Body in Medieval Religion* (New York: Zone, 1992), pp. 79–117, Caroline Walker Bynum simply states (p. 100), 'all ancient biologists thought that the mother's blood fed the child in the womb and then, transmuted into breast milk, fed the baby outside the womb'.

12 See Leviticus 12, for proscriptions surrounding purifying a mother's body after birth, and 15:19–30 for rules dealing with menstrual uncleanness. On the mikveh see Wood, 'The doctors' dilemma', 722–3.

13 Cf. Kristeva, *Powers of Horror*, *passim*, whose focus on Judaeo-Christian traditions of defining sin and evil illustrates this point. Cf. also Gayle Margherita, *The Romance of Origins: Language and Sexual Difference in Middle English Literature* (Philadelphia: University of Pennsylvania Press, 1994), p. 44; and Elaine Scarry, *The Body in Pain* (New York: Oxford University Press, 1985), *passim*.

14 On this point William of Conches in his *Dragmaticon Philosophiae* states the following: 'Sperm is thus the seed of the man, composed of the purest substance of all parts of the body' (quoted in Jacquart and Thomasset, *Sexuality and Medicine*, p. 54). Similarly Thomas Aquinas held that the semen receives the power of the heavenly bodies through which God exercises his power in the world. In his *De Formatione Corporis Humani in Utero*, Giles of Rome equates the ability of the sperm to form so many components out of formless matter with divine virtue and intellect (Jacquart and Thomasset, *Sexuality and Medicine*, p. 57–9). According to Wood, 'The doctors' dilemma', 715, these views were most fully expressed by Albertus Magnus in *De Animalibus*.

15 See vol. 2, p. 628, of Galen, *On the Usefulness of the Parts of the Body*, trans. Margaret Tallmadge May, 2 vols (Ithaca, NY: Cornell University Press, 1968).

16 Galen, however, does not at this point tackle the question of why the female foetus that has formed the correct parts does not have the requisite heat to bring its organs to fruition. The idea is present in the earlier Hippocratic corpus of works (vol. 1, fn 78). Later in book xiv, (vol. 2, pp. 634–5), Galen asserts via empirical evidence that the purest semen is produced by the right side of the body and that the cleanest portion of the uterus lies on that side as well, since this side is fed by arteries that do not pass through other organs before reaching their final destination. According to Jacquart and Thomasset, *Sexuality and Medicine*, pp. 50–1, the Middle Ages tended to accept both Galen's scientific explanations and the taboos about dividing up space upon which they were based and which they supplemented.

17 All references are to the 3rd edn, *Riverside Chaucer*, ed. Larry D. Benson (Boston: Houghton Mifflin, 1987); fragment 1, ll. 410–18.

[18] Jacquart and Thomasset, *Sexuality and Medicine*, pp. 7–47.

[19] Philippa Tristram, *Figures of Life and Death in Medieval English Literature* (New York: New York University Press, 1976), pl. 6. See also Sander L. Gilman, *Sexuality, an Illustrated History: Representing the Sexual in Medicine and Culture from the Middle Ages to the Age of AIDS* (New York: John Wiley & Sons, 1989), pl. 45.

[20] 'Constantinus Africanus' *De Coitu*: a translation', trans. Paul Delany, *Chaucer Review*, 4 (1970), 55–65 (59).

[21] Marie-Christine Pouchelle, *The Body and Surgery in the Middle Ages*, trans. Rosemary Morris (New Brunswick, NJ: Rutgers University Press, 1990), p. 25; Jacquart and Thomasset, *Sexuality and Medicine*, p. 35.

[22] Pouchelle, *Body and Surgery*, p. 84.

[23] Monica H. Green, *The Trotula: A Medieval Compendium of Women's Medicine* (Philadelphia: University of Pennsylvania Press, 2001), pp. 48–51: a female practitioner of Salerno probably had a hand in producing one of the texts associated with the name Trotula in subsequent centuries.

[24] *Medieval Woman's Guide to Health: The First English Gynecological Handbook*, ed. Beryl Rowland (Kent, OH: Kent State University Press, 1981), pp. 3–12; Green, *Trotula*, 48.

[25] Though this text has been roundly criticized for inaccuracies in transcription and translation, it remains the only modern edition of the portion of British Library MS Sloane 2463 available. See Faye M. Getz's review of *Medieval Woman's Guide to Health: The First English Gynecological Handbook*, ed. Beryl Rowland, *Medical History*, 26 (1982), 353–4, for a typical review of Rowland's efforts.

[26] *Medieval Woman's Guide*, p. 3.

[27] See p. 58; all references to the *English Trotula* are to Rowland's edition, *Medieval Woman's Guide*.

[28] Responding to a query concerning whether or not menstruating women should be allowed to attend church, Pope Gregory the Great (540?–604) compared 'this natural overflowing' to any suffering that humans undergo because of the body, like hunger, thirst and fatigue. While he calls menstruation 'an infirmity', it is a result of post-lapsarian depravity of the body, suffering to which all humans are subject in some degree or kind, a specific divine judgement that signifies God's justice and love; see Wood, 'The doctors' dilemma', 713–14. Similarly, our author claims, p. 58, that 'no man shuld dispise oþer for þe disese þat God sendith hym but to haue compassion of hym and releuen hym yef he myght' (no man should despise another for the disease that God sends him but should have compassion for him and relieve him if you might).

[29] See for instance p. 164: 'Divers tymes it happith of diuers women a mischeuous greuaunce in trauaillinge of chyld for defaute of good mydwifes and that greuaunce kepen priue and it nedith for to be holpen.' Also, the term 'prevy membre' used throughout (e.g. pp. 92 and 100) refers to the shameful secrecy of these body parts.

30 See pp. 68; 122–55; 92, 100, 102; and 98–105 respectively.
31 See 'Joseph's Doubt', ll. 55 and 95–7; this and all subsequent reference to *N-Town* plays are from *The N-Town Play: Cotton MS Vespasian D.8*, ed. Stephen Spector (Oxford: Oxford University Press, 1991).
32 See l. 102; this and all subsequent references to *York* plays are from *The Plays Performed by the Crafts or Mysteries of York on the Day of Corpus Christi in the Fourteenth, Fifteenth and Sixteenth Centuries*, ed. Lucy Toulmin Smith (New York: Russell & Russell, 1963).
33 This portion of the cycle is based loosely on *Protevangelium*, 15–16.
34 See 'The Trial of Joseph and Mary', in the *N-Town*, l. 94.
35 See also the *Parson's Tale*, l. 599.
36 *Medieval Woman's Guide*, p. 90.
37 For example, ibid., p. 58.
38 Cf. Margherita, *Romance of Origins*, pp. 43–61.
39 *Seinte Marherete, þe Meiden ant Martyr*, ed. Frances M. Mack (London: Oxford University Press, 1934), p. 25; all subsequent references to *Seinte Marherete* are from Mack's edition and will be given in the text.
40 See Jocelyn Wogan-Browne, *Saints' Lives and Women's Literary Culture c.1150–1300* (Oxford: Oxford University Press, 2001), pp. 124–32, who describes different versions of the virgin/mother type, versions which range from collocating maternity with death to more positive views associated with reproducing heroic values and the heroes that embody them; Wogan-Browne claims (p. 131): 'If the leaky female body requires sealing and enclosure, it must also open as the body of (re-)production. The question of productivity from with the enclosure arouses powerfully ambivalent responses.'
41 Because the Middle English of *Seinte Marherete* is more difficult than any other encountered yet in this project, I have chosen to provide translations for the reader's use.
42 Such imagery was also common in mystical writings of the period. Women mystics especially highlighted a romantic or erotic union with Jesus. For recent studies of this trope see Ulrike Wiethaus (ed.), *Maps of Flesh and Light: The Religious Experience of Medieval Woman Mystics* (Syracuse, NY: Syracuse University Press, 1993).
43 See for other examples, *Seinte Marherete*, pp. 3, 5, 11, 13.
44 See Genesis 3:16.
45 See Wood, 'The doctors' dilemma', 722–3.
46 Cf. 1 Corinthians 13:12.
47 Cf. Julia Kristeva, excerpt from *About Chinese Women*, in *The Kristeva Reader*, ed. Toril Moi and trans. Seán Hand (New York: Columbia University Press, 1986), pp. 138–59.
48 Jacobus de Voragine, *The Golden Legend: Readings on the Saints*, trans. William Granger Ryan, 2 vols (Princeton: Princeton University Press, 1993), vol. 1, p. 370.

49 See Renate Blumenfeld-Kosinski, *Not of Woman Born: Representations of Caesarean Birth in Medieval and Renaissance Culture* (Ithaca, NY: Cornell University Press, 1990), pp. 10, 162, n. 4.

50 See Margaret Ruth Miles, *Image as Insight: Visual Understanding in Western Christianity and Secular Culture* (Boston: Beacon, 1985), pp. 89, 93.

51 See Blumenfeld-Kosinski, *Not of Woman Born*, pp. 91–119.

52 Ibid., pp. 7–47.

53 On how choices were made about whom to save, Blumenfeld-Kosinski, *Not of Woman Born*, p. 27, cites Thomas Aquinas's reading of Romans 3:8: 'Evil should not be done so that good may come.' The *English Trotula*, p. 96, is also quite clear on this point: 'For whan the woman is feble & þe chyld may noȝt comyn out, than it is better that þe chyld be slayne than the moder of þe child also dye.'

54 Blumenfeld-Kosinski, *Not of Woman Born*, p. 24, posits four factors, each with their own numerous components, as the main ones responsible for the increasing practice of Caesarean birth: 'the laicization of surgery; the increasingly explicit directions for Caesareans issued by various church councils; the new definitions of areas of professional competency regarding physicians and surgeons; . . . the performance of autopsies and dissections, which started in the thirteen century'. In this increasingly complex system, we can discern how different institutions gained and/or struggled to maintain authority over areas material, bodily and spiritual they considered within their purview.

55 See Caroline Walker Bynum, 'The female body and religious practice in the later Middle Ages', in *Fragmentation and Redemption: Essays on Gender and the Human Body in Medieval Religion* (New York: Zone, 1992), pp. 181–238 (p. 101 and fig. 6.11); Gail McMurry Gibson, *The Theater of Devotion: East Anglian Drama and Society in the Late Middle Ages* (Chicago: University of Chicago Press, 1989), pp. 144–5 and fig. 6.2.

56 *Seinte Marherete*, p. 49.

57 Mary standing on the dragon is an image still popular today. Being in physical contact with the demon seems to be in Mary's purview, as even Jesus and St George use a weapon to injure him.

58 Luke 1:41 and *Seinte Marherete*, p. 49.

59 See *Seinte Marherete*, pp. 25 and 27.

60 *The Golden Legend*, p. 369.

61 For this version of the story see John J. Delaney, 'Margaret of Antioch,' in *Dictionary of Saints* (Garden City, NJ: Doubleday, 1980).

62 *Seinte Marherete*, p. 53.

63 Ibid., 48.

Chapter 4

[1] Augustine, *De Doctrina Christiana*, 1. 6: 'Ac per hoc ne ineffabilis quidem dicendus est deus, quia et hoc cum dicitur, aliquid dicitur et fit nescio qua pugna verborum, quoniam si illud est ineffabile, quod dici non potest, non est ineffabile, quod vel ineffabile dici potest. Quae pugna verborum silentio cauenda potius quam voce pacanda est.'

[2] Cf. a fourteenth-century religious lyric in Carleton Brown's *Religious Lyrics of the Fourteenth Century*, 2nd edn (Oxford: Clarendon, 1965), no. 16, ll. 1–12. Unless otherwise noted, all lyric citations are from Brown's editions and subsequent references will be given in the text. The following practice is used in reference to lyrics: the number of the lyric in Brown is followed by a colon and the line number(s).

[3] That the poem operates upon the intractable difference between human and divine is the basis of Theodore Bogdanos's thesis in Pearl: *Image of the Ineffable, a Study in Medieval Poetic Symbolism* (University Park: Pennsylvania State University Press, 1983), for example pp. 3–4. On the same basic thesis, see also Marie Borroff, '*Pearl*'s "maynful mone": crux, simile, and structure', in *Acts of Interpretation: The Text in its Contexts, 700–1600: Essays on Medieval and Renaissance Literature in Honor of E. Talbot Donaldson*, ed. Mary J. Carruthers and Elizabeth D. Kirk (Norman, OK: Pilgrim, 1982), pp. 159–72; Morton Donner, 'A grammatical perspective on word play in *Pearl*', *Chaucer Review*, 22 (1988), 322–31; Frances Fast, 'Poet and dreamer in *Pearl*: "hys ryche to qynne"', *English Studies in Canada*, 18 (1991), 371–82 (376–8); Charlotte Gross, 'Courtly language in *Pearl*', in *Text and Matter: New Critical Perspectives of the* Pearl-*Poet*, ed. Robert J. Blanch, Miriam Miller and Julian Wasserman (Troy, NY: Whitston, 1991), pp. 79–91; Wendell S. Johnson, 'The imagery and diction of *The Pearl*', in *The Middle English* Pearl: *Critical Essays*, ed. John Conley (Notre Dame: University of Notre Dame Press, 1970), pp. 27–49 (p. 29); Charles Moorman, 'The role of the narrator in *Pearl*', in *The Middle English* Pearl, ed. Conley, pp. 111–14; Cary Nelson, *The Incarnate Word: Literature as Verbal Space* (Urbana: University of Illinois Press, 1973), pp. 28–30; Howard H. Schless, '*Pearl*'s "Princes Pay" and the law', *Chaucer Review*, 24 (1989), 183–5 (184–5); Anne Howland Schotter, 'Vernacular style and the word of God: the incarnational art of *Pearl*', in *Ineffability: Naming the Unnameable from Dante to Beckett*, ed. Peter S. Hawkins and Anne Howland Schotter (New York: AMS Press, 1984), pp. 23–34; and Anna Torti, '*Auenture, cnawyng*, and *lote* in *Pearl*', in *Literature in Fourteenth-Century England*, ed. Piero Boitani and Anna Torti (Cambridge: D. S. Brewer, 1983), pp. 49–63.

[4] Cf. Roman Jakobson, 'Two aspects of language: metaphor and metonymy', in *European Literary Theory and Practice*, ed. Vernon W. Grass (New York: Dell, 1973), pp. 119–32 (pp. 119–25); Roman Jakobson and Morris Halle, *Fundamentals of Language*, Janua Linguarum, Series Minor 1 (New

York: Mouton, 1980), pp. 90–6; and Paul Ricoeur, *The Rule of Metaphor: Multi-disciplinary Studies of the Creation of Meaning in Language*, trans. Robert Czerny (Toronto: University of Toronto Press, 1977), pp. 9–43.

[5] Bogdanos, *Pearl: Image*, p. 109.

[6] Early readers and editors of the text often understood the poem as strictly autobiographical, a father's story of coming to understand the death of his daughter. Subsequent readers found allegorical or symbolical significance in the work's main images. See René Wellek, 'The *Pearl*: an interpretation of the Middle English poem', in *Sir Gawain and Pearl: Critical Essays*, ed. Robert J. Blanch (Bloomington: Indiana University Press, 1966), pp. 3–36, for a synopsis of such early twentieth-century positions. Wellek himself ultimately concludes that the poem is an elegy with allegorical implications, making the narrator/poet's loss a universal experience. D. W. Robertson, 'The pearl as a symbol', in *The Middle English* Pearl, ed. Conley, pp. 18–26, understands the poem through the four traditional levels of medieval exegesis, while A. C. Spearing, 'Symbolic and dramatic development in *Pearl*', ibid., pp. 122–48, argues that the poem provides its own exegesis, none other being necessary.

[7] Cf. Jacques Derrida, *Of Grammatology*, trans. Gayatri C. Spivak (Baltimore: Johns Hopkins University Press, 1976), pp. 144 and 159, on supplementarity.

[8] See Schotter's Augustinian reading, in 'Vernacular style': 'Words which admitted their own inadequacy were held to be less likely to lead to idolatry than those which took themselves for granted, as Augustine, following Plato and Plotinus, had pointed out' (p. 28).

[9] In this chapter, the following practice is used when Middle English is quoted: all lines from *Pearl* are translated, while only particularly difficult passages from other Middle English texts are glossed. Translations are my own.

[10] Donald Attwater, *A Dictionary of Mary* (New York: P. J. Kennedy & Sons, 1959), p. 267.

[11] See Caroline Walker Bynum, *Fragmentation and Redemption: Essays on Gender and the Human Body in Medieval Religion* (New York: Zone, 1992), fig. 6.11, and Gail McMurry Gibson, *The Theater of Devotion: East Anglian Drama and Society in the Late Middle Ages* (Chicago: University of Chicago Press, 1989), fig. 6.2.

[12] See Bynum, *Fragmentation and Redemption*, fig. 6.10.

[13] Schotter, 'Vernacular style', p. 24.

[14] The image of Mary as glass, undamaged by the light that passes through it, is a common one, exemplified in Brown, *Religious Lyrics*, 32:74.

[15] On this point see Bogdanos, *Pearl: Image*, *passim*, who argues that the poem fails fundamentally to provide a picture of heaven that is human on any level; and, in contrast, Sarah Stanbury, *Seeing the* Gawain-*Poet* (Philadelphia: University of Pennsylvania Press, 1981), pp. 12–41, who argues that the text is organized around the narrator's perception as a way of representing human limitations; the description of heaven can, therefore, only be human.

[16] See ll. 59–65; this and all subsequent reference to *N-Town* plays are from *The N-Town Play: Cotton MS Vespasian D.8*, ed. Stephen Spector (Oxford: Oxford University Press, 1991); all further references will be given in the text.

[17] Susan Groag Bell, 'Medieval women book owners: arbiters of lay piety and ambassadors of culture', in *Sisters and Workers in the Middle Ages*, ed. Judith M. Bennett, Elizabeth A. Clark and Sarah Westphal-Wihl (Chicago: University of Chicago Press, 1989), pp. 135–61 (p. 154), claims that 'Uncountable paintings and sculptures of the Annunciation depict Mary as an avid reader', while Gertrud Schiller, *Iconography of Christian Art*, trans. Janet Seligman (London: Lund Humphries, 1971), vol. 1, p. 42, asserts such an image was popular in western iconography by the fourteenth century.

[18] Bynum, 'The female body and religious practice in the later middle ages', in *Fragmentation and Redemption*, pp. 181–238 (p. 212), observes, however, that such images 'have nothing to do with claiming sacerdotal functions for ordinary women. Mary is priest because it is she who offers to ordinary mortals the saving flesh of God, just as the celebrant does in the mass.'

[19] See *The Apocryphal New Testament Being the Apocryphal Gospels, Acts, Epistles, and Apocalypses*, ed. and trans. Montague Rhodes James (Oxford: Clarendon, 1924), p. 197; all future references to New Testament apocrypha are from this edition. References to books that are divided into chapters and verses will be given in the text, while references to books for which James has provided synopses will be referenced in notes.

[20] Ibid., pp. 198–201.

[21] Ibid., p. 202.

[22] Ibid., p. 207.

[23] For typical accounts, see 'Coptic Texts' (pp. 195–6) 'The Discourse of Theodosius' (pp. 198–9) and 'The Greek Narrative of Saint John the Divine' (pp. 201–7) in James's edition of *Apocryphal New Testament*. All versions of the story agree on the threat Mary offered to Jewish society, the Apostles being collected from their international preaching and Mary's bodily death. However, the texts disagree on how long Mary remains alive between the announcement that she will die and her death. They also disagree on the amount of time her soul was with Jesus before he returned for her body. Also see Marina Warner, *Alone of All her Sex: The Myth and the Cult of the Virgin Mary* (New York: Knopf, 1976), pp. 82–6.

[24] See ll. 37 and 92 in *The Plays Performed by the Crafts or Mysteries of York on the Day of Corpus Christi in the Fourteenth, Fifteenth and Sixteenth Centuries*, ed. Lucy Toulmin Smith (New York: Russell & Russell, 1963); this and all references to the *York* cycle are from Smith's edition and subsequent references will be given in the text.

[25] Again, this drama is very close to apocryphal sources. 'The Latin Narrative of Pseudo-Melito', *Apocryphal New Testament*, p. 214, describes the same scene, while other texts of the Assumption depict the Jews being burned and blinded – as in 'The Discourse of Theodosius' – or just burned – as in 'The Greek Narrative of Saint John the Divine'.

26 'The Latin Narrative of Pseudo-Melito', p. 214.
27 See 'The Death of Mary', l. 147 and 'The Appearance of Our Lady to Thomas', l. 193 in *Plays Performed*, ed. Toulmin Smith.
28 Cf. Luce Irigaray, 'The "mechanics" of fluids', in *This Sex which is Not One*, trans. Catherine Porter (Ithaca, NY: Cornell University Press, 1985), pp. 106–18 (p. 111).
29 See 'The Latin Narrative of Pseudo-Melito', in *Apocryphal New Testament*; Yrjö Hirn, *The Sacred Shrine: A Study of the Poetry and Art of the Catholic Church* (London: Macmillan & Co., 1912), pp. 410–11; and Warner, *Alone of All her Sex*, pp. 81–102.
30 Hirn, *Sacred Shrine*, p. 224.
31 Warner, *Alone of All her Sex*, p. 85, on the Assumption illustrates the way in which popular belief could authorize even the most dubious of sources. Hirn, *Sacred Shrine*, pp. 411–12, notes the way in which the popular belief that there were no relics of Mary, as there were of all other major and minor saints, because she had not left behind a body when she left the earth influenced scholastics and theologians to develop a system of logic that would explain this phenomenon. Jaroslav Pelikan, *Mary through the Centuries: Her Place in the History of Culture* (New Haven: Yale University Press, 1996), in his chapter on the Assumption similarly illustrates the ways that belief and practices authorized various misreadings and the revision of sources.
32 Hirn, *Sacred Shrine*, pp. 416–17, cites pictorial examples of similarities between pictures of this announcement and the Annunciation.
33 See the *Protevangelium*, 13:1–16:3; the *York Plays*, 'Joseph's Trouble about Mary', 102–11; *N-Town*, 'Joseph's Doubt', 108–17 and 'The Trial of Joseph and Mary'.
34 See 'The Greek Narrative of Saint John the Divine', p. 201, and 'Latin Narrative of Pseudo-Melito', 3:1, in *Apocryphal New Testament*.
35 Warner, *Alone of All her Sex*, pp. 83–4.
36 According to Warner, ibid., p. 88, by the last half of the seventh century the notion of the Dormition had arrived in Gaul, and by the ninth some liturgical calendars call the feast day the Assumption. Pope Leo IV (847–55) developed a vigil and an octave for the feast day, celebrated on 15 August, while Pope Nicholas I (858–67) declared Mary's passing to heaven on a par with Christmas and Easter – the Incarnation and the Resurrection. See also Mary Clayton, *The Cult of the Virgin Mary in Anglo-Saxon England* (New York: Cambridge University Press, 1990), pp. 1–40.
37 *Apocryphal New Testament*, ch. 4.
38 Ann W. Astell, *The Song of Songs in the Middle Ages* (Ithaca, NY: Cornell University Press, 1990), pp. 42–72; E. Ann Matter, *The Voice of my Beloved: The Song of Songs in Western Medieval Christianity* (Philadelphia: University of Pennsylvania Press, 1990), pp. 152–64; Warner, *Alone of All her Sex*, p. 126; and Brown, *Religious Lyrics*, 91:95–8: 'Ihesu þat are kynge of lyf / Tech my soule þat is þy wyf / To loue best no þynge in londe / Bot þe, ihesu, hir dere housbonde'.

[39] Matter, *Voice of my Beloved*, p. 163, argues 'According to the allegorical mode Mary becomes here [in the Song of Songs] not only the symbol of the Church, but the embodiment of it.'

[40] See l. 432; this and all subsequent references are from *Pearl*, in *The Poems of the Pearl Manuscript:* Pearl, Cleanness, Patience, Sir Gawain and the Green Knight, ed. Malcolm Andrew and Ronald Waldron (Berkeley: University of California Press, 1978), pp. 53–110.

[41] Quoted in Jefferson B. Fletcher, 'The allegory of the pearl', *Journal of English and German Philology*, 20 (1921), 1–21 (7).

[42] *English Lyrics of the Thirteenth Century*, ed. Carleton Brown (Oxford: Clarendon, 1932); all references to thirteenth-century lyrics are to this edition.

[43] Based on the lyric usages, Gross, 'Courtly language', p. 86, argues that Mary as queen is merely one of several conventional terms of praise of her beauty and dignity, not a description of power. This quotation from *Pearl* is striking, however, for so closely collocating, in the comparison of her to the bailey of the castle, Mary's imperial qualities with her artefactual status, reminding readers of Mary's fluid figurative status in heaven. In his edition of the poem, Richard Morris, *Early English Alliterative Poems in the West-Midland Dialect of the Fourteenth Century* (New York: Oxford, 1869), metonymically glosses this word as 'authority, jurisdiction, dominion', not mentioning the architectural basis of the word.

[44] Hirn, *Sacred Shrine*, p. 416.

[45] Schiller, *Iconography*, p. 108 and figs 279, 280.

[46] See Warner, *Alone of All her Sex*, pp. 268–9; Marta Weigle, *Creation and Procreation: Feminist Reflections on Mythologies of Cosmogony and Parturition* (Philadelphia: University of Pennsylvania Press, 1989), pp. 60–1.

[47] The *York Plays* describe Mary's bliss similarly, saying in heaven she will 'neuere in two . . . be twynnand', or 'sundered' (l. 182).

[48] Bogdanos, Pearl*: Image*, p. 7.

[49] Milton R. Stern, 'An approach to *The Pearl*', in *Middle English* Pearl, ed. Conley, pp. 73–85 (p. 76).

[50] Cf. Ian Bishop, Pearl *in its Setting: A Critical Study of the Structure and Meaning of the Middle English Poem* (New York: Barnes & Noble, 1968), *passim* but particularly pp. 31–9, and 'The significance of the "garlande gay" in the allegory of *Pearl*', *Review of English Studies*, 8 (1957), 12–21.

[51] Patricia Kean, The Pearl: *An Interpretation* (London: Routledge, 1967), pp. 98–113. Also, cf. Song of Songs 4:12.

[52] Bogdanos, Pearl*: Image*, p. 38; *Stanbury*, Seeing, p. 18. R. Allen Shoaf, '*Purgatorio* and *Pearl*: transgression and transcendence', *Texas Studies in Literature and Language*, 32 (1990), 152–68, writes of the influence of eroticism in *Pearl* compared to that in Dante's work.

[53] Bogdanos, Pearl*: Image*, p. 15.

54 *English Medieval Lapidaries*, ed. Joan Evans and Mary S. Serjeantson (London: Oxford University Press, 1933), pp. 107–8.

55 Quoted in Dolores Warwick Frese, *An* Ars Legendi *for Chaucer's* Canterbury Tales (Gainesville, FL: University of Florida Press, 1991), p. 64.

56 Bogdanos, Pearl*: Image*, p. 17.

57 For a sampling of such a critical position, see Bishop, *Setting*, p. 95; Jane Chance, 'Allegory and structure in *Pearl*: the four senses of the *Ars Praedicandi* and fourteenth-century homiletic poetry', in *Text and Matter*, ed. Blanch et al., pp. 31–59; Stanton Hoffman, 'The Pearl: notes for an interpretation', in *Middle English* Pearl, ed. Conley, pp. 86–102; Johnson, 'Imagery', p. 33; D. W. Robertson, 'The "heresy" of *The Pearl*', in *Text and Matter*, ed. Blanch et al., pp. 291–9 (p. 292) and 'The pearl as a symbol', p. 25; Stern, 'An approach', in *Middle English* Pearl, ed. Conley, pp. 73–85.

58 Spearing, 'Symbolic', p. 123.

59 John Conley, '*Pearl* and a lost tradition', in *Middle English* Pearl, ed. Conley, pp. 50–72 (p. 57).

60 Stanbury, *Seeing*, p. 17.

61 For a sampling of essays pertaining to the poem's intertextuality see Maria Bullón-Fernández, '"Byȝonde þe water": courtly and religious desire in *Pearl*,' *Studies in Philology*, 91 (1994), 35–49; Gross, 'Courtly language', *passim*; Gregory Roper, '*Pearl*, penitence, and recovery of the self', *Chaucer Review*, 28 (1993), 164–86 (169); Spearing, 'Symbolic', p. 135.

62 'Articulate' originates from the Latin *articulāre*, 'to joint' and still maintains this sense in modern biological discourse, in which bones are said to articulate with one another at joints.

63 Bogdanos, Pearl*: Image*, p. 3.

64 Sarah Stanbury, 'Feminist masterplots: the gaze on the body of *Pearl*'s dead girl', in *Feminist Approaches to the Body in Medieval Literature*, ed. Linda Lomperis and Sarah Stanbury (Philadelphia: University of Pennsylvania Press, 1993), pp. 96–115 (p. 101).

65 Kevin Marti, *Body, Heart, and Text in the* Pearl-*Poet* (Lewiston, NY: Edwin Mellen, 1991), p. 6.

66 See Bogdanos, Pearl*: Image*, p. 10; Johnson, 'Imagery', p. 31; Marti, *Body*, p. 84; Schotter, 'Vernacular style', p. 30.

67 For a more detailed analysis of stanza construction see Charles Osgood, introduction to The Pearl: *A Middle English Poem* (Boston: D. C. Heath, 1906), pp. ix–lix.

68 Most basically this word means simply 'lady' but the poem allies it with 'make' (759) and its many forms (for example, 'makelez' in 784), 'vyuez' or 'wives' (785) and 'maryage' (414).

69 The glossary in *Early English Alliterative*, ed. Morris, an edition of the poems of the Cotton Nero A X manuscript, including *Pearl*, makes clear the doubled status of this word, glossing it contextually either as 'two' or

'separated', The editions of Osgood and E. V. Gordon, *Pearl* (Oxford: Clarendon, 1953) provide similar glosses.

[70] Fletcher, 'Allegory', p. 6.

[71] Quoted ibid., p. 8. On the lily as a symbol for the Virgin, see also Hirn, *Sacred Shrine*, pp. 438–9, and Brown, *Religious Lyrics*, 10 and 31.

[72] Fletcher, 'Allegory', pp. 11–12.

[73] See Kevin Marti, 'Traditional characteristics of the resurrected body in *Pearl*', *Viator*, 24 (1993), 311–35 (315, 329–32), on aspects of resurrected bodies that would allow them to be individually identified.

[74] On some implications of the term 'luf-longyng' see David Aers, 'The self mourning: reflections on *Pearl*', *Speculum*, 68 (1993), 54–73 (67–8) and Bullón-Fernández, 'Beȝond', pp. 45–7. See also l. 11 in which the narrator complains of being 'for-dolked of luf daungere' or severely wounded by love's danger.

BIBLIOGRAPHY

Primary Sources

Albertus Magnus, *Opera Omnia*, ed. Bernhardo Geyer (Aschendorff: Westfalorum Monastery, 1958).

Alan of Lille, *The Plaint of Nature*, trans. James J. Sheridan (Toronto: Pontifical Institute of Medieval Studies, 1980).

Apocryphal New Testament Being the Apocryphal Gospels, Acts, Epistles, and Apocalypses, ed. and trans. Montague Rhodes James (Oxford: Clarendon, 1924).

Augustine, *Confessions*, trans. R. S. Pine-Coffin (New York: Penguin, 1961).

——*On Christian Doctrine*, trans. D. W. Robertson, Jr. (Indianapolis: Bobbs-Merrill, 1976).

Boethius, *Consolation of Philosophy*, trans. V. E. Watts (New York: Penguin, 1969).

Chaucer, Geoffrey, *Riverside Chaucer*, 3rd edn, ed. Larry D. Benson (Boston: Houghton Mifflin, 1987).

'Constantinus Africanus' *De Coitu*: a translation', trans. Paul Delany, *Chaucer Review*, 4 (1970), 55–65.

Dante Alighieri, *The Divine Comedy*, ed. and trans. Allen Mandelbaum, 3 vols. (New York: Bantam, 1980).

de Lorris, Guillaume, and Jean de Meun, *Le Roman de la Rose,* trans. Charles Dahlberg (London: University Press of New England, 1983).

English Lyrics of the Thirteenth Century, ed. Carleton Brown (Oxford: Clarendon, 1932).

English Medieval Lapidaries, ed. Joan Evans and Mary S. Serjeantson (London: Oxford University Press, 1933).

Galen, *On the Usefulness of the Parts of the Body*, trans. Margaret Tallmadge May, 2 vols (Ithaca, NY: Cornell University Press, 1968).

Jacobus de Voragine, *The Golden Legend: Readings on the Saints*, trans. William Granger Ryan, 2 vols (Princeton: Princeton University Press, 1993).

Malleus Maleficarum, ed. and trans. Montague Summers (1928; repr. New York: Benjamin Blom, 1970).

Medieval Woman's Guide to Health: The First English Gynecological Handbook, ed. Beryl Rowland (Kent, OH: Kent State University Press, 1981).

The Middle English Miracles of the Virgin, ed. Beverly Boyd (San Marino, CA: Huntington Library, 1964).

The N-Town Play: Cotton MS Vespasian D.8, ed. Stephen Spector, (Oxford: Oxford University Press, 1991).

Philo, *The Works of Philo*, trans. C. D. Yonge (Peabody, MA: Hendrickson, 1993).

——*On the Creation*, ed. and trans. F. H. Colson and G. H. Whitaker (Cambridge: Harvard University Press, 1958–62).

The Plays Performed by the Crafts or Mysteries of York on the Day of Corpus Christi in the Fourteenth, Fifteenth and Sixteenth Centuries, ed. Lucy Toulmin Smith (New York: Russell & Russell, 1963).

The Poems of the Pearl Manuscript: Pearl, Cleanness, Patience, Sir Gawain and the Green Knight, ed. Malcolm Andrew and Ronald Waldron (Berkeley: University of California Press, 1978).

Protevangelium, see *Apocryphal New Testament*.

Religious Lyrics of the Fourteenth Century, ed. Carleton Brown, 2nd edn (Oxford: Clarendon, 1965).

Seinte Marherete, þe Meiden ant Martyr, ed. Frances M. Mack (London: Oxford University Press, 1934).

Secondary Sources

Aers, David, 'The self mourning: reflections on *Pearl*', *Speculum*, 68 (1993), 54–73.

Astell, Ann W., *The Song of Songs in the Middle Ages* (Ithaca: Cornell University Press, 1990).

——'Chaucer's "St. Anne Trinity": devotion, dynasty, dogma, and debate', *Studies in Philology*, 94 (1997), 395–416.

Attwater, Donald, *A Dictionary of Mary* (New York: P. J. Kennedy & Sons, 1959).

Bal, Meike, 'Sexuality, sin, and sorrow: the emergence of the female character (a reading of Genesis 1–3)', *Poetics Today*, 6 (1987), 21–42.

Bartlett, Anne Clark, *Male Authors, Female Readers: Representation and*

Subjectivity in Middle English Devotional Literature (Ithaca, NY: Cornell University Press, 1995).

Bell, Susan Groag, 'Medieval women book owners: arbiters of lay piety and ambassadors of culture', in *Sisters and Workers in the Middle Ages*, ed. Judith M. Bennett, Elizabeth A. Clark and Sarah Westphal-Wihl (Chicago: University of Chicago Press, 1989), pp. 135–61.

Bishop, Ian, 'The significance of the "garlande gay" in the allegory of *Pearl*', *Review of English Studies*, 8 (1957), 12–21.

——Pearl *in its Setting: A Critical Study of the Structure and Meaning of the Middle English Poem* (New York: Barnes & Noble, 1968).

Blamires, Alcuin, *The Case for Women in Medieval Culture* (Oxford: Clarendon, 1997).

——'Refiguring the "scandalous excess" of medieval woman: the Wife of Bath and liberality', in *Gender in Debate from the Early Middle Ages to the Renaissance*, ed. Thelma S. Fenster and Clare A. Lees (New York: Palgrave, 2002), pp. 57–78.

Bloch, R. Howard, 'Medieval misogyny', *Representations*, 20 (1987), 1–24.

Blumenfeld-Kosinski, Renate, *Not of Woman Born: Representations of Caesarean Birth in Medieval and Renaissance Culture* (Ithaca, NY: Cornell University Press, 1990).

Bogdanos, Theodore, Pearl: *Image of the Ineffable, a Study in Medieval Poetic Symbolism* (University Park: Pennsylvania State University Press, 1983).

Borroff, Marie, '*Pearl*'s "maynful mone": crux, simile, and structure', in *Acts of Interpretation: The Text in its Contexts, 700–1600: Essays on Medieval and Renaissance Literature in Honor of E. Talbot Donaldson*, ed. Mary J. Carruthers and Elizabeth D. Kirk (Norman, OK: Pilgrim, 1982), pp. 159–72.

Bronfen, Elisabeth, *Over her Dead Body* (New York: Routledge, 1992).

Brooke, Christopher N. L., *The Medieval Idea of Marriage* (Oxford: Oxford University Press, 1989).

Bullón-Fernández, Maria '"Byȝonde þe water": courtly and religious desire in *Pearl*', *Studies in Philology*, 91 (1994), 35–49.

Bullough, Vern L., 'Medieval medical and scientific views of women', *Viator*, 4 (1973), 485–501.

Butler, Judith, *Gender Trouble: Feminism and the Subversion of Identity* (New York: Routledge, 1990).

Bynum, Caroline Walker, *Jesus as Mother: Studies in the Spirituality of the High Middle Ages* (Berkeley: University of California Press, 1982).

——'"And woman his humanity": female imagery in the religious writing of the later Middle Ages', in *Fragmentation and Redemption: Essays on Gender and the Human Body in Medieval Religion* (New York: Zone, 1992), pp. 151–79.

Bynum, Caroline Walker, 'The body of Christ in the later Middle Ages', in *Fragmentation and Redemption: Essays on Gender and the Human Body in Medieval Religion* (New York: Zone, 1992), pp. 79–117.

——'The female body and religious practice in the later Middle Ages', in *Fragmentation and Redemption: Essays on Gender and the Human Body in Medieval Religion* (New York: Zone, 1992), pp. 181–238.

Carruthers, Mary, 'The Wife of Bath and the painting of lions', in *Feminist Readings in Middle English Literature: The Wife of Bath and All her Sect*, ed. Ruth Evans and Lesley Johnson (New York: Routledge, 1994), pp. 22–53.

Cassell's Latin-English and English-Latin Dictionary (New York: Funk & Wagnalls, 1955).

Chance, Jane, 'Allegory and structure in *Pearl*: the four senses of the *Ars Praedicandi* and fourteenth-century homiletic poetry', in *Text and Matter: New Critical Perspectives of the* Pearl-*Poet*, ed. Robert J. Blanch, Miriam Miller and Julian Wasserman (Troy, NY: Whitston, 1991), pp. 31–59.

A Chaucer Glossary, ed. Norman Davis et al. (Oxford: Clarendon, 1979).

Clayton, Mary, *The Cult of the Virgin Mary in Anglo-Saxon England* (New York: Cambridge University Press, 1990).

Coletti, Theresa, 'Purity and danger: the paradox of Mary's body and the en-gendering of the infancy narrative in the English mystery cycles', in *Feminist Approaches to the Body in Medieval Literature*, ed. Linda Lomperis and Sarah Stanbury (Philadelphia: University of Pennsylvania Press, 1993), pp. 65–95.

Conley, John, '*Pearl* and a lost tradition', in *The Middle English* Pearl: *Critical Essays*, ed. John Conley (Notre Dame: University of Notre Dame Press, 1970), pp. 50–72.

Copeland, Rita, *Rhetoric, Hermeneutics, and Translation in the Middle Ages: Academic Tradition and Vernacular Texts* (New York: Cambridge, 1991).

Cotter, James Finn, 'The Wife of Bath and the conjugal debt', *English Language Notes*, 6 (1969), 169–72.

Delaney, John J., 'Margaret of Antioch', in *Dictionary of Saints* (Garden City, NJ: Doubleday, 1980).

de Lauretis, Teresa, *Technologies of Gender* (Bloomington: Indiana University Press, 1987).

Derrida, Jacques, *Of Grammatology*, trans. Gayatri C. Spivak (Baltimore: Johns Hopkins University Press, 1976).

Derrida, Jacques, 'Living on: border lines', in *Deconstruction and Criticism*, trans. James Hulbert (New York: Seabury, 1979), pp. 75–176.

——'Plato's pharmacy', in *Dissemination*, ed. and trans. Barbara Johnson (Chicago: University of Chicago Press, 1981), pp. 61–171.

——'Limited inc a b c . . .', in *Limited Inc*, trans. Samuel Weber and Jeffrey Mehlman (Evanston, IL: Northwestern University Press, 1988), pp. 29–110.

——'Signature, event, context', in *Limited Inc*, trans. Samuel Weber and Jeffrey Mehlman (Evanston, IL: Northwestern University Press, 1988), pp. 1–23.

Dinshaw, Carolyn, *Chaucer's Sexual Poetics* (Madison: University of Wisconsin Press, 1989).

Donner, Morton, 'A grammatical perspective on word play in *Pearl*', *Chaucer Review*, 22 (1988), 322–31.

Dor, Juliette, 'From a crusading virago to the polysemous virgin: Chaucer's Constance', in *A Wyf Ther Was: Essays in Honour of Paule Mertens-Fonck*, ed. Juliette Dor (Liège: University of Liège Press, 1982), pp. 129–40.

Elliott, Dyan, *Spiritual Marriage: Sexual Abstinence in Medieval Wedlock* (Princeton: Princeton University Press, 1993).

Farrell, Robert T., 'Chaucer's use of the theme of help of God in the *Man of Law's Tale*', *Neuphilologische Mitteilungen*, 71 (1970), 239–43.

Fast, Frances, 'Poet and dreamer in *Pearl*: "hys ryche to qynne"', *English Studies in Canada*, 18 (1991), 371–82.

Ferster, Judith, *Chaucer on Interpretation* (New York: Cambridge University Press, 1985).

Fletcher, Jefferson B., 'The allegory of the pearl', *Journal of English and German Philology*, 20 (1921), 1–21.

Fradenburg, Louise O., '"Voice memorial": loss and reparation in Chaucer's poetry', *Exemplaria*, 2 (1990), 169–202.

——'"Our owen wo to drynke": loss, gender and chivalry', in *Chaucer's Troilus and Criseyde: Subgit to alle Poesye*, ed. R. A. Shoaf (Binghamton: Medieval and Renaissance Texts and Studies, 1992), pp. 88–106.

——'"Fulfild of fairye": the social meaning of fantasy in the "Wife of Bath's Prologue" and "Tale"', in *Geoffrey Chaucer: The Wife of Bath: Complete, Authoritative Text with Biographical and Historical Contexts, Critical History, and Essays from Five Contemporary Critical Perspectives*, ed. Peter G. Beidler (New York: Bedford, 1996), pp. 205–20.

Frese, Dolores Warwick, *An Ars Legendi for Chaucer's Canterbury Tales* (Gainesville, FL: University of Florida Press, 1991).

Furrow, Melissa M., 'The Man of Law's St. Custance: sex and the saeculum', *Chaucer Review*, 24 (1990), 223–35.

Getz, Faye M., Review of *Medieval Woman's Guide to Health: The First English Gynecological Handbook*. Beryl Rowland, *Medical History*, 26 (1982), 353–4.

Gibson, Gail McMurry, *The Theater of Devotion: East Anglian Drama and Society in the Late Middle Ages* (Chicago: University of Chicago Press, 1989).

Gilman, Sander L., *Sexuality, an Illustrated History: Representing the Sexual in Medicine and Culture from the Middle Ages to the Age of AIDS* (New York: John Wiley & Sons, 1989).

Gold, Penny S., 'The marriage of Mary and Joseph in the twelfth-century ideology of marriage', in *Sexual Practice and the Medieval Church*, ed. Vern L. Bullough and James Brundage (Buffalo, NY: Prometheus, 1982), pp. 102–17.

Gordon, E. V. (ed.), *Pearl* (Oxford: Clarendon, 1953).

Grabar, André, *Christian Iconography: A Study of its Origins* (Princeton: Princeton University Press, 1968).

Green, Monica H., *The Trotula: A Medieval Compendium of Women's Medicine* (Philadelphia:University of Pennsylvania Press, 2001).

Gross, Charlotte, 'Courtly language in *Pearl*', in *Text and Matter: New Critical Perspectives of the* Pearl-*Poet*, ed. Robert J. Blanch, Miriam Miller and Julian Wasserman (Troy, NY: Whitston, 1991), pp. 79–91.

Hansen, Elaine Tuttle, *Chaucer and the Fictions of Gender* (Berkeley: University of California Press, 1992).

Hirn, Yrjö, *The Sacred Shrine: A Study of the Poetry and Art of the Catholic Church* (London: Macmillan & Co., 1912).

Hoffman, Stanton, 'The *Pearl*: notes for an interpretation', in *The Middle English* Pearl: *Critical Essays*, ed. John Conley (Notre Dame: University of Notre Dame Press, 1970), pp. 86–102.

Irigaray, Luce, 'Commodities among themselves', in *This Sex which is Not One*, trans. Catherine Porter (Ithaca, NY: Cornell University Press, 1985), pp. 192–7.

——'The "mechanics" of fluids', in *This Sex which is Not One*, trans. Catherine Porter (Ithaca, NY: Cornell University Press, 1985), pp. 106–18.

——'This Sex which is Not One', in *This Sex which is Not One*, trans. Catherine Porter (Ithaca, NY: Cornell University Press, 1985), pp. 23–33.

Jacquart, Danielle, and Claude Thomasset, *Sexuality and Medicine in the*

Middle Ages, trans. Matthew Adamson (Princeton: Princeton University Press, 1988).

Jakobson, Roman, 'Two aspects of language: metaphor and metonymy', in *European Literary Theory and Practice*, ed. Vernon W. Grass (New York: Dell, 1973), pp. 119–32.

Jakobson, Roman, and Morris Halle, *Fundamentals of Language*, Janua Linguarum, Series Minor 1 (New York: Mouton, 1980).

Johnson, Wendell S., 'The imagery and diction of *The Pearl*,' in *The Middle English* Pearl: *Critical Essays*, ed. John Conley (Notre Dame: University of Notre Dame Press, 1970), pp. 27–49.

Justman, Stewart, 'Trade as pudendum: Chaucer's Wife of Bath', *Chaucer Review*, 28 (1994), 344–52.

Kean, Patricia, The Pearl: *An Interpretation* (London: Routledge, 1967).

Kiser, Lisa, *Truth and Textuality in Chaucer's Poetry* (Hanover: University Press of New England, 1991).

Kolve, V. A., *The Play Called Corpus Christi* (Stanford: Stanford University Press, 1966).

Kristeva, Julia, *Powers of Horror: An Essay on Abjection*, trans. León S. Roudiez (New York: Columbia University Press, 1982).

——*About Chinese Women*, in *The Kristeva Reader*, ed. Toril Moi and trans. Seán Hand (New York: Columbia University Press, 1986), pp. 138–59.

——excerpt from *Revolution in Poetic Language*, in *The Kristeva Reader*, ed. Toril Moi and trans. León S. Roudiez (New York: Columbia University Press, 1986), pp. 89–136.

——'*Stabat Mater*', in *The Kristeva Reader*, ed. Toril Moi and trans. León S. Roudiez (New York: Columbia University Press, 1986), pp. 160–86.

Leicester, H. Marshall, 'Oure tonges *différance*: textuality and deconstruction in Chaucer', in *Medieval Texts and Contemporary Readers*, ed. Laurie A. Finke and Martin B. Shichtman (Ithaca, NY: Cornell University Press, 1987), pp. 15–26.

——*The Disenchanted Self: Representing the Subject in the* Canterbury Tales (Berkeley: University of California Press, 1990).

Marcuse, Herbert, 'The ideology of death', in *The Meaning of Death*, ed. Herman Feifel (New York: McGraw-Hill, 1959), pp. 64–76.

Margherita, Gayle, *The Romance of Origins: Language and Sexual Difference in Middle English Literature* (Philadelphia: University of Pennsylvania Press, 1994).

Marti, Kevin, *Body, Heart, and Text in the* Pearl-*Poet* (Lewiston, NY: Edwin Mellen, 1991).

Marti, Kevin, 'Traditional characteristics of the resurrected body in *Pearl*', *Viator*, 24 (1993), 311–35.

Matter, E. Ann, *The Voice of my Beloved: The Song of Songs in Western Medieval Christianity* (Philadelphia: University of Pennsylvania Press, 1990).

Miles, Margaret Ruth, *Image as Insight: Visual Understanding in Western Christianity and Secular Culture* (Boston: Beacon, 1985)

——'The virgin's one bare breast', in *The Expanding Discourse*, ed. Norma Broude and Mary D. Garrard (New York: Harper Collins, 1992), pp. 26–37.

Moorman, Charles, 'The role of the narrator in *Pearl*', in *The Middle English* Pearl: *Critical Essays*, ed. John Conley (Notre Dame: University of Notre Dame Press, 1970), pp. 111–14.

Morris, Richard (ed.), *Early English Alliterative Poems in the West-Midland Dialect of the Fourteenth Century* (New York: Oxford, 1869).

Morse, Ruth, *Truth and Convention in the Middle Ages: Rhetoric, Representation, and Reality* (New York: Cambridge University Press, 1991).

Nauman, Jonathan, 'The role of the blessed virgin in the York Cycle', *Philological Quarterly*, 70 (1991), 423–31.

Nelson, Cary, *The Incarnate Word: Literature as Verbal Space* (Urbana: University of Illinois Press, 1973).

Oberembt, Kenneth J., 'Chaucer's anti-misogynist Wife of Bath', *Chaucer Review*, 10 (1976), 287–302.

Osgood, Charles (ed.), The Pearl: *A Middle English Poem* (Boston: D. C. Heath, 1906).

Patterson, Lee, *Chaucer and the Subject of History* (Madison: University of Wisconsin Press, 1991).

——'Feminine rhetoric and the politics of subjectivity: La Vieille and the Wife of Bath' in *Rethinking the* Romance of the Rose, ed. Kevin Brownlee and Sylvia Huot (Philadelphia: University of Pennsylvania Press, 1992), pp. 316–58.

——'"Experience woot well it is noght so": marriage and the pursuit of happiness in the "Wife of Bath's Prologue and Tale"', in *Geoffrey Chaucer: The Wife of Bath: Complete, Authoritative Text with Biographical and Historical Contexts, Critical History, and Essays from Five Contemporary Critical Perspectives*, ed. Peter G. Beidler (New York: Bedford, 1996), pp. 133–54.

Pelikan, Jaroslav, *Mary through the Centuries: Her Place in the History of Culture* (New Haven: Yale University Press, 1996).

Pouchelle, Marie-Christine, *The Body and Surgery in the Middle Ages*, trans. Rosemary Morris (New Brunswick, NJ: Rutgers University Press, 1990).

Ricoeur, Paul, *The Rule of Metaphor: Multi-disciplinary Studies of the Creation of Meaning in Language*, trans. Robert Czerny (Toronto: University of Toronto Press, 1977).

Robertson, D. W., 'The pearl as a symbol', in *The Middle English* Pearl: *Critical Essays*, ed. John Conley (Notre Dame: University of Notre Dame Press, 1970), pp. 18–26.

——'The "heresy" of *The Pearl*', in *Text and Matter: New Critical Perspectives of the* Pearl-*Poet*, ed. Robert J. Blanch, Miriam Miller and Julian Wasserman (Troy, NY: Whitston, 1991), pp. 291–9.

Robertson, Elizabeth, *Early English Devotional Prose and the Female Audience* (Knoxville: University of Tennessee Press, 1990).

Roper, Gregory, '*Pearl*, penitence, and recovery of the self', *Chaucer Review*, 28 (1993), 164–86.

Scanlon, Larry, *Narrative, Authority and Power: The Medieval Exemplum and the Chaucerian Tradition* (New York: Cambridge University Press, 1994).

Scarry, Elaine, *The Body in Pain* (New York: Oxford University Press, 1985).

Schiller, Gertrud, *Iconography of Christian Art*, trans. Janet Seligman (London: Lund Humphries, 1971), vol. 1.

Schless, Howard H., '*Pearl*'s "Princes Pay" and the law', *Chaucer Review*, 24 (1989), 183–5.

Schotter, Anne Howland, 'Vernacular style and the word of God: the incarnational art of *Pearl*', in *Ineffability: Naming the Unnameable from Dante to Beckett*, ed. Peter S. Hawkins and Anne Howland Schotter (New York: AMS Press, 1984), pp. 23–34.

Shoaf, R. Allen, '*Purgatorio* and *Pearl*: transgression and transcendence', *Texas Studies in Literature and Language*, 32 (1990), 152–68.

——'"Unwemmed Custance": circulation, property, and incest in the *Man of Law's Tale*', *Exemplaria*, 2 (1990), 287–302.

Spearing, A. C., 'Symbolic and dramatic development in *Pearl*', in *The Middle English* Pearl: *Critical Essays*, ed. John Conley (Notre Dame: University of Notre Dame Press, 1970), pp. 122–48.

Stanbury, Sarah, *Seeing the* Gawain-*Poet* (Philadelphia: University of Pennsylvania Press, 1981).

——'Feminist masterplots: the gaze on the body of *Pearl*'s dead girl', in *Feminist Approaches to the Body in Medieval Literature*, ed. Linda Lomperis and Sarah Stanbury (Philadelphia: University of Pennsylvania Press, 1993), pp. 96–115.

Stern, Milton R., 'An approach to *The Pearl*', in *The Middle English* Pearl: *Critical Essays*, ed. John Conley (Notre Dame: University of Notre Dame Press, 1970), pp. 73–85.

Storm, Melvin, 'Alisoun's ear', *Modern Language Quarterly*, 42 (1981), 219–26.

——'The miller, the virgin, and the Wife of Bath', *Neophilologus*, 75 (1991), 291–303.

Straus, Ruth Barrie, 'The subversive discourse of the Wife of Bath: phallocentric discourse and the imprisonment of criticism', *ELH*, 55 (1988), 527–54.

Torti, Anna, '*Auenture, cnawyng*, and *lote* in *Pearl*', in *Literature in Fourteenth-Century England*, ed. Piero Boitani and Anna Torti (Cambridge: D. S. Brewer, 1983), pp. 49–63.

Tristram, Philippa, *Figures of Life and Death in Medieval English Literature* (New York: New York University Press, 1976).

Warner, Marina, *Alone of All her Sex: The Myth and the Cult of the Virgin Mary* (New York: Knopf, 1976).

Weigle, Marta, *Creation and Procreation: Feminist Reflections on Mythologies of Cosmogony and Parturition* (Philadelphia: University of Pennsylvania Press, 1989).

Wellek, René, 'The *Pearl*: an interpretation of the Middle English poem', in *Sir Gawain and* Pearl: *Critical Essays*, ed. Robert J. Blanch (Bloomington: Indiana University Press, 1966), pp. 3–36.

Wiethaus, Ulrike (ed.), *Maps of Flesh and Light: The Religious Experience of Medieval Woman Mystics* (Syracuse, NY: Syracuse University Press, 1993).

Wogan-Browne, Jocelyn, *Saints' Lives and Women's Literary Culture c.1150–1300* (Oxford: Oxford University Press, 2001).

Wood, Charles T., 'The doctors' dilemma: sin, salvation, and the menstrual cycle in medieval thought', *Speculum*, 56 (1981), 710–27.

Wood, Chauncey, 'Three Chaucerian widows: tales of innocence and experience', in *A Wyf Ther Was: Essays in Honour of Paule Mertens-Fonck*, ed. Juliette Dor (Liège: University of Liège Press, 1992), pp. 282–91.

INDEX